TAPESTRY

Strategies
for Academic
Communication

TAPESTRY

The **Tapestry** program of language
materials is based on the concepts
presented in *The Tapestry of
Language Learning: The Individual
in the Communicative Classroom* by
Robin C. Scarcella &
Rebecca L. Oxford.

❖

Each title in this program focuses on:

❖

Individual learner strategies and
instruction

❖

The relatedness of skills

❖

Ongoing self-assessment

❖

Authentic material as input

❖

Theme-based learning linked to task-
based instruction

❖

Attention to all aspects of
communicative competence

TAPESTRY

STRATEGIES FOR ACADEMIC COMMUNICATION

Jocelyn Steer

Heinle & Heinle Publishers
An International Thomson
Publishing Company
Boston, Massachusetts, 02116, USA

I T P

The publication of *Strategies for Academic Communication* was directed by the members of the Heinle & Heinle Global Innovations Publishing Team:

Elizabeth Holthaus, Global Innovations Team Leader
David C. Lee, Editorial Director
John F. McHugh, Market Development Director
Lisa McLaughlin, Production Services Coordinator

Also participating in the publication of this program were:

Publisher: Stanley J. Galek
Director of Production: Elizabeth Holthaus
Assistant Editor: Kenneth Mattsson
Manufacturing Coordinator: Mary Beth Hennebury
Full Service Project Manager/Compositor: PC&F, Inc.
Interior Design: Maureen Lauran
Cover Design: Maureen Lauran

Manufactured in the United States of America

ISBN: 0-8384-3961-6

Heinle & Heinle Publishers is an International Thomson Publishing Company.

10 9 8 7 6 5 4 3 2 1

To Jo and Jon

PHOTO CREDITS

1, Steve Vidler/SuperStock; 12, Spencer Grant/FPG International; 23, © Phase Infinity/Ron Jones; 39, Brian Smith/Stock, Boston; 50, left, Judy Gelles/Stock, Boston; 50, right, Tony Freeman/PhotoEdit; 87, upper left, Ron Chapple/FPG International; 87, upper right, Robert Brenner/PhotoEdit; 87, lower left, Richard Hutchings/PhotoEdit; 87, lower right, Jerry Berndt/Stock, Boston; 111, Phyllis Grayber Jensen/Stock, Boston; 119, PhotoEdit; 135, David J. Sams/Tony Stone Images; 138, upper left, Richard Pasley/Stock, Boston; 138, upper right, Brian Smith/Stock, Boston; 138, lower left, David Young-Wolff/PhotoEdit; 138, lower right, Jeff Greenberg/PhotoEdit; 167, Michael Newman/PhotoEdit; 179, John Coletti/PhotoEdit

TEXT CREDITS

6, Samovar, L. A. and R. E. Porter (1991). "How Cultures Teach" in *Communication Between Cultures.* Belmont, CA: Wadsworth Publishing Co., pp. 248-250.

32, Samovar, L. A. and R. E. Porter (1991). Introduction to *Communication Between Cultures.* Belmont, CA: Wadsworth Publishing Co., pp. i–xiv.

62, Porter, R. E. and L. A. Samovar (1991). "Basic Principles of Intercultural Communication" in *Intercultural Communication: A Reader* (6th edition). Belmont, CA: Wadsworth Publishing Co., pp. 5-22.

75, Samovar, L. A. and R. E. Porter (1991). "Nonverbal Communication: The Messages of Space, Time, and Silence" in *Communication Between Cultures.* Belmont, CA: Wadsworth Publishing Co., pp. 213-227.

80, Bulthuis, Jill D. "The Foreign Student Today: A Profile." In K. R. Pyle (ed.), *Guiding the Development of Foreign Students.* New Directions for Student Services, no. 36. Copyright 1986 by Jossey-Bass Inc., Publishers.

89, Stolberg, S. (1993, Dec. 30). "Fears Cloud Search for Genetic Roots of Violence." *The Los Angeles Times.*

90, 93, Copyright, 1993, Los Angles Times. Reprinted by permission.

95, Pincus, J. H. and G. J. Tucker (1985). *Behavioral Neurology.* NY: Oxford University Press, pp. 91-92.

110, Basow, S. (1992). "Power-Related Behaviors" in *Gender: Stereotypes and Roles* (3rd edition). Pacific Grove: Brooks/Cole. pp. 67-70.

112, Basow, S. (1992). "Abuses of Power" in *Gender: Stereotypes and Roles* (3rd edition). Pacific Grove: Brooks/Cole. pp. 311-313.

171, Biagi, S. (1992). "The Psychology of Ads" in *Media/Impact: An Introduction to Mass Media* (2nd edition). Belmont, CA; Wadsworth Publishing Co., pp. 305-307.

175, Basow, S. (1992). "Commercials" in *Gender: Stereotypes and Roles* (3rd edition). Pacific Grove:

WELCOME TO TAPESTRY

*E*nter the world of Tapestry! Language learning can be seen as an ever-developing tapestry woven with many threads and colors. The elements of the tapestry are related to different language skills like listening and speaking, reading and writing; the characteristics of the teachers; the desires, needs, and backgrounds of the students; and the general second language development process. When all these elements are working together harmoniously, the result is a colorful, continuously growing tapestry of language competence of which the student and the teacher can be proud.

This volume is part of the Tapestry program for students of English as a second language (ESL) at levels from beginning to "bridge" (which follows the advanced level and prepares students to enter regular postsecondary programs along with native English speakers). Tapestry levels include:

Beginning
Low Intermediate
High Intermediate
Low Advanced
High Advanced
Bridge

Because the Tapestry program provides a unified theoretical and pedagogical foundation for all its components, you can optimally use all the Tapestry student books in a coordinated fashion as an entire curriculum of materials. (They will be published from 1993 to 1996 with further editions likely thereafter.) Alternatively, you can decide to use just certain Tapestry volumes, depending on your specific needs.

Tapestry is primarily designed for ESL students at postsecondary institutions in North America. Some want to learn ESL for academic or career advancement, others for social and personal reasons. Tapestry builds directly on all these motivations. Tapestry stimulates learners to do their best. It enables learners to use English naturally and to develop fluency as well as accuracy.

Tapestry Principles

The following principles underlie the instruction provided in all of the components of the Tapestry program.

EMPOWERING LEARNERS

Language learners in Tapestry classrooms are active and increasingly responsible for developing their English language skills and related cultural abilities. This self direction leads to better, more rapid learning. Some cultures virtually train their students to be passive in the classroom, but Tapestry weans them from passivity by providing exceptionally high interest materials, colorful and motivating activities, personalized self-reflection tasks, peer tutoring and other forms of cooperative learning, and powerful learning strategies to boost self direction in learning.

The empowerment of learners creates refreshing new roles for teachers, too. The teacher serves as facilitator, co-communicator, diagnostician, guide, and helper. Teachers are set free to be more creative at the same time their students become more autonomous learners.

HELPING STUDENTS IMPROVE THEIR LEARNING STRATEGIES

Learning strategies are the behaviors or steps an individual uses to enhance his or her learning. Examples are taking notes, practicing, finding a conversation partner, analyzing words, using background knowledge, and controlling anxiety. Hundreds of such strategies have been identified. Successful language learners use language learning strategies that are most effective for them given their particular learning style, and they put them together smoothly to fit the needs of a given language task. On the other hand, the learning strategies of less successful learners are a desperate grab-bag of ill-matched techniques.

All learners need to know a wide range of learning strategies. All learners need systematic practice in choosing and applying strategies that are relevant for various learning needs. Tapestry is one of the only ESL programs that overtly weaves a comprehensive set of learning strategies into language activities in all its volumes. These learning strategies are arranged in eight broad categories throughout the Tapestry books:

Forming concepts
Personalizing
Remembering new material
Managing your learning
Understanding and using emotions
Overcoming limitations
Testing Hypotheses
Learning with Others

The most useful strategies are sometimes repeated and flagged with a note, "It Works! Learning Strategy . . ." to remind students to use a learning strategy they have already encountered. This recycling reinforces the value of learning strategies and provides greater practice.

RECOGNIZING AND HANDLING LEARNING STYLES EFFECTIVELY

Learners have different learning styles (for instance, visual, auditory, hands-on; reflective, impulsive; analytic, global; extroverted, introverted; closure-oriented, open). Particularly in an ESL setting, where students come from vastly different cultural backgrounds, learning styles differences abound and can cause "style conflicts."

Unlike most language instruction materials, Tapestry provides exciting activities specifically tailored to the needs of students with a large range of learning styles. You can use any Tapestry volume with the confidence that the activities and materials are intentionally geared for many different styles. Insights from the latest educational and psychological research undergird this style-nourishing variety.

OFFERING AUTHENTIC, MEANINGFUL COMMUNICATION

Students need to encounter language that provides authentic, meaningful communication. They must be involved in real-life communication tasks that cause them to *want* and *need* to read, write, speak, and listen to English. Moreover, the tasks—to be most effective—must be arranged around themes relevant to learners.

Themes like family relationships, survival in the educational system, personal health, friendships in a new country, political changes, and protection of the environment are all valuable to ESL learners. Tapestry focuses on topics like these. In every Tapestry volume, you will see specific content drawn from very broad areas such as home life, science and technology, business, humanities, social sciences, global issues, and multiculturalism. All the themes are real and important, and they are fashioned into language tasks that students enjoy.

At the advanced level, Tapestry also includes special books each focused on a single broad theme. For instance, there are two books on business English, two on English for science and technology, and two on academic communication and study skills.

UNDERSTANDING AND VALUING DIFFERENT CULTURES

Many ESL books and programs focus completely on the "new" culture, that is, the culture which the students are entering. The implicit message is that ESL students should just learn about this target culture, and there is no need to understand their own culture better or to find out about the cultures of their international classmates. To some ESL students, this makes them feel their own culture is not valued in the new country.

Tapestry is designed to provide a clear and understandable entry into North American culture. Nevertheless, the Tapestry Program values *all* the cultures found in the ESL classroom. Tapestry students have constant opportunities to become "culturally fluent" in North American culture while they are learning English, but they also have the chance to think about the cultures of their classmates and even understand their home culture from different perspectives.

INTEGRATING THE LANGUAGE SKILLS

Communication in a language is not restricted to one skill or another. ESL students are typically expected to learn (to a greater or lesser degree) all four language skills: reading, writing, speaking, and listening. They are also expected to develop strong grammatical competence, as well as becoming socioculturally sensitive and knowing what to do when they encounter a "language barrier."

Research shows that multi-skill learning is more effective than isolated-skill learning, because related activities in several skills provide reinforcement and refresh the learner's memory. Therefore, Tapestry integrates all the skills. A given Tapestry volume might highlight one skill, such as reading, but all other skills are also included to support and strengthen overall language development.

However, many intensive ESL programs are divided into classes labeled according to one skill (Reading Comprehension Class) or at most two skills (Listening/Speaking Class or Oral Communication Class). The volumes in the Tapestry Program can easily be used to fit this traditional format, because each volume clearly identifies its highlighted or central skill(s).

Grammar is interwoven into all Tapestry volumes. However, there is also a separate reference book for students, *The Tapestry Grammar,* and a Grammar Strand composed of grammar "work-out" books at each of the levels in the Tapestry Program.

Other Features of the Tapestry Program

PILOT SITES

It is not enough to provide volumes full of appealing tasks and beautiful pictures. Users deserve to know that the materials have been pilot-tested. In many ESL series, pilot testing takes place at only a few sites or even just in the classroom of the author. In contrast, Heinle & Heinle Publishers have developed a network of Tapestry Pilot Test Sites throughout North America. At this time, there are approximately 40 such sites, although the number grows weekly. These sites try out the materials and provide suggestions for revisions. They are all actively engaged in making Tapestry the best program possible.

AN OVERALL GUIDEBOOK

To offer coherence to the entire Tapestry Program and especially to offer support for teachers who want to understand the principles and practice of Tapestry, we have written a book entitled, *The Tapestry of Language Learning. The Individual in the Communicative Classroom* (Scarcella and Oxford, published in 1992 by Heinle & Heinle).

A Last Word

We are pleased to welcome you to Tapestry! We use the Tapestry principles every day, and we hope these principles—and all the books in the Tapestry Program—provide you the same strength, confidence, and joy that they give us. We look forward to comments from both teachers and students who use any part of the Tapestry Program.

Rebecca L. Oxford
University of Alabama
Tuscaloosa, Alabama

Robin C. Scarcella
University of California at Irvine
Irvine, California

PREFACE

DESCRIPTION OF THE BOOK

Strategies for Academic Communication is an advanced academic skills text that prepares ESL students for the rigors of college work. It acknowledges that most ESL students entering a college or university in North America have already developed a number of strategies and techniques for succeeding academically in their own countries. At the same time, however, it recognizes that cultures teach students in diverse and often conflicting ways. Some cultures, for example, emphasize rote learning while others value critical and creative thinking. Thus, a behavior that was treasured in the student's culture may be discouraged in this culture. Students need to find their way through this tangle of confusing and mixed messages and learn how to communicate effectively in an academic setting here.

The approach this text takes, therefore, is to begin the process with the skills and knowledge students bring to class. From there, it guides students through the labyrinth of academic expectations and conventions, helping them to sort through what is helpful, what is not, and what is still needed. Since all students do not follow the same itinerary on this journey, the text leaves considerable room for personal roaming and sidetrips.

The structure that brings students together in this process is the chapter theme, presented through readings and discussion questions. Students explore topics that are likely to come up in college classes, using that content in a range of tasks designed to sharpen their academic communication skills. These tasks range from very basic (marking texts) to more sophisticated and challenging (synthesizing sources).

Uses

The text can be used successfully in a number of contexts. It is ideal as the core text for a study-skills/academic-preparation course for advanced ESL students with TOEFL scores of 500–600 in either an intensive or semi-intensive course. It is appropriate for both matriculated and pre-university students. It could also serve as the text for the study-skills portion of a sheltered or adjunct content class; if desired, the instructor could replace the content in the text readings with the content from a sheltered or adjunct class. It might also serve as the basis for a pre-semester intensive short program in academic skills.

Features of the Book

Each of the five chapters (Exploring College Culture, Tightening the Nuts and Bolts, Thinking and Communicating Critically, Compiling and Communicating Research, and Communicating Orally in Class) has an academic skills focus and a thematic strand that is woven into the chapter exercises and activities. In most cases, the thematic content brings together a number of disciplines. For example, the section on violence in our society combines readings on physiology, psychology, and sociology. The structure of the book permits instructors to substitute alternative content to suit the specific needs of a particular course or group of students. In this way, students are not locked into a content in which they have little interest or previous knowledge.

PREVIEW OF THE CHAPTER

The "Preview of the Chapter" section introduces students to both the theme and the academic topics addressed in that chapter. Often students begin with an oral or written exercise that requires them to think about the chapter theme before they are introduced to the specific academic skills of the chapter. This content then forms the core for that chapter, or a section of that chapter, on which the readings, examples, lectures, and exercises build.

TAKING INVENTORY

Each chapter includes a "Taking Inventory" section that provides students with the opportunity to find out what they *already* know about a theme and/or how proficient they are in an academic skill. The exercises in Taking Inventory range from simple checklists intended to help the student identify strengths and weaknesses to thought-provoking questions for journal writing or discussion. In general, this section is a private tool for the student to use to become aware of previous knowledge and skills and to identify potential areas for improvement. It can also serve as the basis for the student's own goal-setting.

MAKING CROSS-CULTURAL CONNECTIONS

The text places a strong emphasis on cross-cultural comparisons of academic life. More than discussion-starters, these comparisons are designed to help students identify what may be done differently in this country to facilitate their adjustment to and understanding of the academic conventions at work in a college or university in North America.

SURVIVAL TIPS

Brief inserts throughout the book provide students with practical tips for surviving various aspects of academic life. These provide practical information regarding such activities as understanding the professor, using a textbook, participating in a class discussion, and so on.

UP CLOSE

Since so much of a college student's success depends on appropriate use of format and accurate reading of printed material, the "Up Close" sections focus on authentic material, providing a detailed analysis and directing students' attention to important elements.

RESEARCH EXERCISES

College students need to be able to locate information independently, so many of the exercises in the text require students to do research on their own or in pairs. Their research is not restricted to the library but also takes them into the field, where students speak to people in the community in order to gather information.

GAINING EXPERTISE

Each chapter includes a "Gaining Expertise" section that offers suggestions for more challenging activities that usually integrate the skills taught in the chapter. These activities often encourage students to work collaboratively outside the classroom.

EVALUATING YOUR PROGRESS

Each chapter provides students with a tool for evaluating themselves. Some chapters end with questions which are keyed to the questions originally presented in the Taking Inventory section of the chapter. These exercises allow students to compare their answers and assess their progress. Other chapters ask students to compile a portfolio, to comment on their experience in completing their work, and to evaluate the quality of their work in the portfolio.

Strategies for Academic Communication provides the advanced ESL student with readings and assignments that are required of college students in North America. It is an excellent preparation for academic work and it trains students to communicate effectively and appropriately in any academic setting.

Acknowledgments

First of all, I would like to acknowledge my students' contributions. If this text succeeds at all, it will be largely due to their enthusiasm and candid critiques, which taught me to judge my work from their responses and not from my favorite theory or notion.

I'd also like to thank Heinle & Heinle, with special thanks to Dave Lee for encouraging me with the project and to Lynne Barsky for being exceedingly patient throughout the process. I am very grateful to Robert Cohen (Columbia University) and Eileen Roesler (Wichita State University) for their insightful and helpful comments in reviewing the book. I would like to extend special appreciation to Lida Baker (UCLA Extension) for her detailed and careful review of the manuscript. Rebecca Oxford and Robin Scarcella, the *Tapestry* editors, deserve thanks for envisioning this series.

I appreciate the professional support and expertise of Linda Muroi and Phillip White, librarians at San Diego State University, who were very patient with my students as they learned their way through the library maze. Finally, I'd like to extend heartfelt thanks to my friends and colleagues, Sally Cummings, Dawn Schmid, and Cheryl Wecksler, sources of great support during this project.

To the Student

Strategies for Academic Communication is designed to prepare you for the challenges of studying at a college or university in North America. There are five chapters: Exploring College Culture, Tightening the Nuts and Bolts, Thinking and Communicating Critically, Compiling and Communicating Research, and Communicating Orally in Class. Each chapter has two strands—an academic focus and a thematic content.

The academic part of the chapter will introduce you to the academic skills you need to do well in your college work. Some of these skills are taking notes, taking tests, summarizing and paraphrasing, doing library research, compiling a research paper, and giving presentations in class.

Each chapter also introduces you to an interesting theme. Some of the themes in the book are college culture, cross-cultural communication, violence and aggression, and the power of advertising. You will have the chance to learn more about these topics through readings, lectures, research, and group activities.

One important goal of this text is to help you adjust to college culture. Like other cultures, college life has its own rules, conventions, and practices. Throughout the book you will learn important information on how a college functions as well as how you are expected to behave in class and perform in your work. Whenever possible, authentic material from college catalogs and textbooks has been included so that you will know what to expect and be better prepared.

Other features of this text are described.

Journal Writing

You will have ample opportunity to reflect on your own ideas, to make observations, and to respond to readings in your journal. An inexpensive spiral or bound notebook would be excellent for this purpose. Keep your journal with you whenever possible so that when you have an idea you would like to record or a vocabulary word you would like to learn, you can jot it down in your journal.

Assessing Your Needs

You will have the chance to determine your own needs before you begin each chapter. In this way you can decide on your personal goals for a particular chapter. You will find that goal-setting is an excellent way to manage your learning.

Cross-Cultural Comparisons

You will frequently be asked to compare academic life in this country with that in your own culture. This exercise is designed to make you aware of the differences so that you can manage your learning more efficiently.

Research Exercises

An excellent way to find out about your campus and academic life is to explore your college and talk to the people who teach and work there. Throughout the book you will be asked to complete "Exercises" that encourage you to discover the college culture outside your classroom. Although you may feel intimidated by those exercises initially, you will find that such practice will actually make you more confident in the end.

Strategies for Academic Communication is intended for students who want to learn to communicate well in an academic setting—in formal as well as informal situations, in writing and speaking, inside the classroom and out. By providing step-by-step instruction and practical information, this text will help you to overcome your language limitations and foster the confidence you need to be a successful student.

CONTENTS

3 Thinking and Communicating Critically — 87

Exploring College Culture

Chapter Theme: College Culture

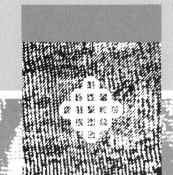

A college in the United States is a small community within a larger one with its own traditions, rules, and ambiance. Thus, it's essential that you become familiar with the workings of this academic community. This chapter introduces you to the many people and services that you are likely to encounter on a college campus. It also explores how academic life in the United States may differ from that in your own culture. If you are planning on entering a university or college in the United States, or if you are already attending one, then you will find the information and exercises in this chapter valuable in helping you to adjust to college culture and to enjoy greater academic success.

ACADEMIC TOPICS

- Understanding College Terminology
- Using Campus Services
- Learning about College Faculty and Administration
- Attending Classes
- Reading Course Descriptions
- Making Cross-Cultural Comparisons of Academic Life

CHAPTER THEME

Understanding College Culture

TAKING INVENTORY: YOUR OWN THOUGHTS

Before you begin this chapter, take a minute to consider what you already know about college life on a campus in the United States. The title of this chapter is "Exploring College Culture." What do you expect to learn from this chapter? What are three things that you would like to know more about? What do you have questions about? Write those down below.

_____

_____

_____

_____

Threads

Make the most of the numerous services that are available at your college. Know and become a part of your campus and you will feel more at home.

Sally Cummings, Associate Professor of ESL

Understanding College Terminology

LEARNING STRATEGY

Overcoming Limitations: Learning specialized academic vocabulary will help you communicate more effectively on campus.

Exercise 1: Knowing the specialized vocabulary of college life can help you adjust to your new environment. Find out what you already know. In the following list, match each term in the first column with a definition in the second column. As you review the answers with your class, make a note of terms that are new for you. Begin to keep a list of this specialized academic vocabulary in your journal or notebook.

1. add/drop deadline
2. class schedule
3. college major
4. to register
5. matriculated
6. credit
7. transcript
8. lecture class
9. seminar class
10. requirement
11. to withdraw
12. to audit
13. GPA

a. course that is necessary to take
b. to sign up for a class
c. accepted into the university
d. main subject for a degree
e. the last day to make course changes to your schedule
f. number of units given for each class hour of a course
g. a booklet listing class meeting times and places
h. type of class in which the teacher does most of the talking
i. list of all coursework and grades completed by a student
j. type of class in which students are expected to talk frequently
k. average grade for all coursework taken
l. to attend a class, but not for a grade
m. to disenroll from a class

LEARNING STRATEGY

Personalizing: Comparing academic life in this country with that in your own will help you become aware of important differences.

Exercise 2: The following chart describes the educational tracking system in the United States. Create a similar chart for the system in your own culture. Then compare and contrast the two systems—in writing or orally with another student, as instructed by your teacher.

THE SCHOOL SYSTEM IN THE UNITED STATES

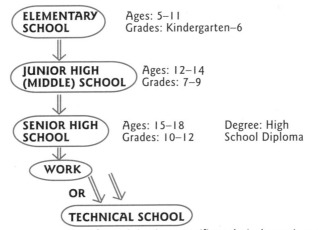

ELEMENTARY SCHOOL
Ages: 5–11
Grades: Kindergarten–6

JUNIOR HIGH (MIDDLE) SCHOOL
Ages: 12–14
Grades: 7–9

SENIOR HIGH SCHOOL
Ages: 15–18
Grades: 10–12
Degree: High School Diploma

WORK

OR

TECHNICAL SCHOOL
Provides training in a specific technical area (e.g. secretarial, data entry, dental) that leads to a certificate.

OR

COMMUNITY COLLEGE
Provides a two-year academic program of primarily general education. Leads to an A.A. (Associate of Arts) or A.S. (Associate of Science) degree. Students often then transfer to a four-year college or university.

COLLEGE/UNIVERSITY— Undergraduate
Provides a four-year academic program of general education and specialized courses in the major subject of study. Leads to a B.A. (Bachelor of Arts) or B.S. (Bachelor of Science) degree.

COLLEGE/UNIVERSITY— Graduate
Students may choose to continue for an advanced degree after their undergraduate work. Programs last from one to three years for a Master's degree in Arts (M.A.), in Science (M.S.), in Education (M.Ed.), or in Business Administration (M.B.A.). A Ph.D. degree represents the highest level of education and usually requires a published dissertation in addition to two years of additional coursework.

TAKING INVENTORY: YOUR OWN BELIEFS ABOUT LEARNING

Personalizing: Identifying what you already know about a topic from personal experiences and knowledge can help you understand a new text more easily.

Exercise 3:   As you may know from your own experience, not all cultures educate people in the same way. The reason is that each culture bases its educational system on a set of different assumptions and beliefs about how and what should be taught. Find out about your own beliefs about education and learning in the following exercise.

Agree or disagree with the following statements, adding comments when necessary. Be ready to share your ideas with another student.

1. Because the teacher knows the most about the subject matter being taught, students should listen quietly in class while the teacher lectures.

   Agree ☐   Disagree ☐   Not Sure ☐

   Comments: _____

2. Disagreeing with a teacher is a sign of disrespect.

   Agree ☐   Disagree ☐   Not Sure ☐

   Comments: _____

3. Teachers should make time available after class for students who need extra help.

   Agree ☐   Disagree ☐   Not Sure ☐

   Comments: _____

4. It's important for me to do better than the other students in the class.

   Agree ☐   Disagree ☐   Not Sure ☐

   Comments: _____

5. It's important for me to help my friends in school, even if that means helping them with their homework or on tests.

   Agree ☐   Disagree ☐   Not Sure ☐

   Comments: _____

6. Religion and education should always be separate.

   Agree ☐   Disagree ☐   Not Sure ☐

   Comments: _____

7. Memorizing a lot of information is *not* an important part of learning. It's more important to learn how to think critically and creatively.

   Agree ☐   Disagree ☐   Not Sure ☐

   Comments: _____

8. My classes are not the important part of college life—the social, athletic, and club activities will teach me more about life than the academic work.

Agree ☐   Disagree ☐   Not Sure ☐

Comments: _____

9. Parents should be responsible for financing their children's education if they are able to.

Agree ☐   Disagree ☐   Not Sure ☐

Comments: _____

10. Although I might respect and like a professor very much, I would not develop a friendship or romantic relationship with one.

Agree ☐   Disagree ☐   Not Sure ☐

Comments: _____

Discuss your answers with the class. Your instructor will indicate what the predominant beliefs are likely to be at your college. Note whether your beliefs are the same or different.

Exercise 4:   Read the following text, "How Cultures Teach," which for the most part, it applies to classes in primary and secondary school, not university or college. However, since our beliefs and assumptions about learning are formed during this time, the information presented is appropriate for the college classroom as well.

As you read, consider how teaching and learning in your own culture is similar to or different from that in the United States. Then discuss the questions that follow, either in writing or orally with another student, as instructed by your teacher.

HOW CULTURES TEACH
by Larry Samovar and Richard Porter

In the United States, teachers talk or lecture to students about 75 percent of the time. Teachers talk more in China, Japan, and Korea. In those cultures, learning is passive, and students are expected to do a great deal of rote memorization. In cultures such as Russia, China, and Japan, teachers will read to the students and then ask questions. In Mexico, students do a great deal of talking and learn through group interaction.

Schools also differ culturally as to how students participate in learning. Participation involves taking part, joining in, and sharing. How one participates, however, is another matter. Japanese students participate by the "silent receipt of information."[1] Discussions are short, with rapid turn-taking. Speaking too much is a sign of conceit and superficiality, and being considered an individual is not desirable in the collectivist Japanese culture. This emphasis upon silence and minimal participation springs from the Buddhist tradition, which values meditation and silence and has led to the incorporation of quiet time into the school curriculum. Silence in the classroom is important to the Vietnamese, Cambodians, and Chinese as well. "Cultures reflecting a Buddhist tradition hold that knowledge, truth, and wisdom come to those whose quiet silence allows the spirit to enter."[2] In the United States, the opposite is true. Classrooms tend to be noisy, and we tend to see talking by each child as a way of promoting individuality. Arab students, with their "emphasis on spoken language, with poetry and oral eloquence being particularly prized,"[3] participate enthusiastically in discussions among themselves; but because they are taught to listen to their teacher, they will speak in class only if given a specific opportunity.

The nonverbal aspects of the classroom also affect how teaching takes place. In Japan, China, and Russia, for instance, students dress in uniforms. In the United States, most students dress as they please, not wanting to look too much like someone else. Space, distance, and time are also cultural variables in the classroom. In the United States, teachers tend to stand at the front of the classroom while they are teaching. In Mexico, teachers move about the room. Russian teachers seem to be rooted to one spot in the classroom. In some cultures, schools follow rigid time schedules, with bells or buzzers announcing the change of activity or classes. In other cultures, time is less rigid, and in some there is no time schedule at all.

Interaction patterns also differ culturally. Vietnamese and Arabic students are taught not to interact with members of the opposite sex. In many instances classes are segregated by gender. This, of course, has produced some problems for international students from these cultures when they come to the United States to study and find themselves in groups of mixed gender. Formality differs also. In Germany, Mexico, and Italy, for instance, students rise when the teacher enters the room. In Russia students sit with their arms folded, holding that school is not the place for fun. American and Israeli schools tend toward informality.

Source: Larry A. Samovar and Richard E. Porter, *Communication Between Cultures.*
Wadsworth Publishing Co., 1991, pp. 248–250

---

[1] L. Damen, *Culture Learning: The Fifth Dimension in the Language Classroom* (Menlo Park, Calif.: Addison-Wesley, 1987), 315.

[2] Janis F. Andersen, "Educational Assumptions Highlighted from a Crosscultural Comparison," in *Intercultural Communication: A Reader* (4th ed.) Eds. Larry A. Samovar and Richard E. Porter (Belmont, Calif.: Wadsworth, 1985), 162.

[3] M. Farquharson, "Ideas for Teaching Arab Students in a Multicultural Setting." Paper presented at the annual meeting of the Teachers of English to Speakers of Other Languages, March 1988, Chicago, Ill. (ERIC Document Reproduction Service No. ED 296 575), 5.

Questions:

1. Think about what a classroom in primary or secondary school in your culture is like. Use your personal experience and the information in the reading to compare your culture with that in the United States.

Amount of time the teacher talks:

The United States _____

My culture _____

Student participation in class:

The United States _____

My culture _____

The role of silence in class:

The United States _____

My culture _____

Student dress:

The United States _____

My culture _____

Position of the teacher:

The United States _____

My culture _____

2. If your own culture was mentioned in the text, do you agree with the statements that were mentioned?

_____

Exercise 5: Using the information in the reading above, your own experience, and the information in the Taking Inventory exercise, formulate a list of three to five *major* differences between education in this country and in your own. Then write a letter to a friend in your country explaining those differences.

Three major differences are:

1. _____

2. _____

3. _____

PART TWO: BECOMING FAMILIAR WITH CAMPUS LIFE

Exercise 6: Read the following narrative, which describes a woman's first days at college.

None of the pictures or the written descriptions in the college catalog prepared me for that first glimpse. The college was much larger, more frightening than I had imagined. I remember my mother, her friend, and me pulling into the tree-lined entrance, in silence, as the importance of the moment struck all of us. I was leaving home. I was going to college. Did this mean I was grown up? What would I do without my family there?

After taking a few wrong turns on poorly marked lanes, we finally found my dorm—a boxy, concrete structure with three floors. Of course, I was on the third floor and there was no elevator. My roommate had not yet come in, so I selected one of the beds, a dresser and a desk. The room had a lovely view of a lake. I remember feeling very comforted by that view.

Then we ventured out on foot—locating the Registrar's office, the Cashier, Admissions, Financial Aid office, and Health Services. My mother wanted to be sure that I could find what I needed, and she managed to retrieve a campus map for me before she left. I don't think she realized at that moment that I would know that campus like the back of my hand in a matter of weeks, and that my whole life would soon center around it. I would later discover other important spots as well, such as the local coffee shop, the student union bookstore, the quieting path through the woods behind my dorm.

We both had tears in our eyes as we hugged and kissed good-bye. We both sensed that neither of us would be the same again.

Questions:

1. This woman describes an important milestone in the lives of many Americans—leaving home to go to college. Describe her feelings about this experience.

2. Do young adults in your culture leave home for college or university? If not, what do they do? When do they leave home?

3. Have you ever had an experience similar to this one? Describe what that was like for you.

Using Campus Services

The previous reading describes a number of offices on campus—Admissions, Financial Aid, etc. Do you know what services these offices provide? Look at the following chart from a university catalog. Ask your instructor to explain any of the services that you are not familiar with.

For additional information on	consult
Admissions	Director of Admissions and Records, AD-1st Floor
Athletics	Director of Athletics, MPE-114
Campus Activities	Student Resource and Information Center, CL-114
Counseling	Counseling Services and Placement, 5850 Hardy
Extension Classes	College of Extended Studies, 5630 Hardy
Financial Aid	Director of Financial Aid, CL-122
Fraternities and Sororities	Director of Housing, 6050 Montezuma
Grades	Admissions and Records, AD-1st Floor
Graduate Study	Dean of the Graduate Division, AD-220
Health Services	Director of Health Services, 5300 Campanile Dr.
Housing	Director of Housing, 6050 Montezuma
Imperial Valley Campus	Dean, 720 Heber Ave., Calexico, CA
Library Facilities	University Librarian, Love Library
Parking	Parking Coordinator, 5850 Hardy
Placement	Counseling Services and Placement, 5850 Hardy
Registration	Admissions and Records, AD-1st Floor
ROTC	
Air Force	Chair, Aerospace Studies, T-56
Army	Chair, Military Science, T-63
Navy	Chair, Naval Science, PSFA-160
Scholarships	Scholarship Office, CL-109
Student Employment	Counseling Services and Placement, 5870 Hardy
Study Abroad (Academic Year)	Division of Undergraduate Studies, AD-223
Summer Study	College of Extended Studies, 5630 Hardy
Teaching Credentials	Credentials Office, College of Education, ED-100
Transcripts	Admissions and Records, AD-1st Floor
Veterans Benefits	Admissions and Records, AD-1st Floor

Exercise 7: Do some research on your own campus. Work with another student and locate the appropriate office on campus for each of the following situations. Use a campus map to help you locate them.

HINT: Consult your college catalog for additional help.

1. Manuel needs to have his academic records sent to another school. What office should he go to?
2. Rebecca wants to get a Master's degree in education. Whom should she talk to?
3. Tranh wants to get a part-time job on campus. Where should he go?
4. Juanita plans to go to the school's basketball game, but she's not sure what time it starts. Where could she call to find out?
5. Hiro's sister wants a sweatshirt from his school. Where can he buy one?
6. Gloria got a parking ticket on campus, and she believes that she didn't deserve it. Where can she go to talk to someone about that?
7. John wants to talk to someone about possible career paths after graduation. Where would you tell him to go?
8. Jeannette's mother just died and she needs to return to her country for the funeral. She is going to miss her final exams. Whom could she talk to so she won't fail her courses?
9. Marlena's professor has been making sexual advances towards her. What should she do?
10. Lee is having student visa problems. Where should he go on campus for advice?

Learning About the Faculty

Not all instructors at your school have the same rank or responsibilities. Most schools follow a system similar to the one described in the chart below.

TITLE	DESCRIPTION
Teaching Assistant (TA)/ Graduate Assistant (GA)	These are graduate students who are hired to teach introductory courses to undergraduate students and/or to assist faculty with non-teaching work.
Lecturer/Instructor/ Adjunct faculty	These are usually part-time faculty who are hired on a temporary basis to teach a few classes per semester.
Professors: Assistant Professor Associate Professor Full Professor	These are full-time faculty who usually begin their career as assistant professors and slowly get promoted to the rank of full professor over time. They form the core of an academic department and make most of the decisions.
Tenured faculty	Tenured faculty are assured job security. Only a select number of faculty members become tenured after many years of teaching and a rigorous selection process.

Exercise 8: Find out who teaches the courses in your selected major at your college or university. If you haven't chosen a major yet, select a subject area that interests you. Work with another student who has the same major as you.

HINT: To help you get this information, consult the college catalog, the course schedule, talk to the department secretary or chairperson, speak with your advisor, and consult with other students.

- What's your major? _____
- Are most of the professors tenured? _____
- Are they mainly men? women? a combination of the two? _____
- Are there many adjunct and part-time faculty teaching classes? _____
- Who are the most popular professors? _____
- Which classes are difficult to get into? _____
- Which professors are "hard"? _____

    "easy"? _____

Learning About College Administrators

It's a good idea to become familiar with the various types of "administrators" on campus. Administrators deal with non-teaching tasks. They hold positions with such titles as College President (also called College Chancellor), Vice Presidents (who take care of such areas as finance, student affairs, academic affairs, etc.), Directors of Student Affairs (e.g., Counseling, Admissions, Campus Life), among others. You probably won't talk to many of these people very often, but you may have contact with "deans," who handle the larger academic departments on campus. For example, if you are a business major, you may need to talk to the "Dean of the Business College" one day.

Exercise 9: Find out the names of the administrators at your school.

College President _____

Vice President for Academic Affairs _____

Vice President for Student Affairs _____

Dean of Undergraduate Studies _____

Dean of (your major department) _____

Attending Classes

TAKING INVENTORY: WHAT DO YOU THINK?

Exercise 10: Explore your own thoughts about what it's like to be in a college class with students from the United States. Be ready to discuss your answers in small groups.

1. How important is class attendance for you? For the professor?
2. How tolerant do you think instructors will be of students who arrive late to class? What should you do if you come in late?
3. Is it important for you to participate in class discussions? Do you think most instructors want you to speak up in class? Are grades affected by such participation?
4. Is it acceptable to ask questions when you don't understand what the professor is saying?
5. Do you think that professors are bothered by students who talk among themselves during class?
6. What should you do if you are unable to complete an assignment on time?

TYPES OF CLASSES

Although each school has its own system of numbering and labeling courses, the underlying concepts are very similar. The following list describes the most common college classes. (See "Up Close: Reading Course Descriptions" on page 13 for more detailed information.)

Seminar classes are usually small and require students to participate in discussions.

• **Introductory classes** (also called "intro" classes) are usually large lecture classes that cover a lot of material. Introductory classes are usually required (e.g., Psych 101).
• **Upper division classes** are intended for students majoring in the discipline. They are more specialized and smaller than the introductory classes. They are often seminar classes that require class discussion and participation.
• **Prerequisite classes** (also called "pre-reqs") must be completed before taking others (e.g., Psych 101 may be a prerequisite for Abnormal Psychology, a more advanced class).
• In **lecture classes** the professor does most of the talking while students take notes. Classes are usually large, and course grades are often based on tests rather than on papers.
• In **seminar classes** students are required to participate and be more active than in a lecture class. These classes often require papers.
• **Laboratory classes** (also called "labs") supplement some classes with an additional hour or more per week. These labs are usually "hands-on" classes (e.g., a chemistry lab).

UP-CLOSE: READING COURSE DESCRIPTIONS

Asian Studies*
In the College of Arts and Letters

Faculty

Asian studies is administered through the Center for Asian Studies, composed of faculty members from the departments of Anthropology, Art, Classical and Oriental Languages and Literatures, Economics, English and Comparative Literature, Geography, History, Linguistics, Philosophy, Political Science, Religious Studies, and Sociology; the colleges of Business Administration, Education, Engineering, and Sciences; and the Library. Professor Daniel D. Whitney is director, Professor Thomas R. Cox is graduate adviser, and Professor David V. DuFault is undergraduate adviser.

Offered by Asian Studies

Master of Arts degree in Asian studies.
Major in Asian studies with the A.B. degree in liberal arts and sciences.
Minor in Asian studies.

Advising

All College of Arts and Letters majors are urged to consult with their department adviser as soon as possible; they are required to meet with their department adviser within the first two semesters after declaration or change of major.

Asian Studies Major

With the A. B. Degree in Liberal Arts and Sciences (Major Code: 03011)

All candidates for a degree in liberal arts and sciences must complete the graduation requirements listed in the section of this catalog on "Graduation Requirements."

Preparation for the Major. Six units in History 105, 106 or Philosophy 101, 102; six units in Anthropology 101, 102, Economics 101, 102, Geography 101, 102, or Political Science 101, 103; and six units in Asian Studies 105, 106 or 107, or History 120, 121. (18 units.) Art 258 and 259 (unless waived by the instructor) are needed if Art 366 is selected in the major. Art 264 and 265 are recommended.

Foreign Language Requirement. Competency (equivalent to that which is normally attained through three consecutive courses of college study) is required in one foreign language as part of the preparation for the major. Asian language recommended. Refer to section in catalog on "Graduation Requirements."

Upper Division Writing Requirement. Passing the University Writing Examination or completing one of the approved writing courses with a grade of C (2.0) or better.

Major. A minimum of 30 upper division units to include six units selected from Asian Studies 458, 459, 499 (maximum three units), 560, 596; from the humanities not less than 12 units from at least two departments selected from Art 366; Comparative Literature 430, 470*, 490*, 495*, 571*; History 496*, 561A–561B, 562, 563, 564A–564B, 565, 566, 567, 568, 569, 570, 596*; Linguistics 496*; Philosophy 351, 575*, 596; Religious Studies 401, 403, 506, 508, 580*, 581* and 499*; and from the social sciences no less than 12 units from at least two departments selected from Anthropology 448, 450, 452, 481*, 496*; Economics 330, 336*, 360, 365*, 465, 489, 496* and 499*; Geography 331, 350, 540*; Political Science 361, 362, 499.

These are the requirements for the major

---

* When relevant.

Asian Studies Minor

The minor in Asian studies consists of a minimum of 21 units to include History 120 and 121, or six units selected from Asian Studies 105, 106, or 107. Other lower division courses acceptable for the minor are Art 264 and 265, and four units of an appropriate Asian language. Twelve units must be in upper division. Upper division courses acceptable for the minor include:

Humanities: Not less than six units selected from History 561A–561B, 562, 563, 564A–564B, 566, 567, 568, 569, 570; Philosophy 351, 575 (when relevant), 596; Religious Studies 401*, 403*, 506*, 508*.

---

* This selection, as well as the one in Exercise 11, is taken from the San Diego State University catalog.

Social Sciences: No less than six units selected from Anthropology 450*; Economics 330, 465; Geography 331, 540 (when relevant); Marketing 376; Political Science 362, 499.

No more than six units may be selected from History 566, 567, 568. No more than six units may be selected from History 569, 570, and Anthropology 452. Three units from Asian Studies 458, 459, 499, 560, or 596.

Courses in the minor may not be counted toward the major, but may be used to satisfy preparation for the major and general education requirements, if applicable. A minimum of twelve upper division units must be completed at San Diego State University.

---

* Additional prerequisites are required for these courses.

LOWER DIVISION COURSES

[handwritten: 100-level courses are often introductory]

105. Intellectual Foundations of Asia   (3) I
An interdisciplinary survey of the philosophical and religious thought of South, Southeast, and East Asia and its application in theory and practice in traditional Asian societies. Not open to students with credit in Asian Studies 105A.

106. Cultural Heritage of Asia   (3) II
Social and cultural heritages of South, Southeast, and East Asian societies as revealed in art, drama, classical literatures, and folk traditions. Not open to students with credit in Asian Studies 105A.

107. Social Foundations of Modern Asia   (3) I, II
Social, economic, and political systems of South, Southeast, and East Asia in modern times. (Formerly numbered Asian Studies 105B.)

UPPER DIVISION COURSES
(Intended for Undergraduates)

[handwritten: Prerequisite courses must be completed before enrolling in this course.]

458. Asian Traditions   (3) I, II
Prerequisite: Six units of Asian-content courses or upper division standing.
Social, cultural, economic, and political traditions of South, Southeast, and East Asia; how they functioned in theory and practice prior to twentieth century. (Formerly numbered Asian Studies 458A.)

[handwritten: 3 credits/units]

459. Contemporary Asian Cultures   (3) II
Prerequisite: Six units of Asian-content courses or upper division standing.
Continuity and change in traditions and values of Asian societies in face of urbanization, modernization, and Westernization since mid-nineteenth century. (Formerly numbered Asian Studies 458B.)

[handwritten: 400-level courses are more advanced]

499. Special Study   (1-3)
Prerequisites: At least six units of upper division work completed toward the major or minor in Asian studies and the consent of the instructor.
Individual study. Maximum credit six units.

UPPER DIVISION COURSES
(Also Acceptable for Advanced Degree)

560. History of Japanese Business and Trade   (3) I, II
Prerequisites: Upper division standing and consent of instructor.
Japanese business and trade from 1600 to present. Emphasis on Japan's rapid economic development since 1868, interplay of social and economic forces, structure of Japanese business system, and problems of international trade.

596. Selected Studies in Asian Cultures   (3)
Topics on various aspects of Asian studies. May be repeated with new content. See Class Schedule for specific content. Limit of nine units of any combination of 296, 496, 596 courses applicable to a bachelor's degree. Maximum credit of six units of 596 applicable to a bachelor's degree. Maximum combined credit of six units of 596 and 696 applicable to a 30-unit master's degree.

GRADUATE COURSES
Refer to the Graduate Bulletin.

Exercise 11: Examine the following course descriptions from the Economics department. Then answer the questions that follow. Refer to the "Up Close: Reading Course Descriptions" for help if necessary.

CATALOG DESCRIPTION OF COURSES IN ECONOMICS

Economics
In the College of Arts and Letters

Faculty

Emeritus: Anderson, Barckley, Chadwick, Flagg, Jencks, Neuner, Turner
Chair: Gifford
Professors: Babilot, Boddy, Clement, Frantz, Gifford, Green, Kartman, Leasure, Madhavan, Name, Popp, Poroy, Sebold, Thayer, Venieris
Associate Professors: Grossbard-Shechtman, Hageman, Hambleton, Stewart
Assistant Professors: Naughton, Seidman, Singh, Villaflor, Vogt
Lecturer: Gerber

Offered by the Department

Master of Arts degree in economics.
Major in economics with the A.B. degree in liberal arts and sciences.
Minor in economics.

LOWER DIVISION COURSES

100. Contemporary Economic Problems   (3) I, II

Investigates economic bases for such current problems as inflation, unemployment, economic power, consumer protection, poverty, discrimination, urban and environmental deterioration, and international domination. Examines such policies as fiscal-monetary policy, tax reform and government controls and provision of services.

101. Principles of Economics   (3) I, II   (CAN ECON 2)

Prerequisites: Satisfactory completion of the English Placement Test, Writing Competency, Entry-Level Mathematics Examination, and Mathematics Competency requirements. Proof of completion of prerequisites required.

An introduction to principles of economic analysis, economic institutions, and issues of public policy. In this semester the emphasis is upon macroanalysis including national income analysis, money and banking, business cycles, and economic stabilization.

102. Principles of Economics   (3) I, II   (CAN ECON 4)

Prerequisites: Satisfactory completion of the English Placement Test, Writing Competency, Entry-Level Mathematics Examination, and Mathematics Competency requirements. Proof of completion of prerequisites required.

An introduction to principles of economic analysis, economic institutions, and issues of public policy. In this semester the emphasis is upon the direction of production, the allocation of resources, and the distribution of income, through the price system (microanalysis); and international economics.

201. Statistical Methods   (3) I, II

Prerequisite: Satisfaction of the Entry-Level Mathematics requirement and qualification on the Mathematics Placement Examination, Part I. Proof of completion of prerequisite required.

Introduction to descriptive statistics, statistical inference, regression and correlation. Students with credit or concurrent registration in another statistics course will be awarded a total of four units for the two (or more) courses.

296. Experimental Topics   (1-4)

Selected topics. May be repeated with new content. See Class Schedule for specific content. Limit of nine units of any combination of 296, 496, 596 courses applicable to a bachelor's degree.

UPPER DIVISION COURSES
(Intended for Undergraduates)

300. Honors Course   (1-3)

Refer to Honors Program.

307. Mathematical Economics   (3) II

Prerequisites: Economics 101, 102, and Mathematics 121 or 141 or 150.

Mathematical concepts as tools in understanding, developing and illustrating economic theories. Applications of calculus and linear equations to constrained optimization, macro models, elasticity, general equilibrium, and input-output analysis.

311. History of Economic Thought   (3)
Prerequisites: Economics 101 and 102.
The development of economics. Contributions of schools of thought and individual writers are examined with regard to their influence on economic theory and policy.

313. Marxian Economic Theory   (3)
Prerequisite: Six units in economics.
Analysis of the theories of Marx, Engels, Lenin, Mao Tse-tung, Baran, Sweezy and others as they pertain to the periods in which they were conceived and to modern times.

320. Intermediate Economic Theory   (3) I, II
Prerequisite: Economics 101, or Economics 100 with approval of department.
Economic theory with special reference to national income analysis and the theory of investment.

321. Intermediate Economic Theory   (3) I, II
Prerequisite: Economics 102 or Economics 100 with approval of department.
Economic theory with special reference to the theory of the firm and the industry; value and distribution.

330. Comparative Economic Systems   (3)
Prerequisite: Economics 100 or 101 or 102.
The economic aspects of laissez-faire and regulated capitalism, cooperatives, socialism, communism, nazism, fascism. Criteria for evaluating economic systems. The individual and government in each system. Planning in a liberal capitalistic society.

332. Capitalist Economy   (3)
Prerequisite: Economics 100 or 101 or 102.
The relationship between the dominant economic and political institutions of capitalist organization and the major social problems of modern capitalism.

336. Economic History of Emerging Nations   (3)
Prerequisite: Economics 100 or 101.
Evolution of economic organization, institutions, and policies of Africa, Asia, and Latin America. Regional emphasis will vary. Maximum credit six units.

338. Economic History of the United States   (3)
Prerequisites: Economics 100 or 101, and 102.
American economic development and national legislation. Studies of agriculture, industry, the labor force, and national output.

347. Research Design and Method   (3)
Prerequisites: Economics 101, 102 and 201. Recommended: Economics 320 and 321 and a computer related course such as Mathematics 107.
Instruction in the practical application of econometric techniques of economic research to range of problems encountered in economics. Independent research project.

360. International Economic Problems   (3)
Prerequisites: Economics 101 and 102. Not open to students with credit in Economics 561.
International problems, economic communities, organizations, and other selected topics.

365. Economics of Underdeveloped Areas   (3)
Prerequisite: Economics 102.
The nature and causes of economic underdevelopment. Problems of and policies for the economic development of underdeveloped areas of the world.

370. Government and Business   (3)
Prerequisite: Economics 100 or 102.
Governmental activities affecting business; the state as an entrepreneur and manager; governmental assistance to business; governmental regulation of business in its historical, legal and economic aspects, including recent developments in the United States and abroad; proposed policies. Not open to students with credit in Economics 476.

380. Labor Problems   (3) I, II
Prerequisite: Economics 100 or 101 or 102.
Labor organizations and their policies, wages, strikes, unemployment, social insurance, child labor, labor legislation, plans for industrial peace, and other labor problems.

Questions:

1. What do you have to do before you can take Econ 102?
2. Gloria is enrolled in a statistics class in the Business department. Can she apply the units from that course to satisfy the requirements of her Economics program?

3. John has taken Econ 296 for two semesters. He has six units. He wants to take Econ 496 this semester. Is this allowed?

4. You want to know more about economic theories for developing countries. What course would you take?

5. You have not yet taken Econ 100, 101, or 102. What course(s) in the Economics department can you take?

6. What are the "intro" classes? Which are most likely to be "seminar classes"?

PART THREE: TROUBLESHOOTING

It's not always easy for American students to adjust to life on a college campus. You can imagine, therefore, that it is doubly difficult for the non–English-speaking student. In addition to coping with the usual challenges of academic life, the ESL student must face the challenge of studying in a different language and culture. This section of the chapter highlights situations that are commonly difficult for ESL students and offers some advice on overcoming these obstacles.

LEARNING STRATEGY

Managing Your Learning: Anticipating potential problems you will face in college can help you deal with them more effectively.

Exercise 12: Think about the following situations and the advice you would give about dealing with them. This will help you to solve the problems that follow the exercise.

1. Roberto has had two years of college in his own country. He's wondering if those years will count towards his Bachelor's degree and what he should do to find the answer.

2. Juanita notices that her roommate is very depressed. She sleeps all day long, she is not eating, she doesn't want to talk, and she seems to be giving up on school. What can you do about that?

3. Shoji is a foreign student who would like to meet more American students. He has tried talking to students in his classes, but they don't really seem interested. He thinks it might be because his English is not good enough.

4. You noticed that a few of the students in your chemistry class were cheating on the mid-term exam. You're wondering if you should report it or not.

5. You're not doing well in your biology class, but you are too embarrassed to talk to a friend about it.

Choosing and Planning a Degree Program

Problem: You're not sure what courses you need, how many units to take, or whether any of your previous work will qualify for "transfer" to this school.

What you need to know:
- Most degree programs are based on credits (or units)—one credit/unit per hour of class attended. This usually amounts to three units per course for a school on the semester system. You need to complete a designated number to obtain a degree.
- Most Bachelor's degrees require about 120 units.
- Most undergraduate degrees require "general education" courses—a variety of courses in math, science, humanities, and social science.
- Many courses in your major will require "prerequisites." Check these very carefully when planning your program.
- Most schools will accept transferred units from another school, but you need to provide good documentation.

Where to go for help:
- Your academic adviser or the advising department
- The chairperson of your major
- The Office of Admissions and Records
- Other students
- The college catalog

Exercise 13:   Consult your college catalog to find the following information:
1. How many units are required for the degree that you want?
2. What prerequisite courses are required for upper division courses?
3. How many "elective" courses can you take?

Dealing with Stress and Depression

Problem: You're experiencing symptoms of stress—panic attacks, headaches, stomachaches, rapid heartbeat, anxiety. You're experiencing symptoms of depression—sleeping too much (or not being able to sleep), lack of appetite, thoughts about hurting yourself, sadness, and loneliness. You wonder what's going on, but you're afraid to tell anyone.

What you need to know:
- College students often experience stress or depression. It's hard being on your own, especially in a new country.
- Although you may feel as though you are "going crazy," you are probably having a normal adjustment reaction.

Where to go for help:
- If you are having physical symptoms, go to the health services office and see a doctor.
- If you are not having physical problems, but you feel sad or anxious, you can go to the counseling office on campus. An experienced professional will be happy to talk to you. Many students use these services.
- Many campuses offer "support groups" for students who have similar problems. Ask at the counseling office.

Exercise 14: Select a member of your class to call the counseling office to find out if individual or group counseling is offered. Then ask that student to report back to the class.

Making American Friends

Problem: You would like to meet other students, but you are not having any success.

What you need to know:
- American students are often very busy. Many of them must work _and_ study. Some of them already have friends here from high school.
- Some American students have not had a lot of experience with people from other cultures, so they may be shy or cautious when they first meet someone from a different culture.
- A university campus has many, many opportunities to interact with other students. Here are some campus groups you can join:

  —a sports club or team
  —a language club (e.g., The French Club)
  —a religious organization
  —a political organization

Where to go for help:
- Consult your college catalog.
- Read the college newspaper.
- Read the bulletin boards on campus for interesting events.

Exercise 15: Find out what social opportunities are available on your campus. Go to at least one organizational meeting of a club or group that interests you. Put together a resource manual for other ESL students that describes these groups.

Dealing with Academic Concerns

Problem: You are failing a course.

What you need to know:
- Your school does not want you to fail your classes, so it offers a number of services to help you pass them.
- Most schools base their grading system on a 4.0 system as follows:

  A = 4.0
  B = 3.0
  C = 2.0
  D = 1.0

  When your grade point average (GPA) falls below 2.0, most schools will place you on "academic probation," which means that you will have one or two semesters to improve your GPA.

Where to go for help:
- Go to the academic skills center on campus or find a tutor for specific help in your subject matter.
- Speak with a school counselor.
- Speak with an advisor to help you choose a better combination of classes so you are not overwhelmed.
- Speak to your instructor. He or she may agree to give you extra help, or have you do an additional assignment to make up for a poor grade.

Exercise 16: Find out what your school's academic probation policy is. Find out where the academic skills center is.

Exercise 17: Compute Megan's GPA for the year based on the following grades. (Each course was a 3-unit course.)

FALL SEMESTER GRADES:		SPRING SEMESTER GRADES:	
English 101	B	Geology 101	C
Psychology 100	C	Economics 201	C
History 200	A	Anthropology 101	D
Chemistry 127	B	Western Civ 175	A

Problem: Cheating during exams

What you need to know:
- Most colleges will penalize students who cheat.
- Usually, the instructor decides what to do about it.
- You could be expelled from school if you are caught cheating.
- Plagiarism is also cheating. (See Chapters 3 and 4 in this book for more details.)

Where to go for help:
- If you want to know your school's policy regarding cheating, consult the catalog.
- If you observe others cheating, you can speak with them directly, talk to the instructor, or consult an advisor or counselor for guidance.

Exercise 18: Find out more about your school's policy on cheating.

Dealing with Housing Concerns

Problem: You live on campus and you are having problems with your roommate. You are a serious student and your roommate is not—she has many friends in the room, and she stays up late listening to music and watching television.

What you need to know:
- You do not need to tolerate this situation. There are many options available to you.
- Many problems like this one can be resolved by discussing them directly with your roommate.

Where to go for help:
- Begin by talking to the Residential Advisor (RA) in your hall.
- If you are unable to work it out at that level, consult the Residential Director (RD) or the Director of Residential Life.

Exercise 19: In small groups, discuss some of the problems that you may have had with roommates, either in this country or in your own, and how these problems were resolved.

Gaining Expertise

1. Organize a "college fair" day. Ask each student in your class to find information about a local or out-of-town college or university in the United States. College catalogs from colleges outside your city are often available in the library. Then ask each student to present a short description of the school to the class.
2. Select one academic discipline and find out the requirements for a degree in that area and the jobs that might be available to a graduate with that degree. Be ready to present that information to the class in writing or orally.
3. Identify both the advantages and the disadvantages of the college experience in the United States. Compare them to those of a college experience in your country. Present this information in writing or orally in small groups.

EVALUATING YOUR PROGRESS

Prepare a brief guide to your college for new, incoming ESL students. Cover the topics presented in this chapter as well as any other information that is pertinent to your school. Provide practical, useful information about professors, degree programs, campus services, campus policies, and nonacademic programs. Be sure to include a glossary of any words or terms that might be difficult for new students to understand.

Tightening the Nuts and Bolts

Chapter Theme: Intercultural Communication

This chapter provides a review of the "nuts and bolts" of academic success—the fundamental skills that every college student needs in order to be successful. You will find explanations and exercises for reading and marking academic texts, for taking useful in-class notes and completing tests. As you work through this chapter, keep in mind that you have probably already acquired many of these skills—either during school in your own country or in an ESL class.

The theme of this chapter is intercultural communication—interacting with people from different cultures. As our world operates more and more on a global level, the ability to communicate effectively with people from cultures that are different from our own will be extremely important. As a person from a different culture in the United States, you have first-hand experience of what it is like to live and study in a foreign culture.

Many of the readings on intercultural communication in this chapter will be "academic," which means that they are written in an objective, scholarly way and intended for use in an academic setting. These types of readings have been chosen to prepare you for college work. Bear in mind, however, as you work through the readings, that your own cross-cultural experiences will help you understand what you read. Thus, you can share your cultural experiences while you become a better reader, note taker, and test taker.

ACADEMIC TOPICS

- Reading for Learning
- Previewing Texts
- Highlighting Texts
- Annotating Texts
- Taking Lecture Notes
- Taking Tests

CHAPTER THEME

Intercultural Communication

TAKING INVENTORY: YOUR EXPERIENCES

IT WORKS!
Learning Strategy:
Identifying
what you
already know

The following questions ask you to think about your own experiences and attitudes about life in the United States. Reflecting on these will also prepare you for the readings on cross-cultural awareness in this chapter. Be honest in your responses—there are no right or wrong answers to these questions. Record your answers in a journal if you wish.

1. What are some of the things that you worry about as a college student in the United States?
2. Describe your own experience making friends in this country. Where are your friends from?
3. Compare the "pace" (how quickly things go) of this country with the pace in your culture. If there are differences, how do they affect you?

4. What does the term "culture" mean to you? How does a person acquire "culture"?

5. What types of strategies have you used to communicate more effectively with people from cultures different from your own?

PART ONE: DEVELOPING STUDY READING SKILLS

LEARNING STRATEGY

Personalizing: Identifying your study habits can help you to recognize your strengths and weaknesses.

TAKING INVENTORY: YOUR TEXTBOOK READING STUDY HABITS

It's important that students develop techniques for reading textbooks efficiently. Before looking at some of those techniques, take inventory of your own study habits. Check Yes, No, or Sometimes after each of the following statements to reflect your current study habits. (If you are not taking a college class at the moment, then think about what you do in your English language classes.) Then consult the following "Feedback" section to learn more about your own study habits.

> **Threads**
>
> When we read too fast or too slowly, we understand nothing.
>
> Blaise Pascal

1. I look at the title page of the textbook or chapter I am reading to determine the author, title, and the date and place of publication.

   Yes ☐   No ☐   Sometimes ☐

2. I look at the text quickly first to find out what it's mainly about before reading it more carefully.

   Yes ☐   No ☐   Sometimes ☐

3. I first read the sections that interest me most.

   Yes ☐   No ☐   Sometimes ☐

4. I prefer not to write in my textbooks.

   Yes ☐   No ☐   Sometimes ☐

5. I read every word of the text carefully, and I look up most of the words I don't know in a dictionary.

   Yes ☐   No ☐   Sometimes ☐

6. I read a text more than once.

   Yes ☐   No ☐   Sometimes ☐

Now compare your answers with the following explanations.

YOUR TEXTBOOK READING
STUDY HABITS: FEEDBACK

1. I look at the title page of the textbook or chapter I am reading to determine author, title, and the date and place of publication.

   It's usually a good idea to read the title page, which provides important information. For example, the date of publication helps you know if the information in the text is up to date. You can also locate other useful information such as the author's academic affiliation, usually printed under his or her name, to find out where that author teaches.

2. I look at the text quickly first to find out what it's mainly about before reading it more carefully.

   Flipping quickly through a chapter and reading the main headings can help acquaint you with the contents of the text. This practice familiarizes you with the text's overall organization and helps you predict what you will be reading later. You can also identify the most important sections by noting the size and boldness of the section headings.

3. I first read the sections that interest me most.

   Many students go directly to the sections that interest them the most. There is nothing wrong with this technique—it gets you interested in the text. Just be sure that you don't forget to read the other sections!

4. I prefer not to write in my textbooks.

   The textbook is a learning device. You will be more engaged and learn more from your reading if you write in your book (that is, provided that the book is your own and not borrowed from the library!). Many students use "highlighters" to mark important passages. Writing notes in the margins of the pages is also useful—a word or two will indicate the main idea of that section or comment on the content. These annotations help you remember what you have read, hold your attention, and help you retrieve information later.

5. I read every word of the text carefully, and I look up all the words I don't know in a dictionary.

   Since it's not unusual to have to read 50-100 pages a day, you can be sure to find many words that are new to you. If you look up each of those words in a dictionary, you will have difficulty finishing your reading assignments, and you will likely have problems keeping the meaning of the text in your memory. It's best to try to guess the meaning of words from the context of the reading. Look up only those words that you need to make the passage clear or those technical terms that are repeated throughout the text.

6. I read a text more than once.

   One of the best ways to learn material from a textbook is to read it more than once. Usually it's a good idea to read for the "gist"—the general idea—the first time you read the text. Then later you can go back and read for details, mark the text more completely, and take notes from it. The types of reading strategies you use will depend on the purpose of your reading—are you reading to prepare for a test? To write a paper? To find the answer to a specific question? For your own knowledge?

Previewing a Text

Previewing a text before you begin reading it carefully is like consulting a map before driving in a new city. It helps you to orient yourself so you won't get lost. Taking a few moments to scan the contents of your reading assignment or textbook quickly can help you navigate through the reading.

Begin with the "front matter" of a text, which includes the title page, the preface, and the table of contents. Turn to the title page of the textbook reading from *Intercultural Communication: A Reader* (p. 61). The title page indicates that there are two authors of this book, and that both authors are affiliated with large universities in California. You may wonder why this information is important, but most Americans know that there are many immigrants living and working in California. The issue of intercultural communication is an important one in California, so the authors' affiliation with a California university is pertinent.

Other important sections to survey before beginning to read a text carefully are the following:

- **The title page:** Look for the author, the academic affiliation, the date of the publication. The date is important because it lets you know how current the information in the text is.
- **The preface:** Skim the preface of the text to determine if the author has selected a specific approach to a text.
- **The table of contents:** This section outlines the text. Skim to find out which topics are covered and which are not.
- **The section headings:** Each chapter will likely have section headings that provide clues to the contents of those sections. Read the initial sentences of each section to determine the main ideas of each.
- **The glossary:** Many textbooks have glossaries that provide valuable definitions for technical vocabulary words.
- **The index:** The index at the end of a text lists topics alphabetically that are treated in the text. If you are looking for specific information, consult the index first to find out if the text covers it.

LEARNING STRATEGY

Managing Your Learning: Previewing a text before reading it helps to identify the organization and the main themes.

Exercise 1: Imagine that you have just bought this textbook, *Strategies for Academic Communication.* Preview the text to answer the following questions.

1. Who is the author? Does she have an academic affiliation?
2. Is this a current textbook?
3. Does this textbook have a specific approach?
4. How many chapters are there?
5. List major skills addressed in the text.
6. Is there a glossary? If so, what kind of vocabulary is included?
7. Are there readings? If so, what are the themes of the readings?

Exercise 2: Preview the reading, "The Foreign Student Today: A Profile," (p. 80) and then answer the questions that follow.

1. Based on the date of publication, would you say the information contained in this article is (a) too old to be useful, (b) outdated, but still valid, or (c) very current and up to date?
2. What is the author's background? Is she qualified to address this topic? How do you know?
3. Name the major topics covered in the article.
4. Note the quote found at the beginning of the article. What is the purpose of the quote?

Identifying Your Purpose in Reading

When you read a novel, you usually do so for pleasure. You can read it quickly, skip parts that don't interest you, and even go to the last page before you have finished it. If you use those reading strategies for your college class assignments, you will probably have some difficulty doing well in the class. That's because study reading requires reading strategies that are quite different from those required of pleasure reading.

When your instructor tells you to read a chapter in a textbook, you need to ask yourself these questions: What am I expected to do with this reading? How will I be required to use this information? Usually, your instructor will make the purpose of your reading clear, or it will be stated clearly on your course outline. But if it's not clear to you, make sure that you find out.

Common purposes for academic reading:
- To prepare for an "objective" (multiple-choice, fill-in-the-blank, matching) test
- To prepare for an "essay" test
- To secure background knowledge, which won't be tested but will be necessary for understanding future readings
- To secure information for a paper
- To secure information for a class presentation
- To secure information for a class discussion

LEARNING STRATEGY

Managing Your Learning: Identifying the purpose of your reading will help you to choose an appropriate strategy for learning the material.

Exercise 3: In pairs or small groups, brainstorm how your reading strategies would be different for each of the purposes stated in the explanation above. For example, how would your study reading differ in preparing for a multiple-choice test and an essay test? What techniques would you use to prepare for each of those tasks?

SURVIVAL TIPS: THE TEXTBOOK

The most common texts for undergraduate students and introductory courses are thick **introductory books** written for a college class. These include a great deal of information, chapter questions, summary sections, illustrations and photos, and glossaries.

Some instructors choose **more scholarly texts** instead of or in addition to a college textbook. These texts are often used for upper division and graduate classes because they represent the work of experts in the subject matters. In contrast to introductory textbooks, these books each present one author's viewpoint, often focus on research, and are more difficult to understand.

Still another type of "textbook" is the **packet of readings**—a collection of articles and chapters selected by the professor from a variety of sources, reproduced in packet form for use in the class.

Be sure to buy your books as early as you can. The bookstore may run out of them if they haven't ordered enough copies.

Highlighting a Text

Once you have previewed your text, the next step is to begin reading more carefully. Highlighting can help you do this. Most university students own and use **highlighters**—markers that are brightly colored and used to set off a portion of a text. When used properly, highlighting can be an excellent study aid for two reasons. First, it helps the reader to prioritize information and to distinguish between what's important to remember and what's not. Second, it makes it very easy later on to retrieve the important information without rereading the entire text.

But there's one serious problem with highlighters. They are so easy to use— they just glide across the page—that some students end up highlighting everything! Then, of course, the highlighting technique is useless because the reader has not made any decisions about what's important and what's not. Also, when it comes time for reviewing that text for the test, there's no way of knowing which sections are important for the test.

Tips for proper highlighting:
- Make sure you know the purpose of your reading. Ask yourself as you begin to highlight: "What do I need to know? What's important for the test or paper?"
- Highlighting can help when you prepare for tests. If you are reading for a multiple-choice test, highlight definitions, names, dates, events, lists, causes and effects, similarities, and differences. (Techniques for test-taking will be discussed in Part Three of this chapter.)
- If you are reading for an essay test, make sure you highlight broad themes, main ideas, summaries, conclusions, definitions, and analyses.
- Avoid highlighting unfamiliar vocabulary.

HIGHLIGHTING FOR FACTUAL AND/OR HISTORICAL INFORMATION

Note how the following text was highlighted for factual information. (Highlighted sections are in italics.)

The Foreign Student Today: A Profile
by Jill Bulthuis

As early as the *Middle Ages students and professors were going abroad in search of academic opportunities* unavailable at home and accepting the challenge of adapting to strange people and customs. *The history of foreign students on United States campuses* can be traced to the colonial colleges, but beginning with *Francisco de Miranda, who studied at Yale as early as 1784, foreign students came to this country as individual sojourners.* Although their *numbers were significant enough to be included in statistics early in this century, they were considered unusual and exotic* due in part perhaps to their English pronunciation or their distinctive styles of dress (Barber, 1985).

Highlight dates, times, and important people

A massive *acceleration of the movement of students and scholars began after World War II, although foreign students did not begin to appear in significant numbers until the 1950s* (Barber, 1985). With this large influx, which represented a wide cross section of society, certain problems became apparent in the adjustment of some students concerning English language skills, and financial support. Their reasons for coming to the United States persist among today's foreign students, and in many cases the challenges they face persist as well. Spaulding and Flack (1976) concluded that the major reasons foreign students come to the United States ① are to get an advanced education or training not available at home, ② to gain prestige with a degree from a U.S. institution, ③ to take advantage of available scholarship funds, ④ to escape unsettled political or economic conditions, ⑤ and to learn about the United States.

Highlight dates

Enumerate reasons

HIGHLIGHTING FOR IDEAS

Note how a student reading for ideas would highlight the same text differently. In this case, trends and conclusions are highlighted. (Highlighted material is in italics.)

The Foreign Student Today: A Profile
by Jill Bulthuis

Highlight causes

As early as the Middle Ages students and professors were going abroad in search of academic opportunities unavailable at home and accepting the challenge of adapting to strange people and customs. The history of foreign students on United States campuses can be traced to the colonial colleges, but beginning with Francisco de Miranda, who studied at Yale *as early as 1784, foreign students came to this country as individual sojourners.* Although their numbers were significant enough to be included in statistics early in this century, they were considered unusual and exotic due in part perhaps to their English pronunciation or their distinctive styles of dress (Barber, 1985).

A massive acceleration of the movement of students and scholars began after World War II, although foreign students did not begin to appear in significant numbers until the 1950s (Barber, 1985). With this large influx, which represented a wide cross section of society, certain problems became apparent in the adjustment of some students concerning English language skills, and financial support. *Their reasons for coming to the United States persist among today's foreign students,* and in many cases the challenges they face persist as well. Spaulding and Flack (1976) concluded that *the major reasons foreign students come to the United States are to get an advanced education or training not available at home, to gain prestige with a degree from a U.S. institution, to take advantage of available* *Highlight conclusions* *scholarship funds, to escape unsettled political or economic conditions, and to learn about the United States.*

Exercise 4: Read the following text on defining culture and then answer the questions that follow.

Some Definitions of Culture
by L. Samovar and R. Porter

If culture were a single thing, we would need only one definition. . . . Because culture is so broad in its scope, scholars have had a difficult time arriving at one central theory or definition of what it is.

Hoebel and Frost see culture in nearly all human activity. They define culture as an "integrated system of learned behavior patterns which are characteristic of the members of a society and which are not the result of biological inheritance." For them culture is not genetically predetermined; it is noninstinctive. . . . All scholars of culture begin with this same assumption—that is, that culture is learned.

. . . From a definition that includes all learned behavior we can move to definitions that propose culture has tangible boundaries. But here again scholars have not agreed on the boundaries. Some, such as Triandis, take an expansive view of culture, suggesting that culture "can be distinguished as having both objective (e.g., roads, tools) and subjective (e.g., norms, laws, values) aspects." Those who define culture in this way look at what a culture does to its environment as well as what it does to its people.

Cole and Scribner offer a definition of culture that ties culture to human cognition. . . . Hofstede has advanced another definition of culture that views culture from a psychological perspective: "Culture is the collective programming of the mind which distinguishes the members of one category of people from another." Both of these definitions stress the mental conditions that cultural experiences impose.

The lack of agreement on any one definition of culture led anthropologists Kroeber and Kluckhorhn to review some five hundred definitions, phrasings, and uses of the concept. From their analysis they proposed the following definition:

> Culture consists of patterns, explicit and implicit, of and for behavior acquired and transmitted by symbols, constituting the distinctive achievements of human groups, including their embodiments in artifacts; the essential core of culture consists of traditional (i.e., historically derived and selected) ideas and especially their attached values; culture systems may, on the one hand, be considered as products of action, and on the other as conditioning elements of further action.

> Larry A. Samovar and Richard E. Porter, *Communication between Cultures.*
> Wadsworth Publishing Co., 1991.

Questions:
1. Highlight the text to prepare for a **brief multiple-choice and matching** test requiring you to recognize the basic ideas of each definition of culture and to identify the author of each.
2. Highlight in a different color to prepare for **an essay** in which you are asked to define the term culture as you see it, drawing on the definitions included in the reading. Be ready to explain your point of view.

Exercise 5: Highlight the section on The Ingredients of Communication in the reading, "Basic Principles of Intercultural Communication" (pp. 65–68). Imagine that you are preparing for a matching test.

Exercise 6: Highlight the section on Culture and Communication from the reading, "Basic Principles of Intercultural Communication" (pp. 71–77). Imagine that you are preparing for a test in which you are required to define key concepts.

Exercise 7: Highlight the section on Context and Communication from the reading, "Basic Principles of Intercultural Communication" (pp. 77–78). Imagine that you are preparing for a seminar class discussion on communication, in which you are asked to discuss the context of your own culture.

Annotating a Text

As you may well know, highlighting is not the only strategy used in study reading. Many students write brief notes called "annotations" in the margins of their books. Like highlighting, these annotations are useful for both identifying important information while reading and also for retrieving key material after reading. Annotating a text can also keep your reading active rather than passive.

The kinds of notes that you will make in the margins of your text will depend on what you are looking for in your reading. Here are some examples:

- **Key information.** If you are reading a text with lots of factual information, you may want to simply note key words to indicate the placement of important information. You can also circle or bracket key terms or signals. These annotations are very useful in preparing for multiple-choice and short-answer tests because your notes identify the placement of key information in a text and make it easier to find later.
- **Main ideas.** In many texts, it is helpful to note the main ideas of passages, paragraph by paragraph.
- **Key concepts, questions, comments.** If you are reading something theoretical or controversial, you may want to make personal responses in the margins, recording a thought or opinion that came into your head while reading. You can also use margin notes to summarize information. Questions that occur to you while reading can also be jotted down in the margin. This type of annotation is valuable in preparing for essay tests and papers.

AN EXAMPLE OF ANNOTATION

Note how this student has used both kinds of annotations in the following text on foreign students. Key words on the left, along with circling and bracketing, indicate major points. Questions and comments on the right reflect the reader's personal reactions.

Key Info/Main Ideas

For stus. more concerned abt. acad. than non-acad.

Profile of most satisf. stu: G.A., good English, Westerner, Am. roommate

Perhaps the most consistent generalizations about foreign students in the United States are those of Iowa State University sociologist, Motoki Lee (1981), who surveyed 2,000 foreign students about their most important and best satisfied needs. Lee developed a profile of the student most likely to have a satisfying educational experience in the United States: A Latin American or European graduate assistant who has good English skills, an American roommate, and a job waiting at home. In general, Lee found that foreign students place much greater importance on their academic and professional goals than they do on nonacademic concerns. Although students were generally satisfied with their progress toward academic goals, their lack of practical work experience and uncertainty about careers were matters of great concern.

Key concepts

Am. roommate? Interesting! How abt contact w/ stus. from own culture?

Acad. & financial probs. greatest

Personal experience lends support to Lee's findings. Even students who have suffered serious problems with housing, for example, or with the banking system, the Internal Revenue Service or with the Immigration and Naturalization Service are inclined to rate academic and financial problems as the most difficult. Foreign student loan funds on many U.S. campuses have kept numerous foreign students afloat while they were waiting for stipends delayed by international conflicts that frequently affect currency transfer controls abroad or when personal or family emergencies have placed unusual demands on their finances.

How true! Money is a problem.

LEARNING STRATEGY

Managing Your Learning: Making annotations (notes) in the margins of a text can help you identify main themes and respond to the information in the text.

Exercise 8: Read and annotate the article, "Definitions of Culture" from Exercise 4 of this chapter. Annotate the main ideas only.

Exercise 9: Read and annotate the section, "Concerns of Foreign Students," from the optional reading, "Foreign Students Today: A Profile" at the end of this chapter. Use the left-right technique demonstrated above to respond to the following tasks.

1. **Key Information:** Imagine that you are preparing for a short-answer test on concerns that foreign students have.
2. **Key Concepts:** Imagine that you are preparing for an essay test on the concerns of foreign students. You know that your professor likes you to think creatively on your own and present your own opinion, even if it is not in agreement with the point of view expressed in the reading.

Exercise 10: Read, highlight, and annotate the selection, "How Cultures Teach," from Chapter 1 (pp. 6–7), using the left/right technique described above.

Managing Vocabulary

Nothing is more frustrating than looking at an assigned reading and being faced with one new vocabulary word after another. Many students resort to their dictionaries for help, writing a definition for each word in the margins. This practice is very time consuming. It also gets in the way of smooth reading, and in the end it's difficult to remember what the main ideas were.

It's important to maintain a balance in dealing with new vocabulary. This means that you can't ignore every word you encounter, but you can't look up every new word either. If you can develop some techniques that will help you quickly assess whether that word is important or not, your reading will likely improve.

Tips on vocabulary management:
- **Use textbook glossaries of technical words and important terms, often found at the end of the book (in the "back matter").** If a word is listed in the glossary of your textbook, it's probably an important one.
- **Look up only essential words.** If you encounter a word only once, and you don't experience confusion or discomfort by not knowing its meaning, don't bother looking it up in the dictionary. If it's an important word, it will reappear and you can decide at that point if it's an essential one.
- **Look up words in topic sentences.** Sentences that contain the main idea of a passage are important.
- **Look up words that appear in a title, a heading, or in bold print in the text.** Words such as these are usually important. Look up these words and write their definitions down in your book.
- **Make a note of any words your instructor uses in class** that you also find in your textbook. These words are important and will likely appear on a test.

LEARNING STRATEGY

Overcoming Limitations: Resisting the temptation to look up every word in a dictionary and developing techniques for determining which words are important will help you increase your reading efficiency.

Exercise 11: The following paragraph on university policy probably contains many words that are new to you. Imagine that you received this notice from your university the day of an important exam. You have very little time to read it (you need to get back to your studying), but you want to make sure that you don't miss important information.

Decide which words you **must** look up, which words would be **useful** to know and which ones are really not that important. Base your decisions on the frequency with which they appear in the paragraph and the degree to which they relate to the main idea of the paragraph.

Auditing Policies

Students who are planning to audit a course this trimester need to keep in mind that auditing a class does not provide them with any credit. Their performance in this class will not be graded, so their GPA for the year will not be affected. It is also vital to know that the professor is not obligated in any way to correct the papers or exams of students who are auditing. With budget cuts augmenting class size, all professors—tenured and adjunct—are teaching very large classes and their time is limited.

It is recommended that **upper division** students refrain from auditing more than one course per academic year to keep class sizes to a minimum. It is further recommended that **lower division** students concentrate on completing general requirements before they begin dabbling in auditing. If you require further information, consult your advisor during office hours or pick up "Guidelines for Auditing" from the Registrar's Office.

Gaining Expertise

Activity One: If you are currently enrolled in a non-ESL college class, photocopy one of the chapters in a textbook that you have read and highlighted or annotated. Include a brief description of how that material is used in the class. Then exchange chapters with a partner. Assess your partner's highlighting and annotating, indicating both strengths and weaknesses.

Activity Two: Highlight, annotate, and look up essential vocabulary for the reading, "Basic Principles of Intercultural Communication" (p. 62). Imagine that you are preparing for a short-answer and essay test on intercultural communication.

PART TWO: TAKING NOTES IN CLASS

In this section of the chapter you will be learning more about listening to class lectures and taking notes.

TAKING INVENTORY: YOUR NOTE-TAKING STUDY HABITS IN CLASS

Before you begin examining specific techniques for improving note-taking in class, find out what your habits are. Check Yes, No, or Sometimes after each of the following statements. (If you are not taking a university class now, think about what you do in your ESL classes.) Then compare your answers with the "feedback" explanations that follow.

1. I take notes when a professor is giving a lecture.

    Yes ☐   No ☐   Sometimes ☐

2. I take notes during a class discussion.

    Yes ☐   No ☐   Sometimes ☐

3. I take notes in complete sentences.

    Yes ☐   No ☐   Sometimes ☐

4. I review my notes after class and add missing details.

    Yes ☐   No ☐   Sometimes ☐

5. I tape-record class lectures.

    Yes ☐   No ☐   Sometimes ☐

YOUR STUDY HABITS: FEEDBACK

1. I take notes when a professor is giving a lecture.

    If you don't take notes in a lecture class, you are missing very important information. Professors often lecture about what they believe is most important—and this means that they may present information in a lecture that they will put in a test or require in a paper. In their lectures professors often present certain information, such as recent research, that you will not find in your readings.

2. I take notes during a class discussion.

    Many students who take careful notes during a lecture put their pencils down when the class is discussing a topic. They stop taking notes because they think that only the professor has something to say worth remembering. It's true that you don't need to take detailed notes during class discussions, but it's still a good idea to write down the general themes and ideas presented. These ideas might appear on tests, and they may also help you to think about the subject material.

3. I take notes in complete sentences.

    There is really nothing wrong with writing notes in complete sentences—if you can write that fast! Students usually find that if they write in complete sentences they can't keep up with the fast pace of the lecture. It's recommended, therefore, that you learn to use abbreviations and symbols in your note-taking. Then after class you can return to your notes and edit them to make them clearer and more complete.

4. I review my notes after class and add missing details.

Studies have shown that students retain information better if they review their notes once after a lecture and then again before the test. Certainly you have noticed how easy it is to forget information. Reviewing your notes is one way to help refresh your memory.

5. I tape-record class lectures.

Many students find that they benefit from this practice, but be sure that you ask the instructor's permission to tape beforehand. Some instructors do not want their lectures taped.

Identifying the Parts of a Lecture

When your professor lectures, he or she has important information to convey, and it is your job to continuously ask yourself, "What am I supposed to learn from this lecture? What's the professor's purpose?" Let those questions guide you as you take your lecture notes.

There are usually three main parts to a class lecture:

1. **Opening remarks** can include information about assignments, review of previous material, questions about the previous lecture, or announcements of community events that are pertinent to the class.

2. The **body of the lecture** develops the information. It accomplishes this in a number of ways, depending on the subject matter, usually by using some or all of the following:

   • **Definitions**—The lecture may be an extended definition of one concept—for example, *culture*, or a series of important, but shorter definitions.

   • **Examples and facts**—The lecturer may provide you with facts and examples in order to clarify a complex topic, such as photosynthesis.

   • **Explanations of theories**—This could be a presentation of competing or complementary theories.

   • **Chronology and/or lists**—The lecturer might provide some historical perspective or lists of component parts.

3. The **wrap-up** is the final part of the lecture, usually very brief; it may include questions, discussion, and last-minute assignments. Important information may be relayed during these final minutes, so don't close your notebook too soon. Professors who run out of time may cram a great deal of information into those final five minutes.

SURVIVAL TIPS: THE COLLEGE LECTURE

An important part of your academic experience will be the college lecture. No doubt you have attended lectures—classes in which a professor does most of the talking and students take notes—in your own country. While not all university classes follow the lecture model, many introductory and required courses do. Here are some tips for coping with the college lecture.

• **Evaluate your lecturer's style.** Not all lecturers are equal. Some are very skillful at communicating their information in an organized and clear fashion. Others, unfortunately, are less organized and less concise, and some move away from the topic—or "digress," as students say. You need to be aware of your professor's lecture style so that you can take appropriate notes.

Threads

Lecture attendance is nearly mandatory for success. Insist on getting a course syllabus—study it, follow it!

George Mansfield, professor

- **Find out if the lecture material will be tested.** Some professors lecture from the textbook, which means you can rely on your textbook to supplement the lecture. Others expect you to learn the textbook material independently, never mention the textbook in class, and instead bring in information from other sources, which will appear on the test. Still other professors never test students on information presented in lectures.
- **Take notes during class discussions.** Lectures sometimes turn into class discussions. Don't turn off your attention at this point, because valuable information often comes from these discussions that may appear on the test.

Law students busily taking notes in a lecture class.

Exercise 12: Pay careful attention to the lecture style of one of your instructors. Note the style—does he or she stay on the topic? Is the class largely lecture, or is there a great deal of discussion? What is (was) your reaction to this style—easy to follow? difficult to follow? why? What strategies can (did) you use to get the most out of the lecture and take notes?

Exercise 13: Read the following transcript from a section on a lecture about business and culture. Identify the sections in the script in which the lecturer "digresses" or moves away from the intended topic. Note how the lecturer then returns to the topic of the lecture.

"Yesterday we looked at general principles of cultural differences. Today, I'd like to talk a bit about the work of Geert Hofstede, who compared employees from 40 countries. All these workers were employed by the same multinational company. From now on we'll be concentrating on culture as it applies to business.

"In his study, Hofstede found that these employees were quite different in four different areas. The first was something he called "power distance." Basically this refers to how easily the employee accepts that power differentials are going to exist within an organization. I often wonder if men and women differ in this regard. It occurs to me that men might be more willing to accept a hierarchy and that women, who tend to work less competitively, may see less of a need for that. But that's just an aside, really. I haven't seen any studies on that.

"Okay. The second criterion is something called uncertainty avoidance, referring to the ability to endure ambiguity and uncertainty. For example, some cultures place more value on having a stable career track and conforming. Other cultures value the individual's ability to move upward in a career by changing jobs, risking job security for advancement.

"The third criterion is individualism. Does anyone have an idea about how the United States ranks on this one? U.S. corporations have been criticized for too much individualism and not enough cooperative group work. You read about it in the news a great deal lately. In fact, last night I was watching Public Television and there was a documentary comparing Japanese, German, and U.S. manufacturing plants. It was an interesting program. Maybe I can bring it in for us to watch."

NOTE: This lecture will be continued later in the chapter.

Learning Abbreviated Note-Taking

One of the gravest errors you can make while you're taking lecture notes is to function as a secretary, writing down everything the professor says, word for word, in complete sentences. Not only is this very difficult to do, but it also requires you to put your full attention on the words rather than the ideas presented in the lecture.

Here are some techniques to avoid this trap and to become a better and more efficient notetaker:

1. **Use abbreviations and symbols whenever possible.** Below are some common abbreviations and symbols. Add your own to this list as you learn them throughout this chapter.

and	&	_____
between	betw	_____
concerning	re	_____
for example	e.g.	_____
important	impt	_____
information	info	_____
international	int'l	_____
said	sd	_____
therefore	∴	_____
with	w/	_____
without	w/o	_____
would	wd	_____
years	yrs	_____

Exercise 14: You will need to invent your own abbreviations and symbols for the specific subject matter of your courses. Practice on the lecture below, which is the continuation of the lecture on business and culture from page 39. Read the script and abbreviate the underlined words. Share your abbreviations with a partner and add any useful ones to the list above.

"The final cultural dimension described by Hofstede is "masculinity." In general, this concept refers to how assertive a society is, how much emphasis the society places on things, money, instead of people.

"Let's look now at the results of Hofstede's research. As you can imagine, Hofstede discovered differences among workers from different cultures. Here's what he found for the United States: below average for power distance, quite a bit below average for uncertainty avoidance, of course, extremely high for individualism and above average for masculinity.

"We're out of time now, but next week we'll look at how other countries fared on this scale of cultural dimensions."

2. **Arrange information on the page** to represent the relationships among ideas and information in a visual way.

Compare the following two examples of student notes. Which example do you find easier and quicker to read? Why?

Student A (a verbatim record of what the lecturer said):

Six ways that we make the personal choices that shape our lives. Six basic ways that people choose their values. Systems based on authority, where one has complete faith in an external authority. Another based on deductive logic, using reasoning. The third is through sense experience. The fourth is by emotion, through feeling that something is right. The fifth is intuition, by unconscious knowing. Finally, some values based on science, by knowing through scientific method.

Student B (a list form of what the lecturer said):

Six ways to choose values:
> *1—authority (faith in ext. autho)*
> *2—deductive logic (reasoning)*
> *3—sense exper.*
> *4—emotion (feeling it's right)*
> *5—intuition (uncons. knowing)*
> *6—science (sci method)*

Note how the list form makes it easier to find important points. You can see how the student indented (moved the margin in several spaces) under the heading, "Six ways to choose values." Indented material is more specific.

Here are some common ways in which lecture material can be arranged on the page other than in paragraph form. Note that in all cases the main topic of the lecture is clearly written at the top of the page.

a. **Use bullets (•) and stars (*)** to outline key points. Stars are a good way to show that a point is especially important. Note how each bulleted item is indented under a more general heading.

Underlying assumptions of value systems based on science:

- *life is problem solving*
- *problem solving requires good managmt, self-improvmt*
- *these demand realism*
- *studying facts = secrets of nature*
- *we can have power and control*
- *experts have access to the knowledge*
- *new techniques are the best*
- *these are complex*
- *change is healthy*
- *technical knowledge can transform world*

*** essential to 20th century American values

b. Chains: Chains can be used to show the position of things in time or in relation to causes and effects.

Stages of adjustment for foreign students:

c. Maps: Maps are a good way to link details with general topics. Since they are not linear on a page, maps allow the notetaker to add information as the lecturer presents it, which may not always be given sequentially.

Stages of adjustment for foreign students:

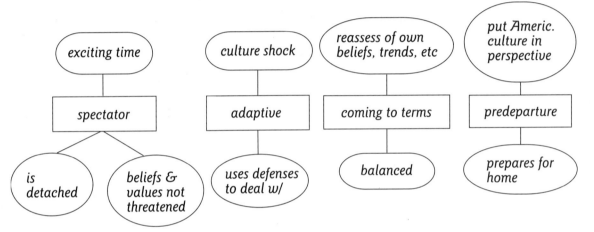

d. Trees: Use trees to show linear relationships, divisions, classifications.

e. Columns and Charts: Use columns and charts to compare and contrast and to show parts of a general topic.

Monochronic Time	_Polychronic Time_
• _does one thg at a time_	• _does many thgs at a time_
• _keeps to schdule_	• _involves people_
• _values punctual._	• _appts. often broken_
• _Time = system for order_	• _emphas. complet. transactions_

Exercise 15: Each of the following statements introduces an academic lecture. Imagine that you are in a class and hear these introductory statements. As you listen to the type of information that is being presented, imagine what your lecture notes might look like on the page. What key words in each sentence indicate the organization of the information presented? Underline them.

- "Now I'd like to trace the process of lateralization of speech functions, which is said to occur before adolescence."
- "Today we're going to examine the major parts of the brain and their functions."
- "There are a number of theories in circulation today to explain the presence of aggression in humans."
- "We'll concentrate on examining the major differences between stocks and bonds."
- "Let's examine how a large corporation can divide up and allocate duties and responsibilities."

Exercise 16: Practice your note-taking. Work in groups of three. Have one student take notes while the other two students carry on a conversation about a topic that interests them (e.g., recent travels, movies they have seen, classes they are in together, etc.). Then have the notetaker read back the conversation to the students.

Exercise 17: Work with a partner. Take turns reading the following lecture to each other and taking notes in the space provided below. Use abbreviations, symbols, and shortened words whenever possible to speed up your note-taking.

(1) Condon and Yousef describe six functions of communication in their book, *An Introduction to Intercultural Communication.* (2) The first is small talk, which is used basically to acknowledge the presence of another person. (3) The next is transmission of information, such as asking for directions, inquiring about how something works, etc. (4) Catharsis means tension relief, and we use communication for this purpose when we laugh or express surprise (as in the expression, "No way!"). (5) Ritual is another function of communication, and this is found in such activities as weddings, funerals, etc. (6) Affective communication is the communication of feelings, of matters of the heart.

1. _____

2. _____

3. _____

4. _____

5. _____

6. _____

Recognizing Signal Words

Lecturers use a variety of words and expressions to signal to the listener the kind of information that will follow and also to connect ideas and parts of a lecture. Below is a brief list of some of these signal words and what they signify. It's a good idea to become familiar with these signal words, because they can help you with your note-taking.

Signal Word/Expression	Explanation
1. Rhetorical Question "What is culture?" "You may wonder if it's easier to learn a third language"	Helps to focus your attention on an important point. The listener is not required to answer.
2. "Let's discuss X and then I'd like to . . ."	To present the plan for the lecture.
3. "Last week, we talked about . . ."	To review and/or summarize important material from a previous lecture.
4. "If you remember . . ." "You already know . . ."	To connect a new idea with an idea from a previous lecture
5. "The important point . . ." "And this is the most important idea . . ."	To signal importance

Exercise 18:   Your instructor will deliver several brief mini-lectures, giving each one twice. As you listen to each lecture the first time, think about how the information is organized and write down what kind of note-taking format (e.g., chains, trees, etc.) would be most appropriate for that lecture. Then take notes the second time the lecture is given, paying attention to the use of signal words.

a. Second Language Acquisition

_____

_____

b. Nondominant Cultures

_____

_____

c. Religions of the World

_____

_____

Exercise 19: Refer to the lecture on business and culture on pages 39 and 40. Underline the signal words in the transcript and be ready to discuss their purpose in the lecture.

Exercise 20: Your instructor will deliver a lecture on culture shock. Use the brief outline below to help you organize your lecture notes.

CULTURE SHOCK

Symptoms
Stages
Advantages
Discussion

Keep the following in mind as you take your notes:

- Use abbreviations and symbols.
- Avoid writing complete sentences.
- Avoid writing in paragraphs—use outlines, graphs, or maps instead.
- Be sure to take some notes during class discussions.

After the lecture, compare your notes with a partner and fill in any gaps that you have. Be ready to write a brief summary of the lecture from these notes.

Gaining Expertise

Activity One: Your instructor will deliver a lecture on the analysis of cultural differences. Before you listen to the lecture, take a moment to reflect on what that topic means to you. If you were to analyze the differences between the United States and your own culture, what elements might you look at to identify how the two cultures differ?

Then, be an active listener as you listen to the lecture. Notice when the three parts of the lecture begin and end. Be conscious of taking notes during any class discussions. Try to use any of the time-saving techniques you already know as well as the new ones you learned in this chapter.

Activity Two: Work in small groups. Prepare a detailed list of abbreviations and symbols to use when taking lecture notes. Ask each person in your group to select a specific discipline (e.g., business, engineering, history, psychology) and prepare abbreviations for the most common terms in those subject areas. Refer to introductory textbooks for help in identifying the relevant words. Compile these lists into a booklet and make copies for all the class members.

PART THREE: TAKING TESTS

TAKING INVENTORY: YOUR TEST-TAKING STUDY HABITS

IT WORKS!
Learning Strategy:
Identifying Your
Study Habits

Exercise 21: What kinds of strategies and techniques do you use when you take tests? Assess your current habits by marking Yes, No, or Sometimes for each of the following statements. Then consult the following "Feedback" section to learn more about your own test-taking study habits.

1. I don't usually have time to study until the night before a test or exam.

Yes ☐   No ☐   Sometimes ☐

2. I look over the test format before I begin answering the test questions.

Yes ☐   No ☐   Sometimes ☐

3. I plan out my time carefully and try to stick to the plan.

Yes ☐   No ☐   Sometimes ☐

4. I answer the easier questions first and then tackle the more difficult ones.

Yes ☐   No ☐   Sometimes ☐

5. I rarely change my answers.

Yes ☐   No ☐   Sometimes ☐

6. I don't review my test; I hand it in when I've finished answering the last question.

Yes ☐   No ☐   Sometimes ☐

YOUR STUDY HABITS: FEEDBACK

1. I don't usually have time to study until the night before a test or exam.

There's no question about it—college students are very busy, and they often find themselves with only the night before a test to study. This is called "cramming for a test." We've all done it. And we all know it's not the best way to study for a test. Studies on memory show that students who study at intervals retain information better and do better on their tests. Try to study a few days prior to the night before a test.

2. I look over the test format before I begin answering the test questions.

This is an excellent idea because it lets you know what kinds of questions are on the test. It will also give you a sense of which sections may be more difficult than others.

3. I plan out my time carefully and try to stick to the plan.

This planning is very important—a key to successful test-taking.

4. I answer the easier questions first and then tackle the more difficult ones.

There is certainly nothing wrong with doing this. Many students find that their self-confidence increases if they answer the easier questions first. Students are often nervous at the beginning of tests, but as they find they can answer some of the questions, they begin to relax. The order in which you answer test questions is really up to you.

5. I rarely change my answers.

   Students often hear that their first answer is usually the best. This actually depends on your own test-taking style. Do you quickly try to answer all the questions first and then go back to review them? If this is your style, then your changed answer may likely be the better one. Or are you the kind of student who thinks a long time before making a choice? In this case, your first answer is likely the better one.

6. I don't review my test; I hand it in when I've finished answering the last question.

   It's always a good idea to review your test if you have time to do so. Then you can make sure you've completed all the questions and you can check spelling, grammar, and punctuation on essay items.

Preparing for the Test

Everybody knows that studying for a test is essential. However, there are some other considerations that good students pay attention to as they get ready for tests. They include the following:

- **Make sure you know what will be covered on the test.** Some questions you may need to ask your professor are: Will the test be on both the lecture and the reading? On just the reading? On just some of the reading?
- **Know the type of test.** Will it be an "objective" test (e.g., a multiple-choice test)? An essay test? A combination of the two?
- **Find out how much this test will count toward your final grade.** Look on your syllabus to find out what percentage of your grade is accounted for by this test. If it's 5 percent, then you know it's not as important as, say, the final, which may count 25 percent. Adjust your studying accordingly.

LEARNING STRATEGY

Managing Your Learning: Planning carefully for a test can help you be more successful.

Exercise 22: You have been studying about intercultural communication in this class. You have had lectures and readings about the subject. Imagine that your instructor says the following to you before the test. After reading this quote, decide what additional information you would need to study properly for the test. Write the questions you would ask in the space provided below.

"We are going to have a test tomorrow on this chapter. Everybody should bring some paper and a dictionary. You will be able to use your dictionaries. The test should take about one hour. It shouldn't be too difficult and will basically cover everything we have been doing in this class for the past month. Any questions?"

Questions I would ask:

_____

_____

SURVIVAL TIPS: TESTS AND YOUR PROFESSOR

There is no escaping taking tests in a college class in the United States. Tests are an integral part of many college classes. Unfortunately, not all professors are good test writers. Not all tests are fair, and you need to be ready for this. Some professors, for example, like to give multiple-choice tests on obscure information that only a small percentage of the students can remember. Other professors give very easy tests—much to your dismay since you've studied hard for several days! Still others write test questions that are vague and seem very subjective. Of course, there are some prized professors who give fair but challenging tests.

Tips to help you succeed in your tests:
- **Talk to students who have taken the course.** If at all possible, talk to more than one student to find out what kind of tests your professor usually gives. This will give you a decided advantage.
- **Review copies of past tests.** Occasionally, professors make copies of previous tests available. These will guide you in your studying and familiarize you with the types of questions likely to appear.
- **Ask questions and listen carefully to the answers.** If you are uncertain about the test, ask the professor directly what it will be like.
- **Study especially hard for the first test.** If you are not sure what kind of test your professor is going to give, study every possible way—learn both the facts *and* the broad concepts, to cover your bases. The second test will be easier, simply because you know what to expect.

ANTICIPATING TEST QUESTIONS

One very useful technique for planning and studying for a test is to anticipate the test questions. You can do this by reviewing your material and formulating questions that you think may appear on the test.

Some ways to anticipate test questions:
- **Use clues from class.** If your professor has favorite topics or has mentioned that certain points are important, these will probably appear on the test more frequently than other information. Review your lecture notes. They will help you identify areas of particular importance from your professor's point of view.
- **Turn your course text into test questions.** As you reread the required material for your course, write questions for important sections. Pay special attention to lists of reasons, results, and characteristics.

- **Use any study guides or sample questions that your professor provides to the class.** These are valuable in helping you identify the kinds of questions that will probably appear on the test.
- **Consider your professor's personality.** Does he or she like details? Encourage creative thinking? Prefer elaborate to simple explanations? Chances are good that your test will in some way reflect the personality of your professor.

LEARNING STRATEGY

Managing Your Learning: Anticipating the test questions can help you prepare more efficiently for the test.

Exercise 23: Form groups of from four to six students. Refer to the section, "Nonverbal Processes" (pp. 75-77), from the reading, "Basic Principles of Intercultural Communication." Divide the text evenly among the students in your group and ask each student to prepare three types of test questions (e.g., one multiple-choice, one short-answer, and one essay) for his or her section. Use your annotations and highlighting to help you focus on important information. Compile these questions and be ready to share them with the entire class.

IDENTIFYING YOUR STUDY HABITS

You may believe that there is only one way to study and that if you could just study that way, you would do well on tests. The truth is that there are many equally effective ways to prepare for tests. The way you choose to study should reflect who you are and include the strategies and techniques that work best for you.

That's why it's very important for you to identify your own interests and tendencies. For example, do you study better in the morning or evening? Do you learn the material better by reading it over several times, or do you remember it better by writing it down? Or perhaps you learn best by teaching someone else. How long can you sit still and concentrate?

The answers to these questions can help you identify the most effective way for you to study. Pay attention to your own needs and what motivates you.

Exercise 24: Work with another student. Compare your styles of preparing for tests. Talk about what works and what doesn't. Be ready to summarize this for the class.

What do you do the night
before a test?

CONTROLLING TEST ANXIETY

A certain amount of anxiety before a test is helpful, because the adrenalin heightens your perception. Too much anxiety, however, can be paralyzing—so much so that some students freeze and "draw a blank," forgetting everything. If you are like that, doing some relaxation exercises before taking a test may prove helpful. Also, creating a mental imagery of success can also enhance your performance.

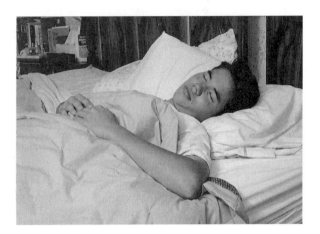

LEARNING STRATEGY

Understanding and Using Emotions: Proper relaxation and positive mental imagery can enhance your performance on a test.

Exercise 25: With your class or in small groups, brainstorm ways to control anxiety before a test. Make a list on the board. Then identify which techniques work best for you.

Taking the Test

Before you begin answering your test questions, take some time to plan how you will budget your time and what strategies you will use to complete the test. Here are some points to consider:

- **Plan your time before you start the test.** Decide how much time you will need to complete each section of the test.
- **Look at the test questions.** Decide how many points each question is worth. Spend more time on the questions that are worth more points.

- **Pace yourself and work evenly.** Look at your watch periodically and be aware of how many more questions are left to answer.
- **Be ready to spend more time on essay questions.** Be aware that as a non-native speaker of English, you will probably take longer than a native speaker would to answer essay questions that require writing sentences and paragraphs. Be prepared to spend more time on these answers, and while you want to write as well as you can, try not to lose time worrying about spelling, grammar, and vocabulary.

LEARNING STRATEGY

Managing Your Learning: Planning your time carefully during the test can help you complete the test more successfully.

Exercise 26:   Examine the sample test below. Imagine that you have one hour to complete this test. Based on the kinds of questions, the points they are worth, and the difficulty they would present for you, plan out your hour carefully. Be ready to discuss your plan with others.

SAMPLE TEST

I. Defining Terms (25 points)
Choose five of the following terms and define each one briefly.
monochronic time
assimilation
acculturation
bicultural
dominant culture
nonverbal communication

II. Multiple Choice (25 points)
Choose the best answer.
1. The stage during which foreigners begin to see both the good and bad aspects of a culture is called
   (a) culture shock
   (b) hostility
   (c) home
   (d) humor
2. Which of the following concerns is greatest for most foreign students in the United States?
   (a) lack of friends
   (b) career
   (c) school work
   (d) b and c
3. Proxemics is
   (a) the study of spatial boundaries
   (b) the study of language
   (c) a statistical analysis of pronunciation differences
   (d) none of the above

4. The religion with the greatest number of adherents is:
   (a) Islam
   (b) Christianity
   (c) Buddhism
   (d) Judaism
5. Which of the following is <u>not</u> a symptom of culture shock?
   (a) concern with cleanliness
   (b) feeling cheated
   (c) anger about not receiving news from home
   (d) not learning the language of the new culture

III. Short Answer (10 points each)
1. Briefly explain two advantages of experiencing culture shock.
2. What is the difference between formal and informal time?
3. What is the systems approach to cultural analysis? What are the systems involved?

IV. Essay Question (20 points)
Choose <u>one</u> of the following questions.
1. List the ten characteristics of culture. Then choose <u>three</u> to explain in depth, analyzing your own culture according to those three characteristics. Finally, compare how the U.S. culture is different from your culture in those three areas.
2. Explain what intercultural communication is and what prevents it. Why is it important to develop good intercultural communication in our world?
3. Compare eastern and western approaches to silence.

UNDERSTANDING TEST PROMPTS

Students usually categorize tests as either **subjective** or **objective. Subjective tests** require you to write sentences, paragraphs, and essays and usually involve some analysis and synthesis of material. These kinds of tests are sometimes called **essay tests**, although you don't always write essays. Essay tests require the application of many skills and can be especially exhausting for the ESL student because of the demands on language skills.

Objective tests are usually multiple-choice, with some matching, fill-in-the-blank, true/false, and labeling questions. Objective tests usually involve more questions and are quicker to complete. Of course, many professors combine the two types—and so it is in your best interest to anticipate which material is likely to appear in the objective part and which in the essay part of the test.

Exercise 27: Discuss your attitudes about taking tests with a partner. Which do you prefer—objective or essay tests? Why? Of the many kinds of objective test questions, which ones do you do best on? Why?

Direction words.   The following direction words are often used in essay test questions. Be sure you understand what these verbs mean and what kind of essay response is expected.

When the test question says . . .	**It often means . . .**
Analyze . . . . *Analyze the process of acculturation to a second culture.*	Examine the parts of a topic, often critically. Provide a moderate amount of detail.
Compare (and/or contrast) . . . . *Compare marriage ceremonies in the United States with those in your culture.*	Show how these items are similar (and/or different). Use examples to support your ideas.
Define . . . . *Define culture shock.*	Provide a description of the essential qualities or characteristics of this term.
Describe . . . . *Describe a nondominant culture in your country.*	Provide a more comprehensive description than a definition and include properties, relationships, key examples.
Discuss (Explain) . . . . *Discuss the concerns of foreign students during their first year.*	Present as much information as you can about this and examine the item from as many viewpoints as possible. Be especially careful about organizing such an answer.
Enumerate (List) . . . . *Enumerate the ten characteristics of a culture discussed in the lecture.*	Make a list of the key parts. Use numbers or bullets to outline these points.
Explain . . . . *Explain the differences between a polychronic and a monochronic culture.*	Provide description or discussion of appearances, process, differences, causes.
Illustrate . . . . *Illustrate how nonverbal communication can cause cross-cultural misunderstandings.*	Give real or hypothetical examples to support something.
Label . . . . *Label the steps involved on the diagram.*	Provide labels on a diagram or illustration.
State . . . . *State the ingredients of communication.*	Provide the facts or main points about a topic, usually in outline form, briefly.
Summarize . . . . *Summarize the theory of high-context/ low-context cultures.*	Present the main points in a very shortened form, without elaboration.
Trace/Outline . . . . *Trace the history of foreign students in the United States.*	Present something historically or sequentially; show time relationships.

54

LEARNING STRATEGY

Overcoming Limitations: Understanding the test prompts and
directions is essential to success on tests.

Exercise 28:   The prompt "describe" can have many different meanings.
Substitute a more precise test prompt for <u>Describe</u> in each of the following test
questions. Refer to the list above for assistance. The first one has been done
for you.

1. <u>Describe</u> the various systems that compose a culture.
    List and explain the various systems that compose a culture.
    _____

2. <u>Describe</u> the obstacles to achieving cross-cultural understanding.
    _____

3. <u>Describe</u> the advantages of living in a foreign culture.
    _____

4. <u>Describe</u> the basic points in Hall's well-known book, *Beyond Culture.*
    _____

5. <u>Describe</u> the processes of acculturation and assimilation.
    _____

Exercise 29:   Work with a partner and examine each of the following test
questions (taken from the sample essay prompts in the chart on page 53) and
answer these questions: What type of answer is required by the direction verb?
What information would you need to include for each and how would you
organize it? Approximately how long would your answer be?

1. Define culture shock.
2. Describe a nondominant culture in your country.
3. Illustrate how nonverbal communication can cause cross-cultural
    misunderstandings.
4. State the ingredients of communication.
5. Summarize the theory of high-context/low-context cultures.

Exercise 30: Choose one of the readings at the end of the chapter and write **five sample essay test questions** using five of the direction words you learned. Think about what the direction word means and the kind of information that would best suit such a question. Be ready to share your questions with a partner, and give and receive feedback. (You don't have to answer the questions!)

Short-Answer Prompts

Many professors include "short-answer" questions on tests. Unlike an essay question, which requires you to combine information and write paragraphs, a short-answer question requires you to write one or two sentences or whatever it takes to provide the information. Sometimes lists or outlines will be sufficient. Here are a few examples of short-answer questions:

> *What are the major religions of the world?*
> *List the stages of culture shock.*
> *Briefly define "caste."*

Hints for Answering Essay Test Questions

1. **Read the question carefully.** Sometimes the question has two parts (e.g., Name the major religions of the world. Summarize the basic beliefs of each.). Other times you have a choice (e.g., Answer either A or B.).
2. **Organize your ideas before beginning to write.** Make notes or write an outline to help you do this. (Spend about one-fifth of your time preparing.) If you run out of time, some professors will give partial credit for the outline.
3. **Answer the question in your first sentence.** Don't worry about fancy introductions—get to the point quickly. Here are some examples:
   Prompt: *Describe a nondominant culture in your country.*
   Answer: *The gay and lesbian community is a very important nondominant culture in my country.*
   Prompt: *Define culture shock.*
   Answer: *Culture shock is the impact of living in a culture that is very different from one's own.*
   Prompt: *Enumerate the symptoms of culture shock.*
   Answer: *There are six symptoms of culture shock, as follows: . . .*
4. After you have given an exact answer in the first sentence or so, provide support through examples, descriptions, or citations. (Spend about three-fifths of your time writing the essay answer.)
5. Leave some blank space after each essay in case you want to add more information later.
6. Be sure to save some additional time (about one-fifth of your time) for editing and checking spelling and grammar.

UP CLOSE: WRITING AN ESSAY EXAM

Essay Question: Describe the symptoms of culture shock.

Informal Outline:

Six symptoms:

Take some time to organize your thoughts on paper.

1. concern for cleanliness (e.g., water)
2. minor pains
3. anger & frustration (e.g., delays)
4. being cheated—esp. about money
5. not learning language
6. desire to be with people from own culture

Test Answer:

use exact numbers

use examples for support

Restate the question in the first sentence.

There are (six) symptoms of culture shock. First is a concern for cleanliness. (For example,) a person may be worried that the water is not clean. Second, foreigners often are worried about minor pains such as cramping in the legs, and believe that something more serious is happening to their bodies. (Another common symptom) is anger over delays and frustration over small things. Anyone who has lived in a foreign country can relate to this symptom—unwarranted anger when the bus or plane is late. (Yet another) very common symptom of culture shock is feelings of being cheated or being taking advantage. This is common, especially when one must deal with exchanging money. Some people in culture shock do not learn the language of the country even though they may live there for an extended period of time. (Finally,) a strong desire to be with people from one's own culture is a symptom of culture shock.

use transition words

no need for an elaborate conclusion

Leave some blank lines at the end for additional ideas

_____

_____

Exercise 31: Write the first sentence for each of the sample essay questions listed in the chart on page 53. Compare your sentences with a partner.

Sample question: *Analyze the process of acculturation to a second culture.*

Answer: *Acculturation to a second culture is a complex process that involves several steps.*

Exercise 32: Read and evaluate the following two answers to the essay question provided. Which answer would you assign a better grade if you were the instructor? What are the strengths and weaknesses of each essay?

Prompt: *Define culture shock.*

Answer #1

Going to a foreign country can be very disturbing. For example, when I came to the United States, I had many problems. I had culture shock. Everything was quite different for me, but I had a fun time at the beginning. This is the honeymoon stage. I think I'm in the hostility stage now, because I don't want to be with Americans and I find American customs annoying. Then after hostility, I will probably experience the humor stage, where I will be able to laugh about my experience and I hope I will speak better English. The last stage, the "home" stage will be before I go, I will have a more objective view of this culture.

My evaluation:

1. The strengths of this answer are:

_____

_____

_____

2. The weaknesses of this answer are:

_____

_____

_____

Answer #2

There are four stages of culture shock and these are: honeymoon, hostility, humor and home. The first stage is when everything is wonderful for the foreigner. The second stage is when everything is irritating to the foreigner. The third stage, when the foreigner begins to learn the language, is the humor stage, because the person can laugh. Finally, the foreigner enters the home stage before returning to his or her culture, in which one sees the good and the bad and has a greater acceptance of the culture. These are the four stages, but they don't always happen sequentially, and they may not be completed totally.

My evaluation:

1. The strengths of this answer are:

_____

_____

_____

2. The weaknesses of this answer are:

_____

_____

_____

Exercise 33: Write the answer to one of the sample essay questions listed in the chart on page 53. Your instructor will give you a time limit and may assign a specific question. Remember to take some time to organize your thoughts and write out the first sentence carefully.

TAKING OBJECTIVE TESTS

Refer to the sample test on page 51. Note the different types of "objective" test questions: **multiple choice, matching, fill-in-the-blank, true/false.** Much has already been written about taking objective tests, so this section will only briefly summarize some of the key points to consider when taking these tests.

Exercise 34: Work in small groups. Look at the sample test on page 51 and make a list of strategies that you would use to answer the test questions. Compare your list with the list below and add any new ones to this list.

1. Work evenly through the questions and put a check or question mark in the margin next to questions you're not sure of. Then you can return to these questions later.
2. Pay attention to these words: *often, sometimes, always, seldom, very often.* Circle them when you read them and note how they may change the meaning of the sentence.
3. In multiple-choice questions, cross off the answers you know with certainty are not correct.
4. If you're not sure how to answer a fill-in-the-blank or a short-answer question, make a guess. Write *something.*

Reviewing the Returned Test

LEARNING STRATEGY

Managing Your Learning: Studying your returned test can help you do better on subsequent tests.

Many students are so relieved to have finished a test that they miss a very important part of the process—reviewing the test when it is returned. Here are some reasons why it's a good idea to study a returned test.

- **Make a note of what you missed** so you can be sure you don't miss it again on a later quiz or examination. If you are not allowed to keep the test, copy the test questions you got wrong on a separate paper so you can review those questions you missed.

- **Pay attention to those questions the whole class missed.** Chances are good that your professor will put those questions on a later test.
- **Take note of what kinds of answers your professor found to be good answers and poor answers.** Did she/he prefer longer, more elaborate essay answers or shorter, more concise ones? Knowing this will help you on the next test. Be sure to read the professor's comments!

Gaining Expertise

Activity One.   Prepare for a test on the reading, "Basic Principles of Intercultural Communication," at the end of the chapter. The test will be based on the reading only and will be a combination of essay and objective questions. Review your highlighting and annotations for that reading. Make notes on a separate sheet of paper, outlining important information and defining key terms. Work with a partner and anticipate the questions that may be on the test. Write out these questions and prepare answers for them.

Activity Two.   Prepare for an essay test on intercultural communication. Refer to your lecture and reading notes. Imagine that the professor has given you the following guidelines for your test:

Your final exam will consist of three essay questions dealing with the topic of cross-cultural communication. You will be required to use the material from your readings and your own cross-cultural experience to respond to questions based on the following topics. Be prepared for the following:

1. An extended definition of culture
2. An explanation of what cultural analysis is and how it is accomplished
3. A cultural analysis of the United States or your home country using one of the models of cultural analysis presented
4. A critical discussion of what interferes with cross-cultural communication and understanding
5. An explanation of how cultures can differ even within a single geographic region or nation
6. An understanding of nonverbal communication

GETTING MORE HELP

You may still feel that you need additional help with some of the academic skills presented in this chapter. Here are some possibilities:

1. Find out where the learning center, or academic skills center, on your campus is. Such centers often offer individual help with study skills.
2. Get a more basic study skills text. Wecksler's *Study Skills for Academic Success* can help fill in the gaps.
3. Get a tutor. If you are financially able, hire a tutor to help you with your study skills or the subject matter.
4. Consult a book that deals specifically with your area of weakness.

EVALUATING YOUR PROGRESS

Find out what you have learned and how your study habits have improved. The following questions were taken from the "Taking Inventory" sections of Parts One, Two, and Three of this chapter. Answer them without looking at your earlier responses, and then compare to see which questions you answered differently.

STUDY READING

1. I look at the title page of the textbook or chapter I am reading to determine the author, title, and the date and place of publication.
Yes ☐   No ☐   Sometimes ☐

2. I look at the text quickly first to find out what it's mainly about before reading it more carefully.
Yes ☐   No ☐   Sometimes ☐

3. I first read the sections that interest me most.
Yes ☐   No ☐   Sometimes ☐

4. I prefer not to write in my textbooks.
Yes ☐   No ☐   Sometimes ☐

5. I read every word of the text carefully, and I look up most of the words I don't know in a dictionary.
Yes ☐   No ☐   Sometimes ☐

6. I read a text more than once.
Yes ☐   No ☐   Sometimes ☐

TAKING NOTES IN CLASS

1. I take notes when a professor is giving a lecture.
Yes ☐   No ☐   Sometimes ☐

2. I take notes during a class discussion.
Yes ☐   No ☐   Sometimes ☐

3. I take notes in complete sentences.
Yes ☐   No ☐   Sometimes ☐

4. I review my notes after class and add missing details.
Yes ☐   No ☐   Sometimes ☐

5. I tape-record class lectures.
Yes ☐   No ☐   Sometimes ☐

TEST-TAKING

1. I don't usually have time to study until the night before a test or exam.
Yes ☐   No ☐   Sometimes ☐

2. I look over the test format before I begin answering the test questions.
Yes ☐   No ☐   Sometimes ☐

3. I plan out my time carefully and try to stick to the plan.
Yes ☐   No ☐   Sometimes ☐

4. I answer the easier questions first and then tackle the more difficult ones.
Yes ☐   No ☐   Sometimes ☐

5. I rarely change my answers.
Yes ☐   No ☐   Sometimes ☐

6. I don't review my test; I hand it in when I've finished answering the last question.
Yes ☐   No ☐   Sometimes ☐

Intercultural Communication: A Reader

Sixth Edition

LARRY A. SAMOVAR
San Diego State University

RICHARD E. PORTER
California State University, Long Beach

Wadsworth Publishing Company
Belmont, California
A Division of Wadsworth, Inc.

Basic principles of intercultural communication

Richard E. Porter
Larry A. Samovar

During the past thirty years, a number of events have led to many changes in worldwide and local interaction patterns. First, changes in transportation technology made the world "shrink" by providing means for people to be almost anywhere within a few hours flying time. (The suborbital aircraft now being designed will cause greater shrinkage. Travel time between China and the United States, for example, will be measured in minutes rather than in hours.) This increase in travel technology was soon followed by changes in communication technology, which made it possible for people to have instantaneous vocal, pictorial, and textual communication anywhere in the world without the need for traveling. Indeed, with a few hundred dollars worth of equipment in the form of a portable facsimile machine and a cellular telephone, it is possible to have instant oral and print communication almost anywhere in the world while driving the freeways in the United States.

These changes have wrought many effects; two, however, stand out as being significant for our purposes. The first is that new communication technology has created an almost free flow of news and information throughout the world and has become so important in the everyday activity of conducting commerce and government that it cannot be set aside. Because of this, it is also impossible to keep communication capabilities out of the hands of the people. Government attempts to censor the free flow of ideas, opinions, and information have been thwarted. In China, for instance, during the Tiananmen Square demonstrations of mid-1989, the Chinese government attempted to ban foreign correspondents from reporting on observed incidents by cutting their access to telephone and television broadcast facilities. American television viewers, however, were shown many incidents of reporters using their cellular telephones to call the United States via the handy communications satellite in stationary orbit over Asia. By the time the government reacted to this technology, the story and information had long since been disseminated to the world. In other parts of the world, similar incidents have occurred; for example, the widespread and multiple changes currently taking place in Eastern Europe are due in part to the availability of news and information.

Communication technology has also broken down our isolation. One hundred years ago it was virtually impossible for the average citizen to have an informed awareness of what was happening in the world. People had to wait for reports to arrive by mail or appear in newspapers, where the news could be up to several months old. Today is quite different. With existing communication technology, we can sit in our living rooms and watch events anywhere on earth, or, indeed, in orbit around the earth, as these events are actually happening. Only a scant few years ago we had to wait hours, days, and even weeks to see who won gold medals in the Olympic Games. Today, we can watch these events as they occur.

This new communication technology has a considerable impact upon us. When we received news and information days and weeks after an event, it was difficult to develop a feeling about or a caring for what was happening thousands of miles away.

But, consider the differences in the impact upon us when we read in the newspaper that the South African police had put down a disturbance in a black township three weeks ago and when we sit today in the living room and watch while a police officer actually clubs someone with a baton. The ability to deny the cruelty of that act is reduced virtually to zero.

The second change has brought us to the brink of a McLuanesque global village. While transportation and communication technology have figuratively shrunk the world, immigration patterns have physically shifted segments of the world population. People from Vietnam, Cambodia, Laos, Cuba, Haiti, Columbia, Nicaragua, El Salvador, and Ecuador, among others, have entered the United States and become our neighbors. As these people try to adjust their lives to this culture, we will have many opportunities for intercultural contacts in our daily lives. Contacts with cultures that previously appeared unfamiliar, alien, and at times mysterious are now a normal part of our day-to-day routine. All of this means that we are no longer isolated from one another in time and space.

While this global phenomenon involving transportation, communication, and migration was taking place, there was also a kind of cultural revolution within our own boundaries. Domestic events made us focus our attention upon new and often demanding co-cultures. Asians, blacks, Hispanics, women, homosexuals, the poor, the disabled, the drug culture, the homeless, and countless other groups became highly visible and vocal as they cried out for recognition and their place in our new global village.

This attention to co-cultures made us realize that although intercultural contact is inevitable, it is often not successful. Frequently, the communicative behavior of the co-cultures disturbed many of us. Their behavior seemed strange, at times even bizarre, and it frequently failed to meet our normal expectations. We discovered, in short, that intercultural communication is difficult. Even after the natural barrier of a foreign language is overcome, we can still fail to understand and to be understood.

These interaction failures, both in the international arena and on the domestic scene, give rise to a major premise: *The difficulty with being thrust into a global village is that we do not yet know how to live like villagers; there are too many of us who do not want to live with "them."* Ours is a culture where racism and ethnocentrism still run deep below the surface. Although there has been a lessening of overt racial violence since the 1960s, the enduring racist/ethnocentric belief system has not been appreciably affected. In many respects, racism and ethnocentrism have become institutionalized and are practiced unconsciously. The result is a structured domination of people of color by the white Anglo power structure. Until this deep-seated antagonism can be eliminated, we will not be able to assume our place in a global village community.

Our inability to yet behave as villagers in the global village is cause for major concern because not only have we not learned to respect and accept one another, we have not learned to communicate with one another effectively, to understand one another, because our cultures are different. Thus, even if we have the strongest desire to communicate, we are faced with the difficulties imposed upon us by cultural diversity and the impact that diversity has on the communication process.

The difficulties cultural diversity poses for effective communication have given rise to the marriage of culture and communication and to the recognition of intercultural communication as a field of study. Inherent in this fusion is the idea that intercultural communication entails the investigation of culture and the difficulties of communicating across cultural boundaries.

To help us understand what is involved in intercultural communication, we will begin with a fundamental definition: *Intercultural communication occurs whenever a message produced in one culture must be processed in another culture.* The rest of this article will deal with intercultural communication and point out the relationships between communication, culture, and intercultural communication.

COMMUNICATION

To understand intercultural interaction, we must first understand human communication. Understanding human communication means knowing something about what happens when people interact, why it happens, the effects of what happens, and finally what we can do to influence and maximize the results of that event.

Understanding and Defining Communication

We begin with a basic assumption that communication is a form of human behavior that is derived from a need to interact with other human beings. Almost everyone desires social contact with other people, and this need is met through the act of communication, which unites otherwise isolated individuals. Our behaviors become messages to which other people may respond. When we talk, we are obviously behaving, but when we wave, smile, frown, walk, shake our heads, or gesture, we also are behaving. These behaviors frequently become messages; they communicate something to someone else.

Before behaviors can become messages, however, they must meet two requirements: First, they must be observed by someone, and second, they must elicit a response. In other words, any behavior that elicits a response is a message. If we examine this last statement, we can see several implications.

The first implication is that the word **any** tells us that both verbal and nonverbal behaviors may function as messages. Verbal messages consist of spoken or written words (speaking and writing are word-producing behaviors) while nonverbal messages consist of the entire remaining behavioral repertory.

Second, behavior may be either conscious or unconscious. We frequently do things without conscious awareness of them. This is especially true of nonverbal behavior, habits such as fingernail biting, toe tapping, leg jiggling, head shaking, staring, and smiling. Even such things as slouching in a chair, chewing gum, or adjusting glasses are frequently unconscious behaviors. Since a message consists of behaviors to which people may respond, we must thus acknowledge the possibility of producing messages unknowingly.

A third implication of the behavior-message linkage is that we frequently behave unintentionally, in some cases uncontrollably. For instance, if we are embarrassed we may blush or speak with vocal disfluencies; we do not intend to blush or to stammer, but we do so anyway. Again, these unintentional behaviors can become messages if someone sees them and responds to them.

This concept of conscious-unconscious, intentional-unintentional behavior relationships gives us a basis to formulate a definition of communication. *Communication may be defined as that which happens whenever someone responds to the behavior or the residue of the behavior of another person.* When someone observes our behavior or its residue and attributes meaning to it, communication has taken place regardless of whether our behavior was conscious or unconscious, intentional or unintentional. If we think about this for a moment, we must realize that it is impossible for us not to behave. Being necessitates behavior. If behavior has communication potential, then it is also impossible for us not to communicate. In other words, we cannot not communicate.

The notion of behavior residue just mentioned in our definition refers to those things that remain as a record of our actions. For instance, this article that you are reading is a behavior residue—it resulted from certain behaviors. As the authors we had to engage in a number of behaviors; we had to research, think, and use our word processors. Another example of behavior residue might be the odor of cigar smoke lingering in an elevator after the cigar smoker has departed. Smoking the cigar was the behavior; the odor is the residue. The response you have to that smell is a reflection of your past experiences and attitudes toward cigars, smoking, smoking in public elevators, and, perhaps, people who smoke cigars.

Our approach to communication has focused on the behavior of one individual causing or provoking a response from another by the attribution of meaning to behavior. Attribution means that we draw upon our past experiences and give meaning to the behavior that we observe. We might imagine that somewhere in each of our brains is a meaning reservoir in which are stored all of the experience-derived meanings we possess. These various meanings have developed throughout our lifetimes as a result of our culture acting upon us as well as the result of our individual experiences within that culture. Meaning is relative to each of us because each of us is a unique human being with a unique background and a unique set of experiences. When we encounter a behavior in our environment, each of us dips into our individual, unique meaning reservoirs and selects the meaning we believe is most likely to be the most appropriate for the behavior encountered and the social context in which it occurred. For instance, if someone walks up to us and says: "If you've got a few minutes, let's go to the student union and get a cup of coffee," we observe this behavior and respond to it by giving it meaning. The meaning we give it is drawn from our experience with language and word meaning and also from our experience with this person and the social context. Our responses could vary significantly depending upon the circumstances. If the person is a friend, we may interpret the behavior as an invitation to sit and chat for a few minutes. On the other hand, if the behavior comes from someone with whom we have had differences, the response may be one of attributing conciliatory good will to the message and an invitation to try and settle past differences. Yet another example could be a situation in which the person is someone you have seen in a class but do not know. Then your ability to respond is lessened because you may not be able to guess fully the other person's intention. Perhaps this is someone who wants to talk about the class; perhaps it is someone who only wants social company until the next class; or perhaps, if gender differences are involved, it may be someone attempting to "put the make" on you. Your response to the observed behavior is dependent upon knowledge, experience, and social context.

Usually this works quite well, but at other times it fails and we misinterpret a message; we attribute the wrong meaning to the behavior we have observed. This may be brought about by inappropriate behavior where someone does or says something they did not intend. Or it could be brought about by the experiential backgrounds of people being sufficiently different that behavior is misinterpreted.

The Ingredients of Communication

In this section we will examine the ingredients of communication; that is, we will look at the various components that fit together to form what we call communication. Since our purpose in studying intercultural communication is to develop communication skills to apply with conscious intent, a working definition of communication must specify intentional communication. *Communication is defined, therefore, as a dynamic transactional behavior-affecting process in which people behave intentionally in order to induce or elicit a particular response from another person.* Communication is complete only when the intended behavior is observed by the intended receiver and that person responds to and is affected by the behavior. These transactions must include all conscious or unconscious, intentional or unintentional, verbal, nonverbal, and contextual stimuli that act as cues about the quality and credibility of the message. The cues must be clear to both the behavioral source of the transaction and the processor of that behavior.

This definition allows us to identify eight specific ingredients of communication. First is a *behavior source.* This is a person who has both a need and a desire to communicate. This need may range from a social desire to be recognized as an individual to the desire to share information with others or to influence the attitudes and behaviors of one or more others. The source's wish to communicate indicates a desire to share his or her internal state of being with another human being. Communication, then, is really concerned with the sharing of internal states with varying degrees of intention to influence the information, attitudes, and behaviors of others.

Internal states of being cannot be shared directly; we must rely on symbolic representations of our internal states. This brings us to the second ingredient, *encoding.* Encoding is an internal activity in which verbal and nonverbal behaviors are selected and arranged to create a message in accordance with the contextual rules that govern the interaction and according to the rules of grammar and syntax applicable to the language being used.

The result of encoding is expressive behavior that serves as a *message,* the third ingredient, to represent the internal state that is to be shared. A message is a set of verbal and/or nonverbal symbols that represent a person's particular state of being at a particular moment in time and space. Although encoding is an internal act that produces a message, a message is external to the source; it is the behavior or behavior residue that must pass between a source and a responder.

Messages must have a means by which they move from source to responder, so the fourth communication ingredient is the *channel,* which provides a connection between a source and a responder. A channel is the physical means by which the message moves between people.

The fifth ingredient is the *responder.* Responders are people who observe behavior or its residue and, as a consequence, become linked to the message source. Responders may be those intended by the source to receive the message or they may be others who, by whatever circumstance, observe the behavior once it has entered a channel. Responders have problems with messages, not unlike the problems sources have with internal states of being. Messages usually impinge on people in the form of light or sound energy, although they may be in forms that stimulate any of the senses. Whatever the form of sensory stimulation, people must convert these energies into meaningful experiences.

Converting external energies into a meaningful experience is called *decoding,* which is the sixth ingredient of communication. Decoding is akin to a source's act of encoding, because it also is an internal activity. Through this internal processing of a message, meaning is attributed to a source's behaviors that represent his or her internal state of being.

The seventh ingredient we need to consider is *response,* what a person decides to do about a message. Response may vary from as little as a decision to do nothing to an immediate overt physical act of violent proportions. If communication has been somewhat successful, the response of the message recipient will resemble to some degree that desired by the source who created the response-eliciting behavior.

The final ingredient of communication we will consider is *feedback*—information available to a source that permits him or her to make qualitative judgments about communication effectiveness. Through the interpretation of feedback, one may adjust and adapt his or her behavior to an ongoing situation. Although feedback and response are not the same thing, they are clearly related. Response is what a person decides to do about a message, and feedback is information about the effectiveness of communication. They are related because a message recipient's behavior is the normal source of feedback.

These eight ingredients of communication make up only a partial list of the factors that function during a communication event. In addition to these elements, when we conceive of communication as a process there are several other characteristics that help us understand how communication actually works.

First, communication is *dynamic*. It is an ongoing, ever-changing activity. As participants in communication, we constantly are affected by each other's messages and, as a consequence, we undergo continual change. Each of us in our daily lives meets and interacts with people who exert some influence over us. Each time we are influenced we are changed in some way, which means that as we go through life we do so as continually changing dynamic individuals.

A second characteristic of communication is that it is *interactive*. Communication must take place between people. This implies two or more people who bring to a communication event their own unique backgrounds and experiences that serve as a backdrop for communicative interaction. Interaction also implies a reciprocal situation in which each party attempts to influence the other—that is, each party simultaneously creates messages designed to elicit specific responses from the other.

Third, communication is *irreversible*. Once we have said something and someone has received and decoded the message, we cannot retrieve it. This circumstance sometimes results in what is called "putting your foot in your mouth." The source may send other messages in attempts to modify the effect, but it cannot be eliminated. This is frequently a problem when we unconsciously or unintentionally send a message to someone. We may affect them adversely and not even know it; then during future interactions we may wonder why that person is reacting to us in what we perceive to be an unusual manner.

Fourth, communication takes place in both a *physical* and *social context,* which establishes the rules that govern the interaction. When we interact with someone, it is not in isolation but within specific physical surroundings and under a set of specific social dynamics. Physical surroundings include specific physical objects such as furniture, window coverings, floor coverings, lighting, noise levels, acoustics, vegetation, presence or absence of physical clutter, as well as competing messages. Many aspects of the physical environment can and do affect communication: The comfort or discomfort of a chair, the color of the walls, to the total atmosphere of a room are but a few. Also affecting communication is the symbolic meaning of the physical surroundings— a kind of nonverbal communication. Social context defines the social relationships that exist between people as well as the rules that govern the interaction. In our culture here in the United States, we tend to be somewhat cavalier toward social hierarchies and pay much less attention to them than do people in other cultures. Nevertheless, such differences as teacher-student, employer-employee, parent-child, admiral-seaman, senator-citizen, physician-patient, and judge-attorney establish rules that specify expected behavior and thus affect the communication process.

Quite frequently, physical surroundings help define the social context. The employer may sit behind a desk while the employee stands before the desk to receive an admonition. Or, in the courtroom, the judge sits elevated facing the courtroom, jurors, and attorneys, indicating the social superiority of the judge relative to the other officers of the court. The attorneys sit side by side, indicating a social equality between accuser and accused until such time as the jury of peers renders a verdict. No matter what the social context, it will have some effect on communication. The form of language used, the respect or lack of respect shown one another, the time of day, personal moods, who speaks to whom and in what order, and the degree of nervousness or confidence people express are but a few of the ways in which the social context can affect communication.

At this point, we should see clearly that human communication does not take place in a social vacuum. Rather, communication is an intricate matrix of interacting social acts that occur in a complex social environment that reflects the way people live and how they come to interact with and get along in their world. This social environment is culture, and if we are to truly understand communication, we must also understand culture.

CULTURE

In all respects, everything so far said about communication applies to intercultural communication. The functions and relationships between the components of communication obviously apply, but what especially characterizes intercultural communication is that sources and responders come from different cultures. This alone is sufficient to identify a unique form of communicative interaction that must take into account the role and function of culture in the communication process. In this section, intercultural communication will first be defined and then discussed through the perspective of a model and then its various forms will be shown.

Intercultural Communication Model

Intercultural communication occurs whenever a message is produced by a member of one culture for consumption by a member of another culture, a message that must be understood. This circumstance can be problematic because, as we have already seen, culture forges and shapes the individual communicator. Culture is largely responsible for the construction of our individual social realities and for our individual repertoires of communicative behaviors and meanings. The communication repertoires people possess can vary significantly from culture to culture, which can lead to all sorts of difficulties. Through the study and understanding of intercultural communication, however, these difficulties at the least can be reduced and at best nearly eliminated.

Cultural influence on individuals and the problems inherent in the production and interpretation of messages between cultures are illustrated in Figure 1. Here, three cultures are represented by three distinct geometric shapes. Cultures A and B are purposefully similar to one another and are represented by a square and an irregular octagon that resembles a square. Culture C is intended to be quite different from Cultures A and B. It is represented both by its circular shape and its physical distance from Cultures A and B. Within each represented culture is another form similar to the shape of the influencing parent culture. This form represents a person who has been molded by his or her culture. The shape of the person, however, is somewhat different from that of the parent culture. This difference suggests two things: First, there are other influences besides culture that affect and help mold the individual, and, second, although culture is the dominant shaping force of an individual, people vary to some extent from each other within any culture.

Message production, transmission, and interpretation across cultures is illustrated by the series of arrows connecting them. When a message leaves the culture in which it was encoded, it carries the content intended by its producer. This is represented by the arrows leaving a culture having the same pattern as that within the message producer. When a message reaches the culture where it is to be interpreted, it undergoes a transformation because the culture in which the message is decoded influences the message interpretation phase of intercultural communication because the culturally different repertoires of social reality, communicative behaviors, and meanings possessed by the interpreter do not coincide with those possessed by the message producer.

The degree of influence culture has on intercultural communication is a function of the dissimilarity between the cultures. This also is indicated in the model by the degree of pattern

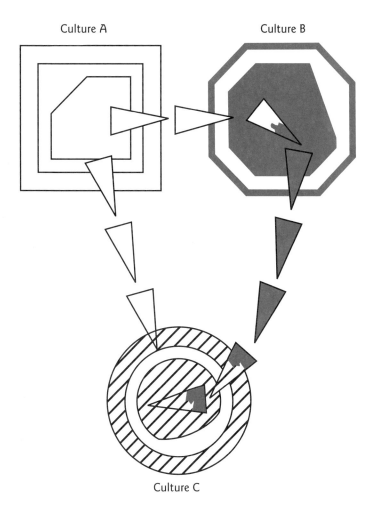

Figure 1 Model of Intercultural Communication

change that occurs in the message arrows. The change that occurs between Cultures A and B is much less than the change between B and C. This is because there is greater similarity between Cultures A and B. Hence, the repertories of social reality, communicative behaviors, and meanings are similar and the interpretation effort produces results more nearly like the content intended in the original message. Since Culture C is represented as being quite different from Cultures A and B, the interpreted message is also vastly different and more nearly represents the pattern of Culture C.

The model suggests that there can be wide variation in cultural differences during intercultural communication, due in part to circumstances or forms. Intercultural communication occurs in a wide variety of situations that range from interactions between people for whom cultural differences are extreme to interactions between people who are members of the same dominant culture and whose differences are reflected in the values and perceptions of subcultures, subgroups, or racial groups. If we imagine differences varying along a minimum-maximum dimension (see Figure 2), the degree of difference between two cultural groups depends on their relative social uniqueness. Although this scale is unrefined, it allows us to examine intercultural communication acts and gain insight into the effect cultural

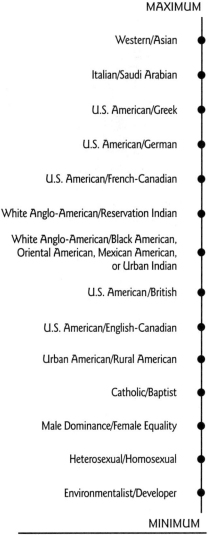

MAXIMUM

Western/Asian

Italian/Saudi Arabian

U.S. American/Greek

U.S. American/German

U.S. American/French-Canadian

White Anglo-American/Reservation Indian

White Anglo-American/Black American,
Oriental American, Mexican American,
or Urban Indian

U.S. American/British

U.S. American/English-Canadian

Urban American/Rural American

Catholic/Baptist

Male Dominance/Female Equality

Heterosexual/Homosexual

Environmentalist/Developer

MINIMUM

Figure 2 Arrangement of Compared
Cultures, Subcultures, and Subgroups
Along a Scale of Minimum to Maximum
Sociocultural Differences

differences have on communication. In order to see how this dimensional scale helps us understand intercultural communication, we can look at some examples of cultural differences positioned along the scale.

The first example represents a case of maximum differences—those found between Asian and Western cultures. This may be typified as an interaction between two farmers, one who works on a communal farm on the outskirts of Beijing in China and the other who operates a large mechanized and automated wheat, corn, and dairy farm in Michigan. In this situation, we would expect to find the greatest number of cultural factors subject to variation. Physical appearance, religion, philosophy, economic systems, social attitudes, language, heritage, basic conceptualizations of self and the universe, and degree of technological development are cultural factors that differ sharply. We must recognize, however, that these two farmers also share the commonality of farming, with its rural life style and love of land. In some respects, they may be more closely related than they are to members of their own cultures who live in large urban settings. In other words, across some cultural dimensions, the Michigan farmer may have more in common with the Chinese farmer than with a Wall Street securities broker.

An example nearer the center of the scale is the difference between American culture and German culture. Less variation is found: Physical characteristics are similar, and the English language is derived in part from German and its ancestor languages. The root of both German and American philosophy are found in ancient Greece, and most Americans and Germans share some form of the Christian religion. Yet there are some significant differences. Germans have political and economic systems that differ somewhat from those found in the United States. German society tends toward formality while in the United States we tend toward informality. Germans have memories of local warfare and the destruction of their cities and economy, of having been a defeated nation on more than one occasion. The United States has never lost a war on its own territory.

Examples near the minimal end of the dimension can be characterized in two ways. First are variations found between members of separate but similar cultures—for instance, between U.S. Americans and English Canadians. The differences are less than those found between American and German cultures, between American and British cultures, or even between American and French-Canadian cultures, but greater than generally found within a single culture. Second, minimal differences also may be seen in the variation between subcultures, subgroups, or racial groups within the same dominant culture. Socio-cultural differences may be found between members of the Catholic church and the Baptist church, between ecologists and advocates of further development of Alaskan oil resources, between middle-class Americans and the urban poor, between mainstream Americans and the gay/lesbian community, between the able and the disabled, or between male dominance advocates and female equality advocates.

In both of these categorizations, members of each cultural group have much more in common than in the examples found in the middle or at the maximum end of the scale. They probably speak the same language, share the same general religion, attend the same schools, and live in the same neighborhoods. Yet, these groups to some extent are culturally different; they do not fully share the same experiences, nor do they share the same perceptions. They see their worlds differently.

CULTURE AND COMMUNICATION

The link between culture and communication is crucial to understanding intercultural communication because it is through the influence of culture that people learn to communicate. A Korean, an Egyptian, or an American learns to communicate like other Koreans, Egyptians, or Americans. Their behavior conveys meaning because it is learned and shared; it is cultural. People view their world through categories, concepts, and labels that are products of their culture.

Cultural similarity in perception makes the sharing of meaning possible. The ways in which we communicate, the circumstances of our communication, the language and language style we use, and our nonverbal behaviors are primarily all a response to and a function of our culture. And, as cultures differ from one another, the communication practices and behaviors of individuals reared in those cultures will also be different.

Culture is an all-encompassing form or pattern for living. It is complex, abstract, and pervasive. Numerous aspects of culture help to determine communicative behavior. These socio-cultural elements are diverse and cover a wide range of human social activity. For the sake of simplicity and to put some limitation on our discussion, we will examine a few of the socio-cultural elements associated with *perception, verbal processes,* and *nonverbal processes.*

These socio-cultural elements are the constituent parts of intercultural communication. When we combine them, as we do when we communicate, they are like the components of a stereo system—each one relates to and needs the other in order to function properly. In our discussion, the elements will be separated in order to identify and discuss them, but in actuality they do not exist in isolation nor do they function alone. They form a complex matrix of interacting elements that operate together to constitute the complex phenomenon called intercultural communication.

Perception

In its simplest sense, *perception is the internal process by which we select, evaluate, and organize stimuli from the external environment.* In other words, perception is the conversion of the physical energies of our environment into meaningful experience. A number of corollary issues arising out of this definition help explain the relationship between perception and culture. It is believed generally that people behave as they do because of the ways in which they perceive the world, and that these behaviors are learned as part of their cultural experience. Whether in judging beauty or describing snow, we respond to stimuli as we do primarily because our culture has taught us to do so. We tend to notice, reflect on, and respond to those elements in our environment that are important to us. In the United States we might respond principally to a thing's size and cost, while to the Japanese color might be the important criterion.

Social Perception. Social perception is the process by which we construct our unique social realities by attributing meaning to the social objects and events we encounter in our environments. It is an extremely important aspect of communication. Culture conditions and structures our perceptual processes so that we develop culturally inspired perceptual sets. These sets not only help determine which external stimuli reach our awareness, but more important, they significantly influence the social aspect of perception—the social construction of reality—by the attribution of meaning to these stimuli. The difficulties in communication caused by this perceptual variability can best be lowered by knowing about and understanding the cultural factors that are subject to variation, coupled with an honest and sincere desire to communicate successfully across cultural boundaries.

Our contention is that intercultural communication can best be understood as cultural diversity in the perception of social objects and events. A central tenet of this position is that minor communication problems are often exaggerated by perceptual diversity. To understand others' worlds and actions, we must try to understand their perceptual frames of reference, we must learn to understand how they perceive the world. In the ideal intercultural encounter, we would hope for many overlapping experiences and a commonality of perceptions. Cultural diversity, however, tends to introduce us to dissimilar experiences and, hence, to varied and frequently strange and unfamiliar perceptions of the external world.

There are three major socio-cultural elements that have a direct and major influence on the meanings we develop for our perceptions. These elements are our *belief/value/attitude systems,* our *world view,* and our *social organization.* When these three elements influence our perceptions and the meanings we develop for them, they are affecting our individual, subjective aspects of meanings. We all may see the same social entity and agree upon what it is in objective terms, but what the object or event means to us individually may differ considerably. Both an American and a Chinese might agree in an objective sense that a particular object is a young dog, but they might see it as a cute, fuzzy, loving, protective pet. The Chinese, on the other hand, might see the dog as something especially fit for the Sunday barbecue. You see, it is an American cultural background that interprets the dog as a pet, and it is the Chinese cultural background that regards dog meat as a delicacy.

Belief/Value/Attitude Systems. Beliefs, in a general sense, can be viewed as individually held subjective probabilities that some object or event possesses certain characteristics. A belief involves a link between the belief object and the characteristics that distinguish it. The degree to which we believe that an event or an object possesses certain characteristics reflects the level of our subjective probability and, consequently, the depth or intensity of our belief. That is, the more certain we are in a belief, the greater is the intensity of that belief.

Culture plays an important role in belief formation. Whether we accept the *New York Times,* the Bible, the entrails of a goat, tea leaves, the visions induced by peyote, or the changes specified in the Taoist *I Ching* as sources of knowledge and belief depends on our cultural backgrounds and experiences. In matters of intercultural communication, there are no rights or wrongs as far as beliefs are concerned. If someone believes that the voices in the wind can guide one's behavior along the proper path, we cannot throw up our hands and declare the belief wrong (even if we believe it to be wrong); we must be able to recognize and to deal with that belief if we wish to obtain satisfactory and successful communication.

Values are the valuative aspect of our belief/value/attitude systems. Valuative dimensions include qualities such as usefulness, goodness, aesthetics, need satisfaction, and pleasure. Although each of us has a unique set of values, there are also values called *cultural values* that tend to permeate a culture. Cultural values are a set of organized rules for making choices, reducing uncertainty, and reducing conflicts within a given society. They are usually derived from the larger philosophical issues inherent in a culture. These values are generally normative in that they inform a member of a culture what is good and bad, right and wrong, true and false, positive and negative, and so on. Cultural values define what is worth dying for, what is worth protecting, what frightens people, what are considered to be proper subjects for study or ridicule, and what types of events lead individuals to group solidarity. Cultural values also specify which behaviors are important and which should be avoided within a culture.

Values express themselves within a culture as rules that prescribe the behaviors that members of the culture are expected to perform. These are called *normative values*. Thus, Catholics are supposed to attend Mass, motorists are supposed to stop at stop signs, and workers in our culture are supposed to arrive at work at the designated time. Most people follow normative behaviors; a few do not. Failure to do so may be met with either informal or codified sanctions. The Catholic who avoids Mass may receive a visit from a priest, the driver who runs a stop sign may receive a fine, and the employee who is tardy too frequently may be discharged. Normative values also extend into everyday communicative behavior by specifying how people are to behave in specific communication contexts. This extension acts as a guide to individual and group behavior that minimizes or prevents harm to individual sensitivities within cultures.

Beliefs and values contribute to the development and content of *attitudes*. An attitude may be defined formally as *a learned tendency to respond in a consistent manner with respect to a given object of orientation.* This means that we tend to avoid those things we dislike and to embrace those things we like. Attitudes are learned within a cultural context. Whatever cultural environment surrounds us helps shape and form our attitudes, our readiness to respond, and ultimately our behavior.

World View. This cultural element, though somewhat abstract, is one of the most important ones found in the perceptual aspects of intercultural communication. World view deals with a culture's orientation toward such philosophical issues as God, humanity, nature, the universe, and others that are concerned with the concept of being. In short, our world view helps us locate our place and rank in the universe. Because world view is so complex, it is often difficult to isolate during an intercultural interaction. In this examination, we seek to understand its substance and its elusiveness.

World view issues are timeless and represent the most fundamental basis of a culture. A Catholic has a different world view than a Moslem, Hindu, Jew, Taoist, or atheist. The way in which native Americans view the individual's place in nature differs sharply from the Euro-American's view. Native Americans see themselves as one with nature; they perceive a balanced relationship between humankind and the environment, a partnership of equality and respect. Euro-Americans, on the other hand, see a human-centered world in which humans are supreme and are apart from nature. They may treat the universe as theirs— a place to carry out their desires and wishes through the power of science and technology.

World view influences a culture at very profound levels. Its effects are often quite subtle and not revealed in such obvious and often superficial ways as dress, gestures, and vocabulary. We can think of a world view as analogous to a pebble tossed into a pond. Just as the pebble causes ripples that spread and reverberate over the entire surface of the pond, world view likewise spreads itself over a culture and permeates every facet of it. World view influences beliefs, values, attitudes, uses of time, and many other aspects of culture. In its subtle way, it is a powerful influence in intercultural communication because as a member of a culture, each communicator's world view is so deeply imbedded in the psyche that it is taken for granted, and each communicator tends to assume automatically that everyone else views the world as he or she does.

Social Organization. The manner in which a culture organizes itself and its institutions also affects how members of the culture perceive the world and how they communicate. It might be helpful to look briefly at two of the dominant social units found in a culture.

The *family,* although it is the smallest social organization in a culture, is one of the most influential. The family sets the stage for a child's development during the formative periods of life, presents the child with a wide range of cultural influences that affect almost everything from a child's first attitudes to the selection of toys, and guides the child's acquisition of language and the amount of emphasis on it. Skills from vocabulary building to dialects are the purview of the family. The family also offers and withholds approval, support, rewards, and punishments, which have a marked effect on the values children develop and the goals they pursue. If, for example, children learn by observation and communication that silence is paramount in their culture, as do Japanese children, they will reflect that aspect of culture in their behavior and bring it to intercultural settings.

The *school* is another social organization that is important. By definition and history schools are endowed with a major portion of the responsibility for passing on and maintaining a culture. They are a community's basic link with its past as well as its taskmaster for the future. Schools maintain culture by relating to new members what has happened, what is important, and what one as a member of the culture must know. Schools may teach geography or wood carving, mathematics or nature lore; they may stress revolution based on

peace or predicated on violence, or they may relate a particular culturally accepted version of history. But whatever is taught in a school is determined by the culture in which that school exists.

Verbal Processes
Verbal processes include not only how we talk to each other but also the internal activities of thinking and meaning development for the words we use. These processes (*verbal language* and *patterns of thought*) are vitally related to perception and the attachment and expression of meaning.

Verbal Language. Any discussion of language in intercultural settings must include an investigation of language issues in general before dealing with specific problems of foreign language, language translation, and the argot and vernacular of co-cultures. Here, in our introduction to the various dimensions of culture, we will look at verbal language as it relates to our understanding of culture.

In the most basic sense, language is an organized, generally agreed-on, learned symbol system used to represent human experiences within a geographic or cultural community. Each culture places its own individual imprint on word symbols. Objects, events, experiences, and feelings have a particular label or name solely because a community of people has arbitrarily decided to so name them. Thus, because language is an inexact system of symbolically representing reality, the meaning for words are subject to a wide variety of interpretations.

Language is the primary vehicle by which a culture transmits its beliefs, values, norms, and world view. Language gives people a means of interacting with other members of their culture and a means of thinking. Language thus serves both as a mechanism for communication and as a guide to social reality. Language influences perceptions, transmits meaning, and helps mold patterns of thought.

Patterns of Thought. The mental processes, forms of reasoning, and approaches to problem solution prevalent in a community make up another major component of culture. Unless they have had experiences with people from other cultures who follow different patterns of thought, most people assume everyone thinks and solves problems in much the same way. We must be aware, however, that there are cultural differences in aspects of thinking and knowing. This diversity can be clarified and related to intercultural communication by making a general comparison between Western and Eastern patterns of thought. In most Western thought there is an assumption of a direct relationship between mental concepts and the concrete world of reality. This orientation places great stock in logical considerations and rationality. There is a belief that truth is out there somewhere and that it can be discovered by following correct logical sequences—one need only turn over the right rocks in the right order and it will be there. The Eastern view, best illustrated by Taoist thought, holds that problems are solved quite differently. To begin with, people are not granted instant rationality, truth is not found by active searching and the application of Aristolelian modes of reasoning. On the contrary, one must wait, and if truth is to be known, it will make itself apparent. The major difference in these two views is in the area of activity: To the Western mind, human activity is paramount and ultimately will lead to the discovery of truth; in the Taoist tradition, truth is the active agent, and if it is to be known, it will be through the activity of truth making itself apparent.

A culture's thought patterns affect the way individuals in that culture communicate, which in turn affects the way each person responds to individuals from another culture. We cannot expect everyone to employ the same patterns of thinking, but understanding that many patterns exist and learning to accommodate them will facilitate our intercultural communication.

Nonverbal Processes

Verbal processes are the primary means for the exchange of thoughts and ideas, but closely related nonverbal processes often can overshadow them. Most authorities agree that the following topics comprise the realm of nonverbal processes: gestures, facial expressions, eye contact and gaze, posture and movement, touching, dress, objects and artifacts, silence, space, time, and paralanguage. As we turn to the nonverbal processes relevant to intercultural communication, we will consider three aspects: *nonverbal behavior* that functions as a silent form of language, the *concept of time,* and the *use and organization of space.*

Nonverbal Behavior. It would be foolish for us to try to examine all of the elements that constitute nonverbal behavior because of the tremendous range of activity that constitutes this form of human activity. An example or two will enable us to visualize how nonverbal issues fit into the overall scheme of intercultural understanding. For example, touch as a form of communication can demonstrate how nonverbal communication is a product of culture. German women as well as men shake hands at the outset of every social encounter; in the United States, women are less likely to shake hands. Vietnamese men do not shake hands with women or elders unless the woman or the elder offers the hand first. In Thailand, people do not touch in public, and to touch someone on the head is a major social transgression. You can imagine the problems that could arise if one did not understand some of the differences.

Another illustrative example is eye contact. In the United States we are encouraged to maintain good eye contact when we communicate. In Japan and other Asian countries, however, eye contact often is not important, and among native Americans, children are taught that eye contact with an adult is a sign of disrespect.

The eyes can also be used to express feelings. For instance, widening the eyes may note surprise for an Anglo, but the feelings denoted by eye widening are culturally diverse. Widened eyes may also indicate anger by a Chinese, a request for help or assistance by a Hispanic, the issuance of a challenge by a French person, and a rhetorical or persuasive effect by a black.

As a component of culture, nonverbal expression has much in common with language: Both are coding systems that we learn and pass on as part of the cultural experience. Just as we learn that the word "stop" can mean to halt or cease, we also learn that an arm held up in the air with the palm facing another person frequently means the same thing. Because most nonverbal communication is culturally based, what it symbolizes often is a case of what a culture has transmitted to its members. The nonverbal symbol for suicide, for example, varies among cultures. In the United States it is usually a finger pointed at the temple or drawn across the throat. In Japan, it is a hand thrust onto the stomach, and in New Guinea it is a hand placed on the neck. Both nonverbal symbols and the responses they generate are part of cultural experience—what is passed from generation to generation. Every symbol takes on significance because of one's past experience with it. Even such simple acts as waving the hand can produce culturally diverse responses: In the United States, we tend to wave goodbye by placing the hand out with the palm down and moving the hand up and down; in India and in parts of Africa and South America, this is a beckoning gesture. We should also be aware that what may be a polite or friendly gesture in one culture may be an impolite and obscene gesture in another. Culture influences and directs those experiences, and is, therefore, a major contributor to how we send, receive, and respond to nonverbal symbols.

The Concept of Time. A culture's concept of time is its philosophy toward the past, present, and future and the importance or lack of importance it places on time. Most Western cultures think of time in lineal-spatial terms; we are time bound and well aware of the past, present, and future. In contrast, the Hopi Indians pay very little attention to time. They believe that each object—whether a person, plant, or animal—has its own time system.

Even within the dominant mainstream of American culture, we find groups that have learned to perceive time in ways that appear strange to many outsiders. Hispanics frequently refer to Mexican or Latino time when their timing differs from the predominant Anglo concept, and blacks often use what is referred to as BPT (black people's time) or hang-loose time—maintaining that priority belongs to what is happening at that instant.

Use of Space. The way in which people use space as a part of interpersonal communication is called *proxemics.* It involves not only the distance between people engaged in conversation but also their physical orientation. We are all most likely to have some familiarity with the fact that Arabs and Latins tend to interact physically closer together than do North American Anglos. What is important is to realize that people of different cultures have different ways in which they relate to one another spatially. Therefore, when talking to someone from another culture, we must expect what in our culture would be a violation of our personal space and be prepared to continue our interaction without reacting adversely. We may experience feelings that are difficult to handle; we may believe that the other person is overbearing, boorish, or even making unacceptable sexual advances when indeed the other person's movements are only manifestations of his or her cultural learning about how to use space.

Physical orientation is also culturally influenced, and it helps to define social relationships. North Americans prefer to sit where they are face to face or at right angles to one another. We seldom seek side-by-side arrangements. Chinese, on the other hand, often prefer a side-by-side arrangement and may feel uncomfortable when placed in a face-to-face situation.

We also tend to define social hierarchies through our nonverbal use of space. Sitting behind a desk while speaking with someone who is standing is usually a sign of a superior-subordinate relationship, with the socially superior person seated. Misunderstandings can easily occur in intercultural settings when two people, each acting according to the dictates of his or her culture, violate each other's expectations. If we were to remain seated when expected to rise, for example, we could easily violate a cultural norm and insult our host or guest unknowingly.

Room furnishings and size can also be an indication of social status. In corporate America, status within the corporation is often measured by desk size, office size, whether the carpet is wall to wall or merely a rug.

How we organize space also is a function of our culture. Our homes, for instance, preserve nonverbally our cultural beliefs and values. South American house designs are extremely private, with only one door opening onto the street and everything else behind walls. North Americans are used to large unwalled front yards with windows looking into the house, allowing passersby to see what goes on inside. In South America, a North American is liable to feel excluded and wonder about what goes on behind all those closed doors.

COMMUNICATION CONTEXT

Any communicative interaction takes place within some social and physical context. When people are communicating within their culture, they are usually aware of the context and it does little to hinder the communication. When people are engaged in intercultural communication, however, the context in which that communication takes place can have a strong impact. Unless both parties to intercultural communication are aware of how their culture affects the contextual element of communication, they can be in for some surprising communication difficulty.

Context and Communication

We begin with the assumption that communicative behavior is governed by rules—principles or regulations that govern conduct and procedure. In communication, rules act as a system of expected behavior patterns that organize interaction between individuals. Communication rules are both culturally and contextually bound. Although the social setting and situation may determine the type of rules that are appropriate, the culture determines the rules. In Iraq, for instance, a contextual rule prohibits females from having unfamiliar males visit them at home; in the United States, however, it is not considered socially inappropriate for unknown males to visit females at home. Rules dictate behavior by establishing appropriate responses to stimuli for a particular communication context.

Communication rules include both verbal and nonverbal components—the rules determine not only what should be said but how it should be said. Nonverbal rules apply to proper gestures, facial expressions, eye contact, proxemics, vocal tone, and body movements.

Unless one is prepared to function in the contextual environment of another culture, he or she may be in for an unpleasant experience. The intercultural situation can be one of high stress, both physically and mentally. The effects of this stress are called culture shock. In order to avoid culture shock, it is necessary to have a full understanding of communication context and how it varies culturally. We must remember that cultural contexts are neither right nor wrong, better or worse; they are just different.

Having determined that cultures develop rules that govern human interaction in specific contexts, we need now to gain some insight into the general concept of context. Anthropologist Edward T. Hall has written extensively about context.[1] Although he categorizes cultures as being either high-context or low-context, context really is a cultural dimension that ranges from high to low. An example of various cultures

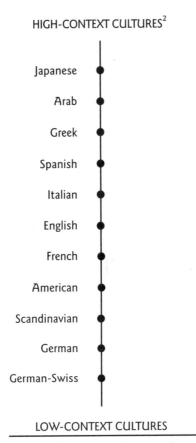

HIGH-CONTEXT CULTURES[2]

Japanese

Arab

Greek

Spanish

Italian

English

French

American

Scandinavian

German

German-Swiss

LOW-CONTEXT CULTURES

Figure 3 High- and Low-Context Cultures

placed along that dimension can be seen in Figure 3.

In high-context cultures most of the information is either in the physical context or is internalized in the people who are a part of the interaction. Very little information is actually coded in the verbal message. In low-context cultures, however, most of the information is contained in the verbal message and very little is embedded in the context or within the participants. In high-context cultures such as those of Japan, Korea, and Taiwan, people tend to be more aware of their surroundings and their environment and do not rely on verbal communication as their main information source. The Korean language contains a word *nunchi* that literally means being able to communicate through your eyes. In high-context cultures, so much information is available in the environment that it is unnecessary to state verbally that which is obvious. Oral

statements of affection, for instance, are very rare—when the context says "I love you," it is not necessary to state it orally.

There are four major differences in how high- and low-context cultures affect the setting. First, verbal messages are extremely important in low-context cultures. It is in the verbal message that the information to be shared is coded; it is not readily available from the environment because people in low-context cultures do not tend to learn how to receive information from the environment through perception. Second, low-context people who rely primarily on verbal messages for information are perceived as less attractive and less credible by people in high-context cultures. Third, people in high-context cultures are more adept at reading nonverbal behavior and reading the environment. And, fourth, people in high-context cultures have an expectation that others are also able to understand the unarticulated communication; hence, they do not speak as much as people from low-context cultures.

SUMMARY

In many respects the relationship between culture and communication is reciprocal—each affects and influences the other. What we talk about; how we talk about it, what we see, attend to, or ignore; how we think; and what we think about are influenced by our culture. In turn, what we talk about, how we talk about it, and what we see help shape, define, and perpetuate our culture. Culture cannot exist without communication; one cannot change without causing change in the other.

We have suggested that the chief problem associated with intercultural communication is error in social perception brought about by cultural diversity that affects the perceptual process. The attribution of meaning to messages is in many respects influenced by the culture of the person responding to the message behavior. When the message being interpreted is encoded in another culture, the cultural influences and experiences that produced that message may have been entirely different from the cultural influences and experiences that are being drawn on to interpret and respond to the message. Consequently, unintended errors in meaning may arise because people with entirely different backgrounds are unable to understand one another accurately.

We have discussed several socio-cultural variables that are major sources of communication difficulty. Although they were discussed in isolation, we cannot allow ourselves to include that they are unrelated—they are all related in a matrix of cultural complexities. For successful intercultural communication, we must be aware of these cultural factors affecting communication in both our own culture and in the culture of the other party. We need to understand not only cultural differences, which will help us determine sources of potential problems, but also cultural similarities, which will help us become closer to one another.

The approach we have taken is also based on a fundamental assumption: The parties to intercultural communication must have an honest and sincere desire to communicate and to seek mutual understanding. This assumption requires favorable attitudes about intercultural communication and an elimination of superior-inferior relationships based on membership in particular cultures, races, religions, or ethnic groups. Unless this basic assumption has been satisfied, our theory of cultural diversity in social perception will not produce improvement in intercultural communication.

At the beginning of this article we mentioned how changes in transportation and communication technology had brought us to the brink of the global village. We also suggested that we, as a people, do not yet know how to live as global villagers. We want to return to this point as we finish here and leave you with some thoughts about it.

The prevailing direction in the United States today seems to be toward a pluralistic, multicultural society. An underlying assumption of this position, one that is seldom expressed or perhaps often realized, is that this requires that we as a society be accepting of the views, values, and behaviors of other cultures. This means that we must be willing to "live and let live." We do not seem able or willing to do this, however, nor are we sure that it is proper to do so in all circumstances. But if we are to get along with one another, we must develop this toleration for others' culturally diverse customs and behaviors—a task that will be difficult.

Even within the dominant mainstream culture, we are unable to accept diversity; for example, we find ourselves deeply divided over such issues as right to life versus freedom of choice. When we must cope with the diversity of customs, values, views, and behaviors inherent in a multicultural society, we will find ourselves in much greater states of frustration and peril. As an example, the CNN News Network carried a story on March 2, 1990 about fundamentalist Christians in a town who were demanding the removal of a statue of Buddha from in front of an Oriental restaurant because "it was the idol of a false God; it's in the New Testament." Also, several months ago the newspapers carried a story about a judge who dismissed wife-beating charges against an Asian man because this form of behavior was appropriate and acceptable in the man's culture. The action by the judge was immediately assailed by the feminist movement. This is not the arena to argue the rightness or the wrongness of the judge's decision, but this is the place to make you aware of the problems that we must face as we move toward a pluralistic, multicultural society. We hope that your thinking about this issue now will prepare you for your life in the global village.

NOTES

1. Hall, E. T. (1976). *Beyond Culture*. Garden City, N.Y.: Doubleday.

2. Copeland, L., and L. Griggs. (1985). *Going International: How to Make Friends and Deal Effectively in the Global Marketplace*. New York: Random House.

The foreign student today: a profile

Guiding the Development of Foreign Students

K Richard Pyle, *Editor*
University of Texas, Austin

**NEW DIRECTIONS
FOR STUDENT SERVICES**

MARGARET J. BARR, *Editor-in-Chief*
Texas Christian University

M. LEE UPCRAFT, *Associate Editor*
Pennsylvania State University

Number 36, Winter 1986

Paperback sourcebooks in
The Jossey-Bass
Higher Education Series

Jossey-Bass Inc., Publishers
San Francisco • London

This is the title page for the book in which the following article appears.

After thorough consideration of the case with our bishops, abbots, princes, dukes, judges, and other noblemen of our high court, we decree this benefit of our grace, that everyone who because of his studies wanders abroad, students and professors of the most divine and holy laws, shall themselves as well as their messengers come in security to places where studies are exercised and live there in peace . . . who of them would not be pitied as they for the love of sciences long exiled, deprived themselves, being already poor of riches, exposed their lives to many dangers and sustain corporal injuries by often very villainous people.

Frederick I, 1158 A.D.,
178 Privilegium Scholasticum

Jill D. Bulthuis

As early as the Middle Ages students and professors were going abroad in search of academic opportunities unavailable at home and accepting the challenge of adapting to strange people and customs. The history of foreign students on United States campuses can be traced to the colonial colleges, but beginning with Francisco de Miranda, who studied at Yale as early as 1784, foreign students came to this country as individual sojourners. Although their numbers were significant enough to be included in statistics early in this century, they were considered unusual and exotic due in part perhaps to their English pronunciation or their distinctive styles of dress (Barber, 1985).

A massive acceleration of the movement of students and scholars began after World War II, although foreign students did not begin to appear in significant numbers until the 1950s (Barber, 1985). With this large influx, which represented a wide cross section of society, certain problems became apparent in the adjustment of some students concerning English language skills, and financial support. Their reasons for coming to the United States persist among today's foreign students, and in many cases the challenges they face persist as well.

Spaulding and Flack (1976) concluded that the major reasons foreign students come to the United States are to get an advanced education or training not available at home, to gain prestige with a degree from a U.S. institution, to take advantage of available scholarship funds, to escape unsettled political or economic conditions, and to learn about the United States. When a student from Mexico City who is studying film at New York University decided he wanted to be a filmmaker, he decided to come to the United States to study. "If I could have stayed in Mexico, I would have," he said, "but there is only one film school there, and it is not a good one" (personal communication). So he enrolled in the program at New York University. A group of Malaysian students are studying computer science at a midwestern university because their government has a training contract with that school. Several students from El Salvador studying at the University of North Carolina at Chapel Hill have continued on into graduate programs to avoid returning to the political unrest at home.

Enrollment Trends

Evangelauf (1985) reported in the *Chronicle of Higher Education* that the number of foreign students attending U.S. colleges and universities has remained relatively steady for the second year in a row. In 1984–1985 the foreign student population was 342,111. According to the results of the annual foreign student census of the Institute of International Education (IIE), the typical foreign student was male, attended a public four-year institution, studied business or a scientific or technical subject, and paid his bills with personal or family resources. More students came from Taiwan than from any other country. The enrollment of students from South and East Asia increased most in the 1984–1985 period, with China experiencing the greatest growth, followed by Malaysia and Korea. Seventy percent of the students were male, 46 percent were studying for bachelor's degrees, and 36 percent were studying for graduate degrees. Of the 65 percent attending public institutions, two-thirds were paying their own education expenses.

The rate of future flow of foreign students into the United States is predicted in a recent IIE research report (Barber, 1985). A relatively small number of countries (fifteen) account for 60 percent of the foreign students in the United States, and this concentration leaves many American institutions vulnerable to the impact of policy changes of a handful of countries that send their students here.

The number of women among foreign students has been increasing steadily. The United States plays an important role in educating foreign students in engineering, the natural sciences, law, and social sciences. Thirty percent of all foreign students in the United States are enrolled in only 1 percent of the institutions, so greater institutional dispersion in the future seems likely, considering the absorption capacity of institutions. A more equal balance between undergraduate and graduate students is also likely to occur in the near future. These trends reflect the condition of educational resources in all parts of the world. In spite of the IIE total enrollment statistics cited above, the firmest of several projections cited here indicates that by 1991 there will be 698,000 foreign students in the United States, almost double the present

number. Since East Asia is gaining economic ground and countries of that region place a high premium on education, wealthy countries with large populations will likely be of far greater significance than small and poor countries. If the People's Republic of China becomes seriously interested in sending students here, the implications for higher education will be dramatic owing to the need for additional services.

Chinese Students. Since Chinese students are generally less prepared for study abroad, they will require comprehensive, balanced support services to ensure adequate adjustment to the language, the educational system, and U.S. culture. College admissions staff will need to develop skill in evaluating credentials from Chinese institutions. Since Chinese people are generally unaccustomed to automobile traffic, safety regulations must be a part of their orientation if they are to avoid accidents. Students in China do not have access to foreign currency exchange, and as a result many have arrived in the United States with insufficient funds to pay their school fees and support themselves adequately. Those who are government sponsored receive lower-than-average stipends; thus their living conditions are frequently substandard and groups live together for reasons of economics and convenience. Institutions with large enrollments of Chinese students and scholars report that support service costs are high and that successful integration of these individuals into the campus community is difficult to accomplish.

Fields of Study. The foreign student population in the United States has grown most rapidly in the fields of business, while the fields of humanities, health, agriculture, and education have shown the smallest relative growth. The fields in which American student interest has dropped most dramatically (humanities and education) are also in relatively low demand by foreign students, while the fields in greatest demand by foreign students are also in high demand by American students (Zikopoülos and Barber, 1985).

Needs of Foreign Students. The influx of foreign students into U.S. colleges and universities in recent years has resulted in countless investigations—some local, others national and international in scope—to study the phenomenon of students sojourners and their experiences in this country. These investigations indicate, however, that it is as difficult to generalize about the expectations, needs, attitudes, experiences, and problems of foreign students as it is to generalize about the schools enrolling them.

The term *foreign student* is clearly too broad for fruitful discussion about students from other countries. The term masks important distinctions based on such matters as country of origin, age, sponsorship, field of study, personal goals in studying abroad, and job opportunities at home. A married graduate student from East Asia is likely to have very different priorities and interests from those of an unmarried Latin American undergraduate. Regarding both as foreign students implies that they have more in common than they do.

Three hundred forty-two thousand students come from more than 150 countries and have dramatically different levels of English language proficiency, academic preparation, financial support, and social skills. These students are attending at least 3,000 schools, each with its own academic program and level of commitment to international education, that are located in communities across the United States (Barber, 1985). A Malaysian graduate student studying engineering at the University of Evansville, Indiana, would describe his or her experiences very differently from an undergraduate German student studying American folklore at the University of Virginia. The financial strain on a student at the University of Southern California is somewhat different from that of a student in a cooperative work-study program at Northeastern University in Boston. Language is a problem for some but not for others. The same disparity is found in the areas of finances, academics, and social life.

Concerns of Foreign Students

Perhaps the most consistent generalizations about foreign students in the United States are those of Iowa State University sociologist, Motoko Lee (1981), who surveyed two thousand foreign students about their most important and best-satisfied needs. Lee developed a profile of the student most likely to have a satisfying educational experience in the United States: a Latin American or European graduate assistant who has good English skills, an American roommate, and a job waiting at home. In general, Lee found that foreign students place much greater importance on their academic and professional goals than they do on nonacademic concerns. Although students were generally satisfied with their progress toward academic goals, their lack of practical work experience and uncertainty about careers were matters of great concern.

Personal experience lends support to Lee's findings. Even students who have suffered serious problems with housing, for example, or with the banking system, the Internal Revenue Service, or with the Immigration and Naturalization Service are inclined to rate academic and financial problems as the most difficult. Foreign student loan funds on many U.S. campuses have kept numerous foreign students afloat while they were waiting for stipends delayed by international conflicts that frequently affect currency transfer controls abroad or when personal or family emergencies have placed unusual demands on their finances.

Given foreign students' diversity of personal experience, cultural distinctions, language experience, and motivations for study in the United States, how can cultural characteristics, attitudes, and patterns about a group as heterogeneous as this be addressed? I will compare and contrast those American values, expectations, and assumptions that cause difficulties and conflicts for students from abroad. (An apology is in order to Canadian and Latin American readers for using the term *American:* I realize that it is an inaccurate and not necessarily inclusive usage.)

Concept of Time. Students from African, Asian, and Latin American countries agree that the pace of life in the United States is fast. Americans are very much on the go, racing from morning to night, frequently taking half an hour to eat lunch while standing up at a counter. Americans are very dependent on the clock, which provides structure in their lives. Movies or other events begin precisely at 7:15 or 9:30, and students rush to make a class that begins at 9:15. New foreign students are amazed when they receive the invitation to the college president's reception in their honor and the invitation reads 7:30–9:30. Whoever heard of telling honored guests when to leave a party? Americans see time as a limited resource, not to be wasted. More university personnel need to realize that there is a different way of viewing the world, a perspective in which time tends to be measured more in days, weeks, and months than in minutes and hours. When invited to a dinner given by West African students, it is a good idea to ask whether it is 7:00 American time or African time, which could mean much later. There is a perspective in others parts of the world that allows for more than a quick "hi" when running into a friend on the street. A Kenyan student points out that in his country there would be more of an exchange of pleasantries when meeting an acquaintance by chance.

Friendships. In this highly mobile society, Americans move an average of fourteen times. When combined with the highly individualistic character for which Americans are well known, the result is a concept of friendship that is less permanent and lasting than friendships in another culture. Americans are described by foreign students at the University of North Carolina as very friendly and approachable but as not following through on their offers. Phrases such as, "Come on over some time," "Let's get together real soon for lunch," "I'll call you," and "Y'all come again real soon," when not followed by a definite invitation, are intended to be meaningless pleasantries. But to many newly arrived foreign students, these exchanges are interpreted as positive signals of sincere interest and friendship.

A five-year study entitled "The Cross-Cultural Student—Lessons in Human Nature" (the "Stick to Your Own Kind" study, as it later became known) conducted at the University of Wisconsin indicated that international students associate most with fellow nationals. These students' warm, intimate, dependent, personally satisfying contacts are almost exclusively limited to their own national group. Their relations with Americans rarely go beyond superficial pleasantries, since they are discouraged about any prospect for deep cross-cultural friendships (Miller, 1971, p. 128).

It appears that despite shared projects, shared picnics, or occasionally shared rooms, the majority of interpersonal contacts fall far short of friendship for these students. Even with the increasing emphasis on internalization and with pressures within the United States for breaking down barriers between different peoples, there is only slight evidence of progress within what should be the most enlightened and tolerant segment of society—the university community.

The result is that foreign students who experience enough interpersonal disappointment or rejection will generally become convinced that the advice to "stick to your own kind," is good.

Foreign student advisers tell the story of Kwame Nkhrumah to demonstrate this isolation. Half a century ago, a poor student from West Africa traveled to this country to attend a university in Philadelphia—a sojourn he would later recall as "years of sorrow and loneliness." He experienced poverty and racism that he had not known in Africa, and he nearly died of exhaustion from working nights and attending class during the day. It was an experience he remembered vividly and often recounted years later after rising to international prominence as the founding father and president of the African nation of Ghana (Herbert, 1981).

Equality. It is not always easy for elite members of hierarchical societies who become graduate students in the United States to see the benefits of an egalitarian system. Accustomed to instantaneous, cordial service at home, they are suddenly faced with making do in the kitchen, grocery store, and laundromat—different territory for many male, and female, students from abroad. To add to the misery, they frequently confront indifferent service people with "I'm as good as you are" attitudes. These experiences, coupled with a reduced standard of living necessitated by small wages or stipends, can result in what sometimes is called status shock. These students may need help in adapting to the American lifestyle, where working women are also housewives and mothers—and without servants.

For some students this egalitarianism may be most noticeable in the classroom. Foreign students are quick to notice the different student-faculty relationships that exist. It is difficult for many of them to adjust to an open classroom environment in which students can criticize a professor's point of view, informal presentations of opinions are part of the grade, and professors remain involved in serious discussions with students after class or occasionally invite students to their homes. This is unusual for many students who are accustomed to speaking in class only when called on or who have had no contact with faculty members outside the classroom.

Pedagogy. Many societies stress memorization in their education systems, and knowledge is conceived of as a body of facts that students memorize. If students acquire this knowledge or a portion of it, they are considered educated. Americans conceive of knowledge, however, as a constant discovery involving an ongoing search, a creative process requiring a different style of pedagogy.

Many foreign students, students from the Middle East, for example, will initially have difficulties studying in our system. They often have not been trained to do independent library research or to write imaginative or even logical essays. Generally they have only experienced the lecture method of teaching and have been required to memorize facts in preparation for exams once or twice a year. Many of these students are unaccustomed to the constant pressure of pop quizzes, frequent exams, classroom assignments, and term papers and may need some coaching to learn how to adapt.

In an educational system such as ours in which professors often leave the classroom during exams and students do not complete study projects cooperatively unless specifically assigned to do so, students new to the honor code system have been accused of cheating and plagiarism. Cheating by foreign students may be partly explained by the pressure to obtain good grades in order to achieve status and prestigious jobs. This pressure, together with culturally reinforced reliance on personal ties, such as those among fellow students, may result in a higher incidence of plagiarism among certain groups of foreign students. Another explanation may lie in not understanding what plagiarism is. If students have never had to write an essay or term paper and if memorization and factual content have been stressed in their educational experience, they may assume that writing a paper means copying material from a published text. One way to reduce such incidents is to ensure that the definitions of plagiarism and cheating are clearly understood in each educational setting, while keeping in mind that these definitions may be different for a computer science course, a physics laboratory, and a business management class.

Adjustment. In discussing the adjustment problems of foreign students, Howard Smith (1955) emphasized four stages that most students pass through while studying abroad: the spectator stage, the adaptive stage, the coming-to-terms stage, and the predeparture stage.

In the spectator stage, foreign students studying in the United States may suffer nervous fatigue, but the excitement of the experience and the adventure is pleasing. Students are somewhat detached in this stage, and their beliefs and values are not threatened. This first stage ends when students are called to participate in activities or endeavors that are rooted in the American culture and that contradict their values and beliefs. The second, or adaptive stage is one of unresolved conflict and culture shock in which individual defenses are rallied to counteract numerous stresses. Coming to terms with a new environment marks the third stage, during which students recognize and reassess their own traditional habits, beliefs, behaviors, and attitudes. Students in this stage reject and criticize American culture more freely and choose the kinds and degrees of conformity that will allow them to adapt to American people and customs. They may become more aggressive, diligent, relaxed, or tolerant, but at least they have reached a state of equilibrium. In the predeparture stage, students put American culture into another perspective as they begin to focus on reestablishing themselves in their home countries.

An awareness of the stages in the adjustment process and of the characteristics of American culture that can hinder the adjustment of students from abroad will be useful to counselors, faculty, and student support services personnel who work with foreign students. It will also be helpful for students to understand how the cultural adjustment process can affect their physical and mental health and how to find and use the support systems available to them.

Conclusion

Many traditional student development theories may not apply to foreign students whose value systems differ dramatically from those of Americans. Americans value independence, self-reliance, autonomy, efficiency, time management, and entrepreneurship. Our theories of student development tend to promote such values, character traits, and life patterns. Many foreign students at U.S. colleges and universities arrive with different values and principles. Many come from countries where such things as young single women living alone or independent of their parents, or competition resulting in someone's failure, is virtually unknown. In their culture paying someone money may be the only way to accomplish something, and definitions of male and female roles are clear and rigid. For some, adapting to an American campus is merely a formidable challenge. To others it presents a serious obstacle to accomplishing educational goals. Sensitivity to different cultural expectations concerning classroom behavior, appropriate roles of faculty and staff, and the way services should be provided may alleviate misunderstanding and frustration for all involved.

The foreign students currently in the United States are from many different countries and of various ages. The represent various socioeconomic levels and study every subject available. This diversity makes a profile of the foreign student today difficult to assess. This population has been likened, however, to a good vegetable soup in which the individual vegetables remain whole and identifiable in appearance and taste, yet blend together to create a flavor that is distinct and enriches what otherwise might be bland and homogeneous.

References

Barber, E. G. (ed). *Foreign Student Flows*. New York: Institute of International Education, 1985.

Evangelauf, J. "Number of Foreign Students in U.S. Rises Less than 1 Percent." *Chronicle of Higher Education*, October 9, 1985, p. 31.

Herbert, W. "Abroad in the U.S.: Foreign Students on American Campuses." *Educational Record*, Summer 1981, pp. 68-71.

Lee, M. Y. *Needs of Foreign Students from Developing Nations at U.S. Colleges and Universities.* Washington, D.C: National Association for Foreign Student Affairs, 1981.

Miller, M. H. "The Cross-Cultural Student—Lessons in Human Nature." *Bulletin of the Menninger Clinic,* 1971, *34* (2), 128.

Smith, H. P. "Do Intercultural Experiences Affect Attitudes?" *Journal of Abnormal and Social Psychology,* 1955, *51,* 469–477.

Spaulding, S., and Flack, M. *The World's Students in the United States.* New York: Praeger, 1976.

Zikopoülos, M., and Barber, E. G. (eds.) *Profiles, 1983 / 1984.* New York: Institute of International Education, 1985.

Jill D. Bulthuis is director of the International Center at the University of North Carolina in Chapel Hill. She has been an active member of NAFSA and has recently served as the NAFSA liaison to ACPA Commission X, "International Dimensions of Student Development."

CHAPTER READINGS

Consult the following sources to learn more about cross-cultural issues.

Condon, J. C., and F. Yousef (1975). *An Introduction to Intercultural Communication.* Indianapolis: Bobbs Merrill.

Hall, E. T. (1976). *Beyond Culture.* Garden City, N.Y.: Anchor Books

Lewis, H. (1990). *A Question of Values: Six Ways We Make the Personal Choices That Shape Our Lives.* San Francisco: HarperCollins.

Prosser, M. H. (1978). *The Culture Dialogue: An Introduction to Intercultural Communication.* Boston: Houghton Mifflin.

Samovar, L. A., and R. E. Porter (1991). *Intercultural Communication: A Reader.* (6th ed.) Belmont, Calif.: Wadsworth.

Samovar, L. A., and R. E. Porter (1991). *Communication Between Cultures.* Belmont, Calif.: Wadsworth.

Stewart, E. C. (1972). *American Cultural Patterns: A Cross-Cultural Perspective.* LaGrange Park, Ill.: Intercultural Network, Inc.

Thinking and Communicating Critically

Chapter Theme: Understanding Aggression and Violence

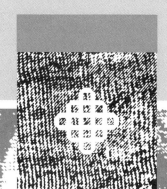

In this chapter, you will be developing sharper critical thinking skills—summarizing, analyzing, interpreting, and synthesizing. These skills will be invaluable to you in your academic work; they will help you become a better reader, writer and speaker. They will also encourage you to think carefully about what you read and how you communicate your own ideas. You will be practicing these skills while learning about a widespread problem in our world—aggression and violence. You will be exploring possible causes and links to violence, and you will soon find out that not all scholars agree.

ACADEMIC TOPICS

- Summarizing Sources
- Paraphrasing Sources
- Analyzing Multiple Sources
- Synthesizing Sources

CHAPTER THEME

Understanding Aggression and Violence

TAKING INVENTORY: YOUR OWN THOUGHTS

You will soon be reading several articles on aggression and violence. Before you find out what other people believe and know about this topic, consider your own ideas. Respond briefly to the following questions in your journal and be ready to discuss your answers in small groups. Be aware that there is no *one* right answer to these questions.

1. How do you explain that some people commit violent acts and others do not? What are some possible reasons?
2. The number of males in U.S. prisons is significantly greater than the number of females. Why do you think this is so? Have you observed differences in the aggressive behavior of males and females? If so, what are they?
3. Do you believe there is a "cure" for violent behavior? What would that be?

Exercise 1:   Preview the following article on violence and the brain. **Skim for important clues** to the contents of the article, looking at the title, illustrations, date of publication, information about the author, the main ideas, headings, and so on. Be ready to share what you find out with your class.

Then read the text more carefully, interacting with it by **highlighting important points** and **annotating questions and comments** in the margin. If there are words that are unfamiliar to you, make a note of them—without stopping to consult a dictionary unless it is absolutely necessary. (If you are unsure about marking your text, refer to Chapter 2 for help.) Answer the questions at the end of the text and be ready to discuss your responses with the class.

FEARS CLOUD SEARCH FOR GENETIC ROOTS OF VIOLENCE

Many say studies could open the door to abuses and racism. Scientists are sharply divided.

by Sheryl Stolberg
Times Medical Writer

As gun detectors become standard furniture in schools and some children learn to fire automatic weapons before they learn to drive, Dr. Markku Linnoila is struggling to unravel a great mystery of human behavior: What transforms innocent little children into brutal teenagers and adults.

Across America, hundreds of other scholars are on a similar quest, frantically searching for the roots of modern violence. Most are pursuing the obvious leads: poverty, parental neglect, lack of education, drugs, guns and TV violence.

Not Linnoila. He is hunting for clues in genes—and triggering great controversy while he is at it.

In his laboratory at the National Institutes of Health, the soft-spoken native of Finland has spent 13 years immersing himself in the intricacies of the brain chemical serotonin. By examining the spinal fluid and blood of more than 1,000 Finnish prisoners—including 300 violent offenders—he says he has proved over and over again that people with low levels of this neurotransmitter are prone to impulsive, violent acts, especially when they abuse alcohol.

Now Linnoila is searching for "vulnerability genes" that create this serotonin deficit. His goal: to be able to predict who might become violent, and then to prevent it—either with programs to help these people change their behavior or, if that doesn't work, new drugs.

At a time when the U.S. Centers for Disease Control has declared that violence is America's most pressing public health threat, Linnoila's work raises some of the most intriguing—and politically volatile—questions in medical research today. Are some people biologically or genetically predisposed to violence? Could traditional medicine hold clues, even tiny ones, to making streets safe again?

"We are trying," Linnoila explains simply, "to address this public health problem with an open mind."

But not everyone's mind is so open.

His work challenges long-held assumptions that social and environmental factors—poverty, joblessness, discrimination, lack of education—are the sole causes of crime and violence. And there is bitter controversy over whether science should even attempt to answer the questions raised by his research.

Critics say research like Linnoila's is dangerous, that it holds too much potential for abuse. The biggest fear is that the studies will be used to discriminate against people of color, particularly African Americans. This is because blacks are disproportionately represented in arrest statistics; the federal government reports that African Americans, who make up about 12 percent of the population, account for 45 percent of all arrests for violent crimes such as homicide, rape and robbery.

Thus, scientific pursuits have become entangled in delicate discussions of race, social tensions are spilling over into the laboratory. Not surprisingly, the debate sometimes gets emotional.

"We know what causes violence in our society: poverty, discrimination, the failure of our educational system," said Dr. Paul Billings, a clinical geneticist at Stanford University who has spoken out against such research. "It's not the genes that cause violence in our society. It's our social system."

Counters Adrian Raine, a USC psychologist who has reviewed all published research that attempts to link biology to violence: "It is irrefutably the case that biologic and genetic factors play a role. That is beyond scientific question. If we ignore that over the next few decades, then we will never ever rid society [of violence]."

Many Factors at Work

. . . Although rational voices agree that biology and genetics probably play a role in causing violence, what they cannot agree on is this: How much of a role? Or is this intellectual territory better left unexplored?

. . . Yet over the years, science has developed a significant—if scattered— body of evidence that indicates some people are indeed biologically prone to violence. For instance, studies have shown that a disproportionate number of murderers have suffered from head injuries. Hypoglycemia—low blood sugar levels—has been linked to violent and aggressive behavior. So has the male hormone testosterone, in high concentrations.

Sophisticated brain imaging has pinpointed differences in the prefrontal cortex—the region of the brain believed to control social behavior—of violent criminals. Other studies have suggested that people with low levels of "arousal"—heart rate, sweat rate and electrical activity of the brain—are more likely to commit violent crimes.

Controversial History

Not all of these biological differences have their roots in genes.

. . . So far, just one study has made a connection between a specific gene and violence. In October [of 1993] a team of Dutch scientists reported that they had found a genetic mutation in a family whose men had a long history of

Violence and the Brain

Dr. Markku Linnoila of the National Institutes of Health has spent the past 13 years researching serotonin, a neurotransmitter—or brain chemical—that modulates emotion. Linnoila's research has repeatedly shown that people with low levels of serotonin (pronounced SER-uh-TOE-nin) are prone to impulsive, violent acts. Linnoila is now looking for genes that create this serotonin imbalance. Finding these genes could help scientists predict who might become violent—and give them preventive treatment.

Background

The brain has 10 billion to 100 billion nerve cells. Messages between cells are communicated by both electrical and chemical processes. Here is a look at how the chemical process works:

The Messengers

A. Nerve cells, called neurons, contain tentacle-like structures known as axons that carry messages. Others, known as dendrites, receive messages.

B. The axons of one nerve cell are separated from the dendrites of another by a tiny gap called a synaptic cleft, or synapse.

C. Messages are transmitted across the synapse by the various neurochemical transmitters.

D. Many researchers believe that the neurotransmitter known as serotonin plays a key role in a number of emotions. Imbalances in serotonin levels have various effects; low levels have been tied to depression, suicidal behavior and aggression while large amounts can bring on emotional highs, including mania.

What Is Serotonin?

Serotonin, which is converted from an amino acid called tryptophan, is a naturally occurring chemical found in the brain, blood and other parts of the body. It can also be produced synthetically. In the brain, it is one of at least 40 chemicals that serve as messengers between nerve cells.

Research by NONA YATES/Los Angeles Times
Sources: World Book Encyclopedia, Times files.

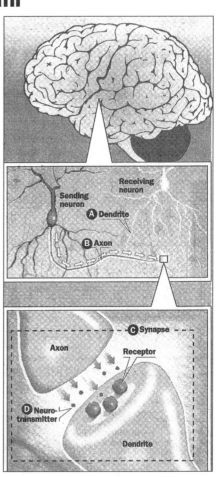

violence—including a rape that occurred 50 years ago, two arsons and an incident in which a man tried to run down his boss with a car after receiving a negative performance evaluation.

These men, the researchers found, had abnormal genes that code for enzymes that help break down the brain chemical monoamine oxidase, which could cause someone to respond violently to stress if allowed to build up in high concentrations. But the study's authors—well aware of the controversy their work might engender—were quick to caution that their discovery of the so-called aggression gene applied only to the one family they studied, and that the genetic defect was probably not widespread.

The serotonin deficit that Linnoila is investigating is far more commonplace; he estimates it may be present in as many as one out of every 20 men. But, Linnoila adds, there are more than 20 genes that could control the manufacture of this brain chemical. And it will be at least another decade before he understands how they work together—in connection with other factors, such as alcohol abuse or poor parenting—to make people violent.

"The low serotonin turnover as such does not make anybody a violent criminal," Linnoila said. "It is simply a predisposing factor. . . . The challenge is really to understand how the genes and environment interact."

Adapted from an article in the *Los Angeles Times,*
December 30, 1993.

Questions:
1. What did Linnoila find from his studies on Finnish prisoners?
2. What is Linnoila's current area of study? How is this different from his serotonin studies?
3. What are some of the critics' arguments? Why do critics fear Linnoila's research?
4. What do opponents of Linnoila's theories believe is at the root of violence? What would they say is likely a cure for violence? What would Linnoila say?
5. The title of the article is "Fears Cloud Search for Genetic Roots of Violence." What does the title mean? What are the "fears" referred to in the article?

PART ONE: SUMMARIZING STEP-BY-STEP

As a college student, you will be asked to write summaries for a variety of academic situations: on essay exams, in papers, in formal oral presentations, or as a study technique. A **summary** is a condensed version of a text; it presents the main ideas and often the principal supporting ideas.

Summarizing requires a number of skills and takes a good deal of practice to do well. First, you need to have good reading skills in order to understand well the ideas in your source. It also requires that you know how to distinguish between main and supporting ideas and select only the key ideas in the text. Finally, since you cannot copy the author's words, you will need to restate, or *paraphrase*, the text in your own words. (Paraphrasing will be dealt with in detail later in this chapter.)

These are the steps in writing a summary:

1. Identify the central idea.
2. Identify key supporting ideas.
3. Use reporting phrases to acknowledge the source.
4. Add linking devices.

UP CLOSE: SAMPLE SUMMARY

Note how the following source has been summarized.

reporting phrase used

author acknowledged

paraphrased

Aggressiveness*
by Susan Basow

"We see that the largest gender differences in aggression occur during childhood when physical aggression is observed in a naturalistic setting. As children get older, attitudinal and situational factors appear to play a greater role in modifying the display of aggression. However, even among adults, men tend to be more physically aggressive than women. How do we explain these modest but consistent findings? Most explanations for this gender difference center either on physiological or social factors although it is probably more accurate to say that these factors interact."

Aggressiveness
by Susan Basow

(According to) Susan Basow, the discrepancy in aggression between males and females is largely an interaction between the biological and environmental. (This) difference is greater in childhood (since) the socialization process tempers the expression of aggression in adults.

controlling idea

linking devices used

*Source: *Gender: Stereotypes and Roles* (1992), 3rd edition, Brooks Cole Publishing: Pacific Grove, Calif., p. 67

LEARNING STRATEGY

Forming Concepts: Distinguishing among the central ideas, main supporting ideas, and details in the text will help you to write a more concise summary.

Step One: Identifying the Controlling Idea

The first step in writing a summary is to identify the author's central idea—the one point in the text that is the most important, the one about which, if asked, the author would say, "Yes, that's the one idea I want everyone to remember." As you can see, this ability to identify the central, also called the **controlling,** idea is a question of reading well and separating the main idea from secondary details.

Some students believe that they can find the controlling idea in the first paragraph, in one sentence. This is rarely true. Usually you will have to pull main ideas from different sections of a text and combine them. For example, if you were going to write one sentence to describe the controlling idea of the article, "Fears Cloud Search for Genetic Roots of Violence," from the Preview section of this chapter, you would only find a part of the controlling idea in the first paragraph:

"Dr. Markku Linnoila is struggling to unravel a great mystery of human behavior: What transforms innocent little children into brutal teenagers and adults."

This sentence tells you what Dr. Linnoila is investigating, but the sentence under the title of the article tells you that these investigations compose only a part of the article's message.

> "Many say studies could open the door to abuses and racism. Scientists are sharply divided."

This sentence indicates that some controversy exists dealing with racism and potential abuse. Your one-sentence summary of this article, then, would include all of these ideas, in a very general way. Here is an example:

> **The controlling idea:** "Linnoila is looking for a "vulnerability gene" to explain serotonin deficits in humans as an explanation for violent behavior, but there are many opponents who believe that such research will lead to discrimination against populations with high criminal rates."

Exercise 2: Formulate a one-sentence summary that reflects the controlling idea of the following paragraph (taken from "Fears Cloud Search for Genetic Roots of Violence" found in the Preview section of this chapter). Make sure you write this sentence in your own words. (Refer to the section on paraphrasing in this chapter if you are unsure about using your own words.)

> **Source:** Critics say research like Linnoila's is dangerous, that it holds too much potential for abuse. The biggest fear is that the studies will be used to discriminate against people of color, particularly African Americans. This is because blacks are disproportionately represented in arrest statistics; the federal government reports that African Americans, who make up about 12% of the population, account for 45% of all arrests for violent crimes such as homicide, rape and robbery.

Exercise 3: Write a one-sentence summary of paragraph 2A on page 109 of the "Gaining Expertise" section for Part Two: Paraphrasing Sources.

Exercise 4: Write a one-sentence summary of paragraph 2B on page 109 of the "Gaining Expertise" section for Part Two: Paraphrasing Sources.

Exercise 5: Summarize the plots of two of your favorite movies in one or two sentences. Compile these brief summaries from all members of the class to create a movie directory. Do the same for your favorite novels.

Exercise 6: Even visual information can be summarized in one sentence. Look at the political cartoon. What is the cartoonist's main point? What idea is he trying to convey? Write a one-sentence summary to capture this idea.

The Law Breaker

Step Two: Identifying Key Supporting Ideas

The next step in summarizing a text is to identify **key supporting ideas.** The number of supporting ideas you include in a summary depends on the purpose of your summary. A brief mention of an article in a paper you are writing would require only the most important ideas. However, if you are planning on refuting a theory, you will need to present a fairly thorough summary of that theory.

Imagine that you are using the article, "Fears Cloud Search for Genetic Roots of Violence," found in the Preview section of this chapter for a paper you are writing on the "Roots of Violence." You wish to summarize the debate about a genetic determinant of violence described in the article. Your paper is only five pages long, so you need to condense the information. What would you include?

One way to manage this task is to **make a list or outline of the important points of the source on a separate sheet of paper.** Refer to the highlighting and annotating you did when you first read the article. Most likely your text markings reflect important information. Use the information you noted to help you outline the key points to include in your summary. Some of the major points in the article cover the following topics:

- Linnoila's serotonin studies
- Linnoila's current research on a "vulnerability gene"
- The implications of this research
- The dangers of this research
- The critics' response

Exercise 7: Summarize the key supporting points from the article, "Fears Cloud Search for Genetic Roots of Violence," found in the Preview section of this chapter. Use the main topics listed above to guide you, writing one sentence for each. Do not copy anything from the article; write the sentences in your own words. Keep these sentences for later use in the chapter.

Exercise 8:
1. Read the following article, "The Etiology of Violence," highlighting and annotating the text for main points.
2. Complete the outline, following the reading paragraph by paragraph.
3. Write a one-sentence summary capturing the controlling idea of the source.
4. Write several sentences expressing the supporting ideas of the text. Be sure to use your own words.
5. Compare your sentences with those of a partner and revise them if necessary.

ETIOLOGY OF VIOLENCE

1   It is likely that the "dyscontrol syndrome" described by Mark and Ervin is the same syndrome that Detre calls "explosive personality disorder" and others "criminal sociopathic personality." The combination of a characteristic past history of violent behavior with commonly associated **electroencephalographic** abnormalities that often involve the **temporal lobe** certainly suggests that the **antisocial behavior** may be determined or at least influenced by neurological, if not by **limbic abnormality**.

2   Some studies have suggested that habitual acts of antisocial behavior involving physical violence are **genetically determined**. While the point remains very controversial, it appears that an XYY chromosome abnormality may be associated with tall stature and aggressiveness (Hook and Kim, 1970; Jacobs et al., 1971). But, this association may be distorted. In the original studies, the relationship was observed mainly in **mental-penal institutions**, whereas more recent data seem to indicate that as much as 90 percent of the XYY population remains outside mental hospitals and prisons (Gerald, 1976).

3   In **twin studies**, the **concordance** rates for **delinquency** are higher in monozygotic than in dizygotic twins; but, such evidence for a genetic influence in episodically violent behavior is not conclusive (Slater and Crowie, 1971), and the dominant view today is that an unfavorable environment in childhood is the major determining factor in episodic violence.

4   There is considerable evidence that associates a disruption of family life with the development of **episodic** violence. Troubled family life, including **brutality**, alcoholism and **marital discord**, is such a constant feature in the background of chronically violent persons that it is possible to predict the development of delinquent behavior on the basis of certain personality and family factors. When all of the five following factors are found in two- to three-year-old children, it seems likely that delinquency can be predicted with the same degree of accuracy (90%) as it can in five- and six-year-olds (Glueck and Glueck, 1966): (1) **psychopathology** of either or both parents (alcoholism, delinquency, emotional disturbance, or mental retardation); (2) indifference or hostility to the child by one or both parents; (3) extreme **restlessness** in the child; (4) nonsubmissiveness of the child to parental authority; (5) unusual destructiveness in the child.

5   On the basis of this association, it would be a mistake to attribute violence in the **offspring** to purely environmental factors, since brutality, alcoholism, and marital discord in parents may themselves be expressions of a genetic defect. This is supported by Heston's report (1966) that criminality and other associated sociopathic disorders were significantly more **prevalent** in the offspring of schizophrenics raised in **foster homes** than in the offspring of nonschizophrenics raised in foster homes. Another factor to be considered in the association of environmental stress and violence is the effect of a violent juvenile delinquent on his parents. The child's problem may be so severe that it disrupts the life of the whole family (Bell, 1968).

6   On the basis of the evidence, it is not possible to determine whether "nurture" or "nature" is more important in the development of episodic violent behavior. What does seem clear, however, is that episodic violence is not a simple functional psychological disorder. Neurological determinants are present, and the syndrome cannot be reversed by any known therapeutic means. To the extent that episodic violence is a learned behavioral pattern, it is one that is learned at a very early age (Detre et al., 1972). It appears to be at least as difficult to alter episodic violence in the adult human being as it is to alter the abnormal socialization of adult monkeys that is the result of early social deprivation (Harlow, 1971).

Source: *Behavioral Neurology* (1985) by J. H. Pincus and G. J. Tucker, Oxford University Press, N.Y,. pp. 91–92

Vocabulary

electroencephalograph: a graphic representation of brain activity

temporal lobe: part of the brain

antisocial behavior: behavior that is destructive to people or things

limbic abnormality: some defect in the limbic system of the brain

genetically determined: present at birth in a person's genes (as opposed to something that develops from experience)

mental-penal institutions: places where those who are severely disturbed mentally and who have committed crimes are sent

twin studies: research done on twins

concordance: similarity

delinquency: psychological tendency to engage in unlawful behavior

episodic: not regular or habitual

brutality: physical violence

marital discord: serious problems between husband and wife

psychopathology: psychological dysfunction

restlessness: agitation, inability to relax

offspring: children

prevalent: present everywhere

foster homes: home in which child is raised by parents who are not biologically the child's

Comprehension Questions:
1. What is the XYY theory?
2. What is the "dominant view" today regarding the major determining factor in episodic violence according to the article?
3. Describe which environmental factors contribute to the development of violence.
4. What are the author's conclusions regarding the "nature/nurture" controversy and the development of violence?

Etiology of Violence

Paragraph 1: A history of violence is often paired with abnormal EEGs, which indicates that _____

_____

_____

Paragraph 2: Past research was thought to show that violence is caused by _____. However, this was later disputed because the population sample the research was based on was in _____

Paragraph 3: Even though studies using twins showed that _____

_____ today, most researchers agree that _____

_____

Paragraph 4: One of the most persistent characteristics of the violent person's profile is _____

_____

In fact, it is possible to predict delinquency for two- or three-year-old children as accurately as for five- or six-year-old children if the following features are present:

1. _____

2. _____

3. _____

4. _____

5. _____

Paragraph 5: It would not be correct to say that violence in children is due to *only* the environment, since some of those elements in the environment are

_____

_____

_____

Another contributing aspect would be _____

_____

Paragraph Six: In conclusion, _____

_____

_____

Step Three: Using Reporting Phrases to Acknowledge the Source

LEARNING STRATEGY

Managing Your Learning: Introducing summaries with appropriate reporting phrases helps to avoid plagiarism and acknowledges the source.

Whenever you include paraphrased or summarized material, you need to acknowledge your source. One way to do this is by using a reporting phrase. Here are some examples:

According to Linnoila, low serotonin in the brain predisposes an individual to violent behavior.

(Use the preposition **according to** *+ the name of the author or source, followed by the controlling idea.)*

In Linnoila's view, low serotonin in the brain predisposes an individual to violent behavior.

*(Begin your sentence with the preposition **in** + the author's name + **view**, followed by the controlling idea.)*

In the article, "Fears Cloud Search for Genetic Roots of Violence," Linnoila states that low serotonin in the brain predisposes an individual to violent behavior.

*(Begin with the phrase, **in the (article, book, speech),** add the title of the source, and then state the author's name and a reporting verb (e.g., "states") followed by the controlling idea.)*

Linnoila argues that low serotonin in the brain predisposes an individual to violent behavior.

(Begin with the author's name and an appropriate reporting verb, followed by the controlling idea.)

Here are other verbs that can be used in place of "argues" in the sentence above. Add others that you know to this list.

claims	describes	notes
contends	points out	concurs
insists	illustrates	agrees
maintains	writes	supports the view that

UP CLOSE: ACKNOWLEDGING SOURCES

NOTE: Refer to the section on using quotations in Chapter 4 for more detailed information on citing and documenting sources.

Underline or italicize the titles of books, plays, journals, and movies.

According to Tannen in her book, *You Just Don't Understand,* women make decisions by consensus, and men prefer to act independently without discussion. (italics)

> *Capitalize titles of books.*

Tannen states in her book, *You Just Don't Understand*, that women make decisions by consensus, and men prefer to act independently without discussion. (underline)

Use quotation marks around the titles of articles, poems, short stories, and songs.

Place punctuation inside quotation marks.

In her article, "You Have to Believe You Can Make a Difference," Carla White describes a touching story of her friend who dies in gang activity.

Add the author's credentials and background when it is appropriate:

Include information about author's credentials and background.

According to Tannen, a linguistics scholar who has studied the difference in communication styles between men and women, women make decisions by consensus, and men prefer to act independently without discussion.

Exercise 9: Add a reporting phrase to the one-sentence summary of the article, "Fears Cloud Search for Genetic Roots of Violence" (page 89).

Step Four: Adding Linking Devices

A written summary is like any other piece of writing that you produce—it must have a topic sentence or thesis (the controlling idea of the source), supporting details (the supporting ideas in the source), and transitions between ideas. Note how adding the transitions (in bold) to the following summary of the paragraph from page 92 has made the summary easier to follow.

Summary without transitions:

According to Susan Basow, the discrepancy in aggression between males and females is largely an interaction between biological and environmental factors. There is a greater difference in childhood. The socialization process tempers the expression of aggression in adults.

Summary with transitions:

According to Susan Basow, the discrepancy in aggression between males and females is largely an interaction between biological and environmental factors. **This difference** is greater in childhood **because** the socialization process tempers the expression of aggression in adults.

Exercise 10: Write a longer summary (100–150 words) from the outline you completed of the article, "The Etiology of Violence." Be sure to use your own words; underline the transitions you have included to connect ideas.

Exercise 11: Now complete the summary for the Preview article, "Fears Cloud Search for Genetic Roots of Violence." Use your one-sentence summary with reporting phrase, your supporting sentences, and added transitions. Check to make sure you have not copied from the original source. Proofread the summary for errors in grammar and punctuation.

Gaining Expertise

Find a source from the library on one of the following topics or choose one of your own, with your instructor's permission. Summarize the source using the step-by-step procedure described in this chapter.

Topics related to the chapter theme:

1. The use of handguns in the United States
2. Domestic violence
3. The link between drug use and violence
4. The effect of TV violence on children

PART TWO: PARAPHRASING SOURCES

As you learned in Part One of this chapter, you must use your own words when you write a summary. If you copy from the source directly, then you are "stealing" that author's words. This is called **plagiarism**. To avoid plagiarizing, you will need to learn how to paraphrase, which means to restate the source in your own words. In some ways, paraphrasing is like translating—you don't change any ideas or leave any information out, but you do change the language in which it is presented. Although the words are your own, the ideas and information still "belong" to the original author.

You will paraphrase in writing and speaking when you want to explain another author's ideas in detail and when quoting doesn't seem appropriate. Of course, you always acknowledge the author of the ideas. Paraphrase can also be used as a check to determine whether you have understood a text or not. It's very difficult to paraphrase a text if you don't understand it.

Description of a Good Paraphrase

- The paraphrase has the same meaning as the source; nothing has been added or deleted by the paraphraser.
- The original words and structures of the source have been rephrased, except for technical words or very common words, called "public domain" words.
- The length of the paraphrase and the source are about the same.
- The writing style of the paraphrase reflects the style of the paraphraser and not that of the author of the source.

Exercise 12:   Read the following original source on aggression in teenage boys and compare it with the paraphrased version next to it. Then answer the questions that follow.

Original Source

Aggressiveness, present in many male teenagers, has often been characterized as having a biological base. However, social learning theorists Bandura and Walters (1959) did a study which indicated that aggressiveness might be a product of environmental factors and especially, social reinforcement. In this study, they found that aggressive boys had encouragement from their parents to be aggressive outside the home. Since their fathers experienced indirect pleasure from hearing about their son's aggressive behavior, this provided reinforcement for the boys.

Paraphrase

Social scientists have often described aggressiveness, which is evident in many adolescent boys, as having a biological component. Nevertheless, research completed by social learning theorists Bandura and Walters (1959) showed that aggressiveness might result from factors in the environment and, in particular, social reinforcement. It was found in the study that young males who were aggressive had been encouraged by their parents to be aggressive away from the home. Their fathers received vicarious gratification from learning of their sons' aggressive behavior; consequently, the boys' behavior was reinforced by their fathers' experience.

Threads

Plagiarism does nothing to improve your writing and besides, it's transparent to your instructor.

George Mansfield, professor

Questions:

1. How did the paraphraser change the following words and expressions?
   male teenagers   indirect pleasure   hearing about
2. Find at least two examples of words which were not changed. Why do you suppose they were not?
3. Find at least one example in which the sentence structure was changed significantly. How has it been changed?
4. List some of the other ways in which the original source has been changed.

LEARNING STRATEGY

Forming Concepts: Applying specific techniques can help you become a better paraphraser.

Learning Techniques for Paraphrasing

You will use a variety of techniques when you paraphrase a source. In this chapter you will learn some of the most common ones. Keep in mind as you learn these specific techniques that just using one of them to paraphrase a source (e.g., replacing some of the words in a text with synonyms) is rarely sufficient. Although you may not use all of these techniques in a single paraphrase, you will likely use them all at one time or another.

Here are the techniques you will study in this chapter:

1. Using appropriate synonyms
2. Changing the sentence type
3. Reducing the clause to a phrase
4. Changing the voice (active or passive)
5. Changing the part of speech

USING APPROPRIATE SYNONYMS

Using a thesaurus: One of the most common techniques for paraphrasing is to replace a word from the source with a synonym of your choice. This is an important technique, but as a non-native speaker of English you must exercise extreme caution in finding a word which has a similar meaning and tone to the original word. Some students use a *thesaurus,* a "synonym dictionary," which provides several synonyms for one word. Many word processors include a thesaurus as well. (See "Up Close: Using a Thesaurus" on page 102 for more explanation.) A thesaurus can be very helpful, but it can also be dangerous, for if you are not familiar with the synonyms, you may end up by selecting a word that makes no sense.

Words can have many different connotations. Consider, for example, the word *large.* Synonyms for this word include: *fat, big, huge, monstrous, gigantic, enormous, spacious.* These words do not have precisely the same meanings. In the sentence, "She settled into a large house," you could not replace *large* with the word *fat,* which is usually used to describe people. You would choose *big, huge,* or *spacious* instead, which are words that describe space.

Therefore, it is best to use words with which you are familiar or words for which you have an exact definition. Do not simply look up a synonym in the thesaurus and replace the source word with the first synonym listed. It is a good idea to check the exact definition of the synonym in an English dictionary.

Also, some students think that if they find a synonym for every word in a source, then they will have a good paraphrase. This is far from true! Using synonyms is only one technique and it should be used with the other techniques listed above. Otherwise, your final paraphrased version will sound strange and incoherent. Use this technique carefully.

Sometimes using a synonym is not necessary. Notice from the sample paraphrase above that some words were not changed—e.g., *aggressiveness, social learning theorists, reinforcement*. These are **technical words** from the social sciences, and should not be changed. When you become familiar with the vocabulary from your field of study, then you will know which words are technical words and which words can be changed.

Words in the public domain do not need to be changed. For example, *girl* is a common word which does not "belong" to any one author. If you looked this word up in a thesaurus, you might find a synonym such as *damsel*, which is an old English word often found in fairy tales. While there is no specific rule for determining if a word is public domain or not, you can always ask a native speaker if a word is a very common one. Or rely on your own judgment. Chances are if you learned the word very early on in your language learning process, it's probably in the public domain.

UP CLOSE: USING A THESAURUS

The following is a sample thesaurus entry for the word *form*. Since *form* can be both a verb (They *formed* a group) and a noun (The *form* of that tree is beautiful), you will note that there is a separate entry for each. Pay careful attention to the part of speech of the word you are looking for and refer to the appropriate entry.

NOTE: The verb entry is not complete; it is included here only as an example.

Indicates the part of speech.

form, *n* **1.** [Shape]—*Syn.* figure, appearance, plan, arrangement, design, outline, conformation, configuration, formation, structure, style, stance, construction, fashion, mode, scheme, framework, *Gestalt* (German), contour, profile, silhouette, skeleton, anatomy, articulation.

This is a cross reference to another entry.

2. [The human form]—*Syn.* body, frame, torso; see **figure 2.**

Categories of synonyms.

3. [The approved procedure]—*Syn.* manner, mode, custom; see **method 2.**
4. [Anything intended to give form]—*Syn.* pattern, model, die; see **mold 1.**
5. [A standard letter or blank]—*Syn.* mimeographed letter, duplicate, routine letter, pattern, form letter, data sheet, information blank, chart, card, reference form, order form, questionnaire, application; see also **copy.**
6. [A rite]—*Syn.* ritual, formality, custom; see **ceremony.**
7. [Type]—*Syn.* make, sort, class; see **kind 2.**
8. [Arrangement]—*Syn.* organization, placement, scheme, see **order 3.**
9. [Convention]—*Syn* habit, practice, usage; see **custom 1, 2.**
synonyms

Note that there is a separate entry for each part of speech.

form, *v.* **1.** [To give shape to a thing]—*Syn.* mold, pattern, model, arrange, make, block out, block, . . . (etc.)

Source: *Webster's New World Thesaurus* (1985), by Charlton Laird, Simon and Schuster, New York.

Exercise 13: Read the following paragraphs. Several possible synonyms for the underlined words in the original passage have been provided. Using a thesaurus and a dictionary, choose the synonym that you think is the most appropriate one based on the context of the source. Be ready to say why the other synonyms are not appropriate. (The first underlined word has been done for you and explained in detail. Refer to "Up Close: Using a Thesaurus" on page 102 as you study this example.)

1. "The <u>plain</u> truth is that modern American women, liberated or not, have little economic security as wives and mothers, or as workers. They are <u>squeezed</u> between the traditional and modern <u>forms</u> of financial security to an extent which is <u>unknown</u> in other societies."

Source: Sylvia Ann Hewlett, *Lesser Life: The Myth of Women's Liberation in America.* Warner Books, 1986 (p. 13)

An example of choosing a synonym:

a. forms: figures, arranges, patterns, sorts

Explanation: First, you determine that in this sentence *forms* is a noun, not a verb, so you look at only the first entry. (You know that this entry is for the noun because of the *n* located after the word *form*.)

Next, you must decide which of the nine categories under *forms* is appropriate for this sentence. You see that you can easily eliminate "the human form," "a standard letter or blank," "a rite." The other three categories require more careful thought.

Looking at the choices of synonyms given in the example above, you decide to examine each one individually. (Refer to "Up Close: Using a Thesaurus" on page 102 for a thesaurus entry of the word *form*.) "Figures" refers to the category, "the shape of something," and so it is not appropriate. "Arranges" is a verb, and this sentence requires a noun. "Patterns" is better, but notice that it appears under the two categories of "anything intended to give form" and "blanks, standard letter," both of which seem inappropriate for a discussion of financial security. "Sort" is the most appropriate because it refers to the category "type." Further, it is likely that you are familiar with this word, and it's always best to choose a word you are comfortable using in a sentence.

Now continue in a similar fashion for the remainder of the exercise.

b. plain: modest, clear, average, obvious
c. squeezed: wedged, forced, pinched
d. unknown: undiscovered, hidden, unheard of
e. Which words in the above source belong to "public domain" and do not need to be changed?

_____

_____

2. Aggressive children are <u>unpopular</u>, and because their <u>relations</u> with their <u>peers</u> tend to be <u>unsatisfying</u>, they spend more time watching television than their more popular peers. (L. D. Eron, 1982, p. 210)

a. unpopular   despised, disliked, obnoxious, abhorred
b. relations   siblings, connections, similarities
c. peers   gazes, rivals, age group
d. unsatisfying   inadequate, shocking, disquieting, vexing

Exercise 14: Read the following text. Then use a thesaurus to find at least two synonyms for the following underlined words. Consult an English dictionary to choose the most appropriate synonym based on the context of the sentence. Circle that synonym.

Adolescence has <u>typically</u> been described as a <u>tumultuous time</u> of development in which the teenager is especially subject to difficulties related to an identity crisis (Erikson) and a change of focus from the family to peers (Freud). Some researchers (Bandura) now <u>suggest</u>, however, that this <u>characterization</u> of adolescence is exaggerated and that <u>severe</u> psychological <u>disturbances</u> are not greater during adolescence. If suicide is an indication of these disturbances, the fact that suicide is the third, after accidents and homicides, <u>cause of</u> teenage death, supports this. Self-esteem <u>decreases</u> during the 12–14 age period, but <u>increases</u> shortly after that. If a <u>strong</u> self-concept existed before those years, the <u>chances</u> are quite strong that the teenager will return to a more stable state after adolescence. Thus, it is not <u>advisable</u> to overestimate the rate of emotional disturbances in teenagers.

typically: _____

tumultuous time: _____

suggest: _____

characterization: _____

severe: _____

disturbances: _____

cause of: _____

decreases: _____

increases: ____ _____

strong: _____

chances: _____

advisable: _____

Now circle any words in the text that belong to the public domain. Underline technical words that do not need to be changed.

CHANGING THE SENTENCE TYPE

A second technique for paraphrasing involves **changing the sentence type** by using an equivalent form of a transition word, as in these examples below.

- Boys learned competition, **but** girls learned cooperation at school. *(coordinating conjunction)*
- **While** boys learned competition, girls learned cooperation at school. *(subordinating conjunction)*
- Boys learned competition; **however,** girls learned cooperation at school. *(sentence transition)*
- **Unlike** girls, who learned cooperation at school, boys learned competition. *(preposition)*

Exercise 15: Refer to the sample paraphrase on page 100. Find one example of changing the sentence type, using the following List of Equivalent Forms as a guide. Suggest other equivalent forms that could have been used to paraphrase this sample.

LIST OF EQUIVALENT FORMS

Coordinating Conjunctions	Subordinating Conjunctions	Sentence Transitions	Prepositions
but yet	although though even though while, whereas in spite of the fact that	however nevertheless	despite in spite of in contrast to unlike
so for	because due to the fact that since as now that	as a result consequently therefore thus	because of due to
and		moreover in addition furthermore also	in addition to
or		otherwise if not	

Exercise 16: Apply the two paraphrasing techniques studied so far to write a partial paraphrase of the following sentences.

1. Recent research has shown that watching violent television increases violence among viewers, but 80 percent of the TV that American children watch has at least one violent scene.

   _____

   _____

   _____

2. Some researchers believe that TV viewing of violent programs increases violence because young children learn by observation, which can be real or filmed.

   _____

   _____

   _____

3. One study showed that children who watched *Batman* or *Superman* on TV demonstrated more violent behavior than children who watched *Mister Rogers' Neighborhood.*

_____

_____

_____

REDUCING A CLAUSE TO A PHRASE

A third technique involves changing clauses (a clause is a group of words with a subject and a verb) to phrases, or the reverse. The following chart summarizes some of the possibilities for reducing clauses to phrases.

NOTE: This technique must be used in conjunction with other techniques such as finding synonyms.

Type of Reduction	Clause	Phrase
Adjective clause	Aggressiveness, **which is evident in many adolescent boys,** has often been described as having a biological base.	Aggressiveness, **evident in many adolescent boys,** has often been described as having a biological base.
	Social learning theorists Bandura and Walters (1959) did a study **which indicated** that aggressiveness might be a product of environmental factors. . . .	Social learning theorists Bandura and Walters (1959) did a study **indicating** that aggressiveness might be a product of environmental factors. . . .
Adverb clause	In this study, they found that **boys who were aggressive** had encouragement from their parents to be aggressive outside the home.	In this study, they found that **aggressive boys** had encouragement from their parents to be aggressive outside the home.
	Because they received reinforcement from their fathers, these boys became more aggressive.	**Receiving reinforcement from their fathers,** these boys became more aggressive.
	Because their fathers encourage it, young boys develop aggressive behavior.	**Due to their father's encouragement,** young boys develop aggressive behavior.

CHANGING THE VOICE (ACTIVE OR PASSIVE)

A fourth technique involves changing the voice from active to passive, or passive to active. Not all sentences can be paraphrased in this way; look at the context of the sentence to decide if this is an appropriate technique.

Active Voice

In this study, **they found** that socialization plays an important role.

Passive Voice

It was found in this study that socialization plays an important role.

CHANGING THE PART OF SPEECH

Another technique involves changing the part of speech of the word. For example, note how the parts of speech have been changed below.

- **Increased** viewing of **violence** on television may lead to
  (adj)   (noun)
  aggressiveness in children.
- An **increase** in viewing **violent** television . . .
  (noun)   (adj)
- When children **increase** the amount of **violent** television
                (verb)   (adj)
  they view . . .

Exercise 17:   Rewrite the partial paraphrases you completed in Exercise 16 and change the parts of speech when possible.

SURVIVAL TIPS: PARAPHRASING

Avoid these common errors when paraphrasing:

- **Not understanding the passage being paraphrased**. It's not enough to have a vague notion of the "main idea"; you need to be absolutely certain of what the author is saying. If you are having trouble paraphrasing, then you probably don't understand the passage well enough.
- **Including personal opinion in the paraphrase.** Be careful not to include any ideas or information not presented in the original source. Be especially careful that the ideas you paraphrase are the author's—and not your own.
- **Writing paraphrases that make little sense**. Read your paraphrase over to make sure that you can understand it; then check it for spelling and grammar.

Exercise 18: Of the two paraphrases below, which one is better? Why? What's wrong with the other paraphrase? How would you make it better?

Original source:

"Students obsessed with A's tend not to get them. Certainly, A students care a great deal about their grades and a few are among the obsessed. But, unlike other grade-conscious students, better students spend more time thinking about their studies than their grades."

Source: *Acing College* by Joshua Halberstam, Penguin Books, New York, p. 171.

Paraphrase #1

Students who are overly concerned with getting A's don't usually receive them. It's definitely true that students who do get A's are concerned about them, and some even obsess over getting them. However, the best students worry more about learning than grades, which is not necessarily true of students who worry only about their grades.

Comments:

_____

_____

_____

Paraphrase #2

If you are obsessed with getting As in college, then you will never get them. Sure, A students worry about their grades, and some even are between those who are obsessed. Nevertheless, different from evaluation-aware learners, good students pass their time pondering their learning and not their grades. Anyway, it's very hard for us to get good grades.

Comments:

_____

_____

_____

Gaining Expertise

1. Refer to the article, "Etiology of Violence" on page 95 in Part One of this chapter. Decide which technical words in the first three paragraphs of that text should not be changed. Circle these words. Underline words in the fourth paragraph that are part of the public domain and wouldn't need changing in your paraphrase.

2. Using the suggested techniques described above, write a paraphrase for each of the following paragraphs. Follow these steps:
   (1) Read and understand the passage.
   (2) Look up any words that are not clear to you.
   (3) Underline words that you need to change.
   (4) Identify specific techniques which you can use.
   (5) Be sure that your final version is well-written and coherent.

   a. On the differences in communication styles between men and women.

   "Many women feel it is natural to consult with their partners at every turn, while many men automatically make more decisions without consulting their partners. This may reflect a broad difference in conceptions of decision making. Women expect decisions to be discussed first and many by consensus. They appreciate the discussion itself as evidence of involvement and communication. But many men feel oppressed by lengthy discussions about what they see as minor decisions, and they feel hemmed in if they can't just act without talking first. When women try to initiate a freewheeling discussion by asking, "What do you think?" men often think they are being asked to decide."

   Source: *You Just Don't Understand: Women and Men in Conversation* by Deborah Tannen, Ballantine Books, New York, 1990, p. 27.

   b. On the mind-body connection.

   "We don't yet understand all the ways in which brain chemicals are related to emotions and thoughts, but the salient point is that our state of mind has an immediate and direct effect on our state of body. We can change the body by dealing with how we feel. If we ignore our despair, the body receives a "die" message. If we deal with our pain and seek help, then the message is: 'Living is difficult but desirable,' and the immune system works to keep us alive."

   Source: *Love, Medicine, and Miracles* by Bernie Siegel, Harper & Row, New York, 1986, p. 69.

   c. On violence

   "There is considerable evidence that associates a disruption of family life with the development of episodic violence. Troubled family life, including brutality, alcoholism and marital discord, is such a constant feature in the background of chronically violent persons that it is possible to predict the development of delinquent behavior on the basis of certain personality and family factors."

   Source: *Behavioral Neurology* (1985) by J. H. Pincus and G. J. Tucker, Oxford University Press, N.Y., pp. 91–92.

3. Select a brief article that interests you from your local newspaper or favorite news magazine. Prepare notes on the article and paraphrase it orally for a classmate.

4. Write a 150-word summary of one of the longer sources from Chapter 2, being sure to use all the techniques you have learned for paraphrasing. Use your annotations of the chapter to help you with the summary. Be sure to include appropriate reporting phrases and transition words.

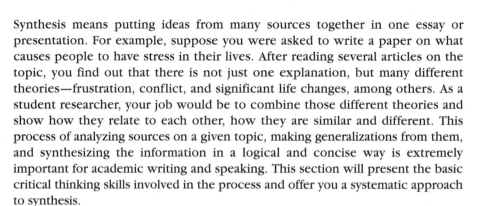

Synthesis means putting ideas from many sources together in one essay or presentation. For example, suppose you were asked to write a paper on what causes people to have stress in their lives. After reading several articles on the topic, you find out that there is not just one explanation, but many different theories—frustration, conflict, and significant life changes, among others. As a student researcher, your job would be to combine those different theories and show how they relate to each other, how they are similar and different. This process of analyzing sources on a given topic, making generalizations from them, and synthesizing the information in a logical and concise way is extremely important for academic writing and speaking. This section will present the basic critical thinking skills involved in the process and offer you a systematic approach to synthesis.

Consider the following selection on "Social Explanations" for gender differences in the expression of aggression. Note how the author has combined ideas and information from a number of different sources (usually cited in parentheses). Note also how those ideas *support* her thesis, stated in the first sentence, that "society plays the determining role in the development of aggressive behavior."

Social Explanations

Regardless of any physiological predisposition, society plays the determining role in the development of aggressive behavior, a point dramatically illustrated by the classic cross-cultural studies of Margaret Mead (1935). Rather than males always being more aggressive than females, she found one New Guinean tribe where both sexes were aggressive as adults (Mundugumor); one where both sexes were nonaggressive (Arapesh); and one, where females were aggressive and males passive (Tchambuli). In more modern Western cultures as well, norms regarding aggressiveness by males vary (J. H. Block, 1973). Compared to England and Scandinavia, the United States particularly encourages aggression in males. Parents seem more tolerant of certain forms of aggression in their sons than in their daughters (for example, physically defending oneself in a fight with a same-sex peer) although they generally discourage other forms (such as picking fights with someone younger or weaker or, for boys, with girls). Peers, too, appear to reinforce boys more than girls for their aggressive behavior, even at the toddler stage (Fagot & Hagan, 1985). The male role in the United States incorporates expectations of both aggressiveness and chivalry (Eagly, 1987b), a complexity that may account for the moderate effect size found for gender in aggregated research on aggressive behavior. Many stereotypically male activities, such as team sports and military service, deliberately encourage aggressive behavior. Thus, differential gender roles may give rise to gender differences in aggressive behavior.

Source: *Gender Roles and Stereotypes* (1992) by Susan A. Basow,
Brooks Cole, Pacific Grove, Calif.

Exercise 19: Read the above selection, outlining the key points and details the author uses to support those points. Determine the number of sources the author uses.

Managing Your Learning: Following a systematic procedure for dealing with multiple sources will help you analyze and synthesize information more easily.

Here is a step-by-step procedure for writing with synthesis:

1. **Read** each of your sources carefully; **summarize** main ideas.
2. **Analyze** your sources to identify the similarities and differences.
3. Group similar ideas together; **generalize** from these similar ideas.
4. **Assemble** your various generalizations in a logical and coherent way.

Step One: Summarizing Your Sources

The first step in synthesizing is to understand your sources well. Summarizing them is an excellent way to ensure your understanding. You have already learned this skill in Part One of this chapter.

Exercise 20: Practice your summarizing skills by preparing an outline which summarizes the main and supporting points in the following essay on the abuses of power. After summarizing the source, think about how this author's point of view is similar to or different from the other readings in this chapter. Be ready to engage in a discussion in class.

Male athletes who play contact sports in college tend to have more violent attitudes and to behave more aggressively.

Abuses of Power

Inherent in the preceding discussion regarding different forms of power is the observation that not only are men more likely than women to have structural power, but they are also more likely to abuse such power—as seen in economic greed, political corruption, self-serving legal maneuvering, and military massacres. Perhaps power leads to abuse, especially absolute power ("Power tends to corrupt and absolute power corrupts absolutely" —Lord Acton, 1887). Thus, men's greater abuse of power simply may be a function of their greater likelihood of being in positions of power. Yet gender is not incidental to men's having greater structural power than women, nor is it incidental to the use of violence, the major form of abuse. As we saw in Chapter 3, males are expected and encouraged to act aggressively. Although males, in general, do seem to have a greater predisposition toward aggression than females, aggressive behavior is definitely learned and is responsive to a wide range of situational conditions. In our culture, far more than in most others, male aggressiveness appears to be viewed ambivalently. While violence and its social effects (crime, rapes, wars) are overtly condemned, aggression and violence are covertly glorified in the media (films, books, and especially TV) and in daily interactions. Action films like the "Rambo" series are box-office hits mainly because the "action" is violent.

Because of the link between masculinity and violence, one way of "proving" one's masculinity is by some form of aggression or violence. We have seen how male political leaders may try to prove their masculinity through macho talk and military intervention. In this sense, war may be viewed as the ultimate proof of manhood. This may explain in part, the strong resistance to allowing women in combat. Terrorism, too, whether by the Right or the Left, whether officially sanctioned or officially punished, can be viewed as a consequence of the cultural linkage of masculinity and violence since it is an act overwhelmingly committed by men (R. Morgan, 1989). Indeed, the terrorist—aggressive, dedicated, passionate, risk-taking—may be a male cultural idol.

In sports as well, masculinity is tied to aggression and violence. The greater the danger of injury and the more combative the activities, the more likely it is that the sport and its players will be viewed as masculine (Fasteau, 1974; Raphael, 1988). Thus, contact sports (such as football, hockey, boxing, wrestling, basketball, and soccer) are viewed as more masculine than sports such as golf or swimming, which are neither combative nor extremely competitive. Perhaps not coincidentally, athletes in the contact "masculine" sports tend to be more violent in their attitudes and behaviors than comparable groups of nonathletes or than athletes in noncontact sports, at least on college campuses (J. M. Brown, 1982; J. M. Brown & Davies, 1978). In particular, male high school and college athletes in contact sports have been implicated in a disproportionate number of rapes and other sexual assaults (Eskinazi, 1990; Neimark, 1991). (See Miedzian, 1991, for further discussion of the link between masculinity and violence.)

As this last finding suggests, criminal activities too reflect gender roles; in particular, men's crimes are more likely than women's to involve violence. Men constitute more than 80% of those who commit crimes and more than 90% of those who commit violent crimes ("Status Report," 1988). This pattern holds true around the world (Seager & Olsen, 1986). Most crimes are committed by men between the ages of 13 and 24, mostly poor. Criminal behavior is often a way for a young man to prove his masculinity at a time when such proof is important—that is, during adolescence and young adulthood. Violence in particular may be a way for young men to display their "toughness" and gain peer approval when more acceptable paths of attaining status (such as via money, a prestigious job, athletic success) are unavailable due to poverty, racism, lack of education, and lack of hope (Freiburg, 1991a; Messerschmidt, 1986). The use of violence by powerless men to prove their masculinity may explain why nearly one in four young Black men is in jail, on probation, or on parole.

Violent street crime tends to be committed by powerless men, but powerful men also commit crimes, although they are less likely to be charged or convicted of them (Messerschmidt, 1986). Corporate crime, which may involve deliberate corporate neglect of workplace and product safety (for example, the defective Ford Pinto and the unsterilized Dalkon shield), may result in injury and death far exceeding that which results from street crime. Although appearing to be far removed from violent street crime, corporate crime reflects masculine stereotypes too, especially those relating to ambition, competition, and lack of concern for others.

Females predominate only with respect to crimes of prostitution and juvenile running away, both of which are considered "victimless crimes" and both of which may result from female sexual victimization (U.S. Department of Commerce, 1989b). Female criminals usually are interested more in improving their financial circumstances than in violence or dominance, and women's motives are more "need-based than greed-based" (Daly, as cited in "Women's Booty," 1987). The crimes that have increased the most for females have been embezzlement, larceny, forgery, and fraud—all nonviolent crimes—although violent crime committed by young, urban girls may be on the rise as well (F. Adler, 1981; F. R. Lee, 1991; Mann, 1984). As women's work experiences become more similar to men's, their temptations may be similar as well. For example, with more women working in banks, embezzlement by women becomes more possible, However, most of women's crimes are unrelated to their paid work. As with men, powerlessness in the form of poverty and racism is strongly associated with crime and especially with criminal convictions (Redmond, 1990). Men not only are more likely than women to use violence, but they are more likely to be victims of violence as well, at least in terms of police statistics. Race also is a factor, mediated by the greater likelihood of Blacks and Hispanics than Whites to be poor and live in crime-infested neighborhoods.

One out of ten Black males between ages 15 and 24 were homicide victims in 1988, the highest rate of any group ("Dangers," 1990). In their lifetime, non-White males have a 1 in 38 chance of becoming a murder victim, non-white females a 1 in 138 chance, White males a 1 in 204 chance, and White females a 1 in 437 chance ("Non-white," 1989). The homicide rate in the United States is higher than in 21 other industrialized countries, largely due to the easy availability of firearms, the violence of the crack trade, and the glorification of violence (by men) in the media ("Report: Homicide Rate," 1990).

Although men, at least minority men, are more likely to be murder victims than women, violence against women has escalated since the early 1960s (Caputi & Russell, 1990). The magnitude of the violence committed against women is enormous—murder, rape, sexual abuse, assault, robbery, sexual slavery (forced prostitution), sexual harassment—yet much of it never gets officially reported or classified. A probability sampling of 930 San Francisco-area women aged 18 or older revealed that nearly one out of three women had been a victim of rape or attempted rape, more than one out of three had been a victim of childhood sexual abuse, and one out of five had been a victim of marital violence (D. E. H. Russell, 1984). Fewer than 10% had reported these crimes to the police. Even more chilling than the magnitude of the violence committed by men against women is the fact that most of it is committed by men known to the victim. For example, more than half of all female homicide victims are killed by current or former partners, compared to a minority of male homicide (L. E. A. Walker, 1989b).

Source: Gender Roles and Stereotypes, 3rd ed. (1992), by Susan A. Basow, Brooks Cole, Pacific Grove, Calif.

Step Two: Analyzing Your Sources

Imagine that you are going to prepare a brief, one-page essay on the "Roots of Violence." Your task is to present a coherent explanation for the various points of view you have learned about in your research review.

To do this, you need to **analyze** the information you have gathered from your sources. Then you can identify the diverse explanations for the presence of violence. Consider the three sources you have read so far in this chapter ("Fears Cloud . . . " on page 89, "The Etiology of Violence" on page 95, and "The Abuses of Power" on page 112). What explanations for violence and aggression are offered in these readings? If you were to brainstorm a list of them, you might come up with a preliminary list that looks like this:

- serotonin
- vulnerability gene
- testosterone
- gender roles
- poverty
- powerlessness
- violence in the family

Exercise 21: Formulate sentences for each of the topics listed above. Add any other ideas that you find in your readings. Then put the last name of the author supporting each idea in parentheses next to the sentence. If more than one author supports an idea, list both. Here is an example of the first one:

> Serotonin: An overload of the neurotransmitter, serotonin, predisposes an individual to violent behavior (Linnoila).

Step Three: Formulating Generalizations

Once you have analyzed your sources and identified key ideas, you are ready to examine your information and group ideas together in a logical way. In the above example, for instance, the terms *serotonin, testosterone*, and *vulnerability genes* seem related. They all deal with a biological or genetic explanation, so you might group these together and label them as such.

From this grouping, you might come up with a generalization similar to the following:

> Some researchers believe that the roots of violence can be found in the biolgical and chemical workings of the human body.

Of course, you would then support this generalization with specific data from your sources.

Deciding how to group information can be very difficult. For example, an explanation for violence based on testosterone could belong to the general category of "biological explanations" (testosterone is a hormone) and "gender explanations" (it is found in men). There is no one right answer to this question; as long as your category is logical, your choice will depend on how you wish to present your information.

At other times, you may find that you have information that does not group easily with other ideas. What do you do then? You can list it in its own group; if it is trivial or lacks substance, you can choose to omit it from your final synthesis.

Exercise 22: Group the various sentences that you wrote for Exercise 20 into logical categories (at least three). Write a generalization statement for each group.

Step Four: Assembling Your Information

The final step in the process of synthesis is to combine your generalizations and supporting details in a logical and coherent way. First, you must decide the order in which to present your ideas. For example, how will you order your synthesis essay on the "Roots of Violence"? Once again, the decision is yours—there are many logical ways to do this. One possibility is to present the two extreme views first (only biological causes or only social causes) and end with what might be your own view, based on your research, that violence is the result of an interaction of the two.

Here are some additional tips for writing your synthesis essay:

- **Begin the essay with one general statement that covers the ideas you will present**. For example: "The roots of violence are not easily identifiable; great controversy over this question exists."
- **Be sure to put the name of the author of the information in your synthesis in parentheses after the idea.** For example: "An overload of the neurotransmitter, serotonin, can predispose an individual to violent behavior (Linnoila)."
- **Focus on the ideas and not the authors of those ideas**. Be sure that your essay does not sound like a list of unrelated ideas such as: "Linnoila thinks Y and Pincus and Tucker think X and Basow says Z."

Exercise 23: Write a one-page synthesis essay explaining "The Roots of Violence." Draw on the three sources you read for this chapter and bring in others if you have access to them.

Gaining Expertise

1. Form small groups of four or five students and brainstorm definitions for the term *stress*. Make a list of all the group's ideas, with the author's name listed next to each one.

   Analyze your group's ideas. Group similar ideas together in categories and give each category a label. Reduce most of the ideas into three or four categories. Write those categories in the chart below. Be sure to acknowledge each member who contributed an idea to each of the categories.

WHAT IS STRESS?	SOURCE(S)
1._____	_____
_____	_____
2._____	_____
_____	_____
3._____	_____
_____	_____
4._____	_____
_____	_____

Write a brief synthesis essay in which you define stress. Draw from your classmate's ideas, as well as the Additional Sources provided below.

Additional Sources

"We will define stress as a complex set of reactions made by an individual under pressure to adapt. Stress is a response made to a perceived threat to one's well-being. Stress is something that happens inside people. There are physiological reactions and unpleasant feelings (distress, discomfort) associated with stress." (from *Psychology: An Introduction*, p. 540)

"It's often said that stress is one of the most destructive elements in people's daily lives, but that's only a half truth. The way we react to stress appears to be more important than the stress itself. (Bernie Siegel, *Love, Medicine,* and *Miracles*, p. 70)

"Whether or not you *choose* to have a stressful experience determines the response to that stress that you will have. If you feel helpless, the stress response will be more harmful." (Hans Seelye)

"On the available evidence, it can only be said that the mind working through the immune system may tip the balance between health and illness in certain situations, possibly by way of stress hormones. Reduced immune functioning associated with emotional stress slightly increases the chance of catching a cold, and it might reduce the chance of recovering from more serious illnesses." (The *Harvard Mental Health Letter*, February 1992, p. 3)

"The new understanding of the mediating mechanisms involved in the body's response to stress suggests that the inability to cope may affect the immune system in a way that causes white blood cells to lose some of their ability to fight off disease, resulting in repeated infections, allergies, and perhaps even cancer." (Judy Foreman, *Boston Globe,* 1986)

2. Prepare a short survey to give to your classmates on a topic that interests you. The survey can be written or oral. Then analyze the results of the survey and compile them in a short essay, in which you synthesize what your classmates say. Following is a sample survey.

   Survey on Program Satisfaction

   a. Are you happy with the program you are enrolled in?
   b. What parts of the program would you *not* change?
   c. What parts would you change?

3. Select an issue or event that has been in the news recently. Read several (at least three) newspaper and/or magazine articles about the issue. Watch for television coverage of the event as well. Gather several different viewpoints or analyses of the event or issue. Make a synthesis chart and then summarize these viewpoints, synthesizing all the information in a short essay.

4. Work with a partner and find a topic that interests both of you. Find two articles each on that topic from the library. Write summaries of your articles and exchange them. Then write a synthesis essay in which you discuss your topic and include your partner's sources, as well as the ones you read yourself.

EVALUATING YOUR PROGRESS

Prepare a portfolio of your best work from this chapter. Include a summary, paraphrase, and synthesis. Write a brief (no more than one page) introduction to the portfolio. Describe the problems you encountered in writing these pieces, things you are proud of, and areas you believe require additional attention. Be ready to share your portfolio with another student.

Compiling and Communicating Research

Chapter Theme: Steve Jobs (right), the Founder of Apple Computer, Inc.

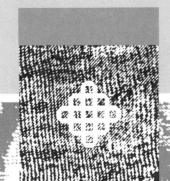

Many of your college assignments will require writing that involves library research. This chapter will assist you in locating and evaluating appropriate source material for such written work. It will also guide you step-by-step through the process of compiling that information into a piece of writing that is acceptable as academic work. You will follow the steps of a hypothetical business student as he researches, reads about, and gathers information on Steve Jobs, the founder of Apple Computer, Inc.

ACADEMIC TOPICS

- Using the Library
- Finding and Evaluating Sources
- Choosing and Limiting a Research Topic
- Organizing a Research Paper
- Citing and Documenting Sources

CHAPTER THEME

Steve Jobs, the founder of Apple Computer, Inc.

TAKING INVENTORY: YOUR RESEARCH PAPER EXPERIENCE

Think about the kind of academic writing you have done in the past either in this country or in your country of origin. How long were these pieces of writing? What were they about? Where did you find the information for your paper? Was your experience a good one? Why or why not?

In small groups, share your past experiences doing library research and writing about it. Discuss the questions above as well as any other relevant ones that come up during your group discussion.

PART ONE: GETTING STARTED

Imagine that on the first day of a Business Strategy and Integration course, the professor informs the students that they will be writing two papers for the course. Other than the length of the papers (5–10 pages), he does not provide any additional information. Since this is your first semester at a college in the United States, you will likely have a number of questions about writing these "papers."

To begin with, what is a "paper"? A paper, which might also be called **a research paper** or a **term paper** or sometimes a **report,** usually involves some sort of investigation—gathering information from scholarly sources or original data from experimental research—which the student will compile and write up in an organized fashion.

You may also have questions about the form of the paper. The specific length, format, organization, and purpose of each paper you write will largely be determined by the instructor and/or the conventions of the discipline. A paper for a Business class, for example, usually follows APA (for American Psychological Association) format. A literary analysis for a literature course will likely follow MLA (for Modern Language Association) format. It's always a good idea to ask the instructor of the course what type of format is preferred.

You might also wonder why an instructor, who is probably already well acquainted with the subject of your paper, may require you to go through such a process. The goals of writing a paper are not simply to learn about a topic. They are also to teach you something about **critical thinking**—the ability to analyze, interpret, and evaluate information and ideas.

It's important to remember that the final product—the actual five or ten pages that you turn in to the professor—is not the only evidence of your learning. The process of finding and refining a topic of interest to you, of searching through reams of material to locate appropriate support for that topic, and finally of compiling an intelligent and well-written paper is really the reward for your hard work. The skills you acquire in mastering this process are essential—not only for your college work, but for your career later on.

Before you begin checking books out of the library and writing your paper, you will need to set a few things in order. The first section of this chapter will look at some preliminary matters—getting acquainted with your library, setting up a schedule you can follow, and brainstorming for topics to write about.

Getting Acquainted with Your Library

LIBRARY TERMINOLOGY

IT WORKS!
Learning Strategy:
Learning
Specialized,
Academic
Vocabulary

Exercise 1: Read the following sentences and try to define or describe the meaning of the library word in bold from the context.

1. All the history books are shelved in the **stacks** on the fourth floor of the library.

   _____

2. Before you can find that book in the library, you need to have the **call number.**

   _____

3. Most of the material in the **reference area** (e.g., encyclopedias, indexes, college catalogs) cannot be taken out of the library.

   _____

4. Students need a library card to **check out** books from this library.

   _____

5. Be sure to return your library books by the **due date;** otherwise, you will have to pay a **fine** of 25 cents per day.

6. If you need to find me, I'll be in the **current periodicals** room reading the most recent issue of *People* magazine.

Compare your answers with the Library Terminology on page 163. Scan that list for other words you may not know, and make a point of learning them.

LIBRARY BASICS

You will find books, periodicals and a broad collection of reference materials in a library. Books **can** be checked out of the library; periodicals (magazine and journal articles) and reference materials (e.g., encyclopedias, fact books, atlases) **cannot** be checked out and must be used in the library. You will be learning more about using these three types of sources in greater detail in Part Two of this chapter.

Card catalogs. A library has a very precise system of cataloguing its resources. For example, all books and periodicals are given a specific number, called a **call number,** which is the "address" for that book. Most college libraries use the Library of Congress card catalog system. The Dewey Decimal system is used by many public libraries.

Look in the "card catalog" under the **author, title,** or the **subject** of the book to find a book's call number. (See "Up Close: Catalog Cards" for an illustration of each one.) It used to be that each book had at least one card and these cards were filed alphabetically in drawers. Students had to flip through these cards and find the one they were looking for. Today, most libraries have computerized their card catalogs, which makes the process of finding a call number much easier. Students can now enter the author's last name, the title of the book, the subject of the book, key words in the title of the book, and the call number to pull up an entry for the desired source on the screen.

Author Card

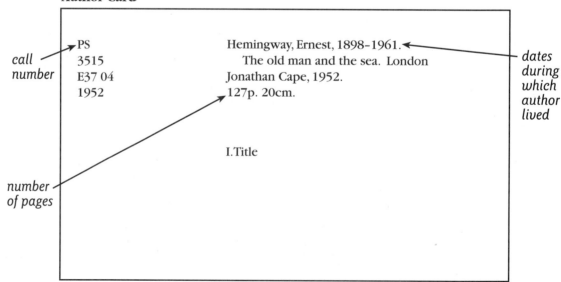

Title Card

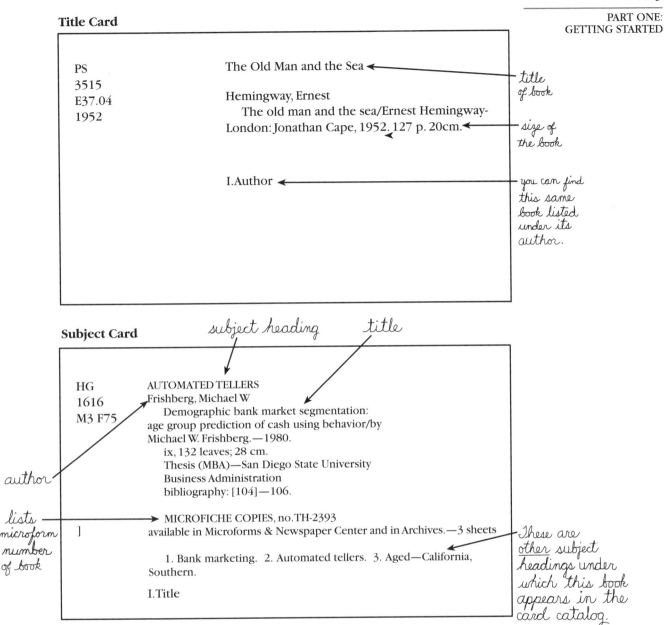

Subject Card

Electronic databases. Another new addition to most college libraries today is the **electronic database** index. Instead of looking through heavy printed indexes with very small print, students can search for periodical and newspaper articles quickly by simply typing a few key words into a computerized electronic database. The titles of articles on these topics, along with the authors, dates of publication, names of the journals in which they appear, and page numbers appear on the computer screen. For a small fee, students can print out these entries. Below are some of the most common electronic databases:

- **ABI/Inform** provides an index of business articles.
- **Applied Science and Technology Index** is an index of articles published in major technology and applied science periodicals.
- **Dissertation Abstracts** lists doctoral and masters' theses.

- **ERIC** is an index with abstracts of educational documents and journal articles collected by a central clearinghouse for educational information.
- **INFOTRAC** indexes articles on topics in the social sciences, humanities, and nontechnical general science area from general-interest periodicals.
- **Lexis/Nexus** allows full-text searching of magazines, newspapers, newsletters, law reports, television and radio transcripts, and more.
- **Medline** is an index with abstracts of journal articles published in health, medicine, nursing, and dentistry.
- **Newspaper Abstracts** indexes articles from 25 major newspapers.
- **Periodical Abstracts** lists general interest, academic, and business periodicals and provides abstracts.
- **PsycLit** is an index with abstracts (an abstract is a summary) of articles in the world's periodicals on psychology and related disciplines.
- **Wilson Business Abstracts** is an index with abstracts of material published in major business periodicals.

Exercise 2: Where would you search for articles on the following topics? Write down the name(s) of the electronic database(s) you would use for the following. (There may be more than one possible answer.)

1. 1994 Superbowl Football Game
2. Laser optical surgery
3. Ford Motor Company's new management policy
4. Second-language acquisition
5. Your professor's Ph.D. dissertation
6. The Gulf War
7. The NAFTA agreement
8. Nelson Mandela and apartheid in South Africa
9. Prozac (an antidepressant medication)
10. American Disabilities Act of 1990

LIBRARY TOUR

Learning your way around your library will save you a great deal of time when you start looking for sources later on. Before beginning a paper, take some time to visit your library and get acquainted with key sections. (You will be learning more about specific functions of the library in Part Two of this chapter.)

When you need information about the library, consult these sources:

- Ask reference librarians. They are there to help you.
- Look for free printed material about the library.
- Read the signs posted in the library.
- Ask other students.

Exercise 3: Find out the answers to the following questions about your school's library. If your school doesn't have a library, go to the nearest college library.

1. What are the library's hours of operation?

2. How long can you check out a book?

3. How much is the fine per day if a book is not returned on time? Is there a grace period?

_____

4. Does the library have a card catalog or computerized system for cataloguing books?

_____

5. Where are the following located?
  • current periodicals
  • bound periodicals (magazines and journals in book form)
  • photocopy machines
  • reserve book room
  • audio and video materials
  • microfilm or microfiche

6. Does your library have any electronic databases? What are they?

_____

7. Does your library give tours? Does it have a "term paper clinic"?

_____

Making Cross-Cultural Connections

*IT WORKS!
Learning Strategy:
Comparing
Academic Life*

Exercise 4: Libraries can be very different from one country to another. After visiting your library, compare it with libraries in your country. On one side of the following chart, make a list of how libraries operate in your culture. On the other side, describe how the library at your school works. If you're not sure about some of the answers, ask someone from your own country, another student, or a librarian.

	MY CULTURE	THIS UNIVERSITY
Who finds the materials?	_____	_____
Is library use free?	_____	_____
Are there periodicals?	_____	_____
Can you take the materials home?	_____	_____
Can you walk around freely?	_____	_____
Is it computerized?	_____	_____
Is there a separate reference room?	_____	_____
Do people study there?	_____	_____
Other points	_____	_____

Compare your answers with a student from a culture that is different from your own. Find out what's similar and what's different.

Setting a Schedule for Your Research Paper

Managing Your Learning: Setting a realistic schedule for your research paper will help you complete it before the deadline.

One of the most common mistakes students make when they write a research paper is procrastinating—putting it off until the very last minute. It's nearly impossible to write a good research paper the day before it is due. Research takes time and persistence. One way to avoid the procrastination problem is to make a schedule for yourself and adhere to it.

Below are the basic steps in writing a research paper, along with some suggestions for how long it might take to complete a 10-page paper over a 15-week semester. Other papers may take longer or shorter amounts of time, but these suggestions will give you a sense of how much time to allot for each step. (Parts Two and Three of this chapter will take you through these steps in detail.)

1. **Preliminary thinking about your topic**—two to three weeks
   It takes some time to decide on a topic. It's not uncommon to change your mind several times before making a firm decision.
2. **Surveying the topic**—one week
   Once you have decided on your topic, spend a week in the library reading general reference material (e.g., encyclopedias, general periodicals, books) on the topic. This will help you decide on your specific search strategy.
3. **Searching for sources**—three weeks
   During this time, you will be looking for books and journal articles relevant to your paper topic. Be aware that the book you want may be checked out or the journal you need may not be part of the library's collection. Start this process as early as possible in the semester to avoid last-minute crises.
4. **Reading and taking notes**—five to six weeks
   Allow yourself plenty of time to read your sources carefully and to take notes. You may have to do Steps 3 and 4 several times over—you will read a source and then return to the library to find a text mentioned in that source.
5. **Writing the first draft of the paper**—three to four weeks
   Once you have decided on a topic and have located and read your sources, the actual writing of your paper should not take too much time.
6. **Editing and proofreading the paper**—one week
   Be sure to set aside a week to make final revisions to the paper.

Exercise 5:   Your instructor will assign a due date for your paper. Make up a schedule and include (1) the step, (2) a deadline for completion of that step, and (3) a concrete outcome for that step to show that you have completed it (e.g., for Step 1 you might write down a brief description of your topic).

STEPS	DUE DATE	OUTCOME
1. Preliminary thinking	_____	_____
2. Surveying the topic	_____	_____
3. Searching for sources	_____	_____
4. Reading and taking notes	_____	_____
5. Writing the first draft of the paper	_____	_____
6. Editing and proofreading the paper	_____	_____

Brainstorming for Topic Ideas

Students often complain, "I just don't know what to write about!" A good paper topic rarely falls out of the sky; rather, it requires some prior thought. Students use a variety of techniques for the initial exploring of a topic—through discussions with other students or with the professor and by reading their textbook.

Brainstorming will help you to discover your interests. You can make a list of possible topics that appeal to you. Or, use a "mapping" or "webbing" system to find out what your interests are. Begin by writing the general topic given by the professor in the middle of a piece of paper and putting a circle around it. In the Business class example above, the student wrote "Business Paper" in the middle of his map as follows:

Then he drew "bubbles" from that center circle to show areas in business that interested him, as follows:

Then the student drew more bubbles to narrow down his areas of interest even further. This time, he concentrated only on "Computers" and "International Business" because those topics interested him the most.

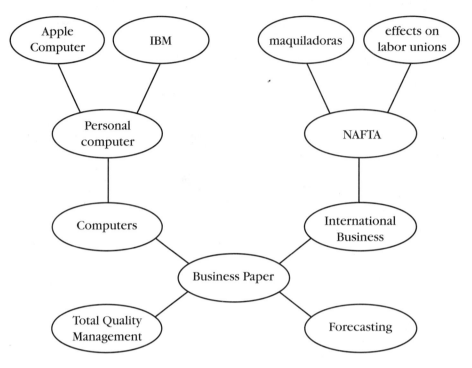

After the student had completed his brainstorm map, he decided that he was interested in doing a paper on "Apple Computer." Although this initial topic idea is still very general, he can begin reading and searching for information for his topic now.

Exercise 6: Complete a brainstorming "map" like the one above to help you find a topic for your research paper. Select a key word from the list below to begin your brainstorm. (Or use one provided by your instructor.)

health	learning a second language
advertising	technology
immigration	American culture
education	Hollywood
nutrition	alcoholism

SURVIVAL TIPS: PAPER TOPICS TO AVOID

It's best to avoid the following types of topics when selecting a paper topic:

- **Very current topics.** It's difficult to find published material on events that are very current.
- **Obscure international topics.** It may be appealing to write about a situation in your country, but you may find it very difficult to find information on your topic.

- **Controversial topics.** You may find it difficult to write an objective research paper on a controversial topic such as abortion or capital punishment.
- **Topics that are too broad or too specific.** Keep the length of your paper in mind when you select a topic. If your topic calls for gathering a lot of information, you will find it difficult to fit it into a short paper. If your topic is too specific, you will have to spend a lot of time searching for information.

Exercise 7: Imagine that you are writing a 5–10 page paper. Evaluate the following topics with a partner, using the suggestions listed above in "Survival Tips" as a guide. Decide whether the topic is appropriate or not. If it is not, indicate why. Then revise the topics that you decided were inappropriate.

1. A history of the Great Depression

_____

2. Images of Asian women in contemporary American cinema

_____

3. Deregulation of banking in Indonesia in the 1980s

_____

4. Prayer in the public schools

_____

5. 1994 First-quarter earnings of IBM

_____

PART TWO: CONDUCTING A SEARCH

The next step in the process of writing a research paper is to conduct a search for appropriate sources and do preliminary reading so that you can begin to limit your topic. You will usually go to a library to find appropriate material, but electronic databases and computerized full-text information services are becoming more affordable and accessible. Regardless of whether you are sitting at home, connected to these databases through a modem on your computer, or searching through indexes in the library, you will need to map out a general plan of action for finding your sources. The following sections of this chapter describe a common sequence of steps in the search.

Surveying Your Topic

The starting point for your search will depend on how much you already know about your topic. If it is something about which you know very little, you will want to begin by reading some general information about your topic. If you are already knowledgeable on the topic and familiar with the literature, you may not need this step.

Let's return to the student in the Business class who wants to do a paper on Apple computers. Clearly, this topic is much too broad for a short paper of 5–10 pages, so he will need to do some background reading to help him limit the topic. One useful source of general information is an **encyclopedia.** Encyclopedias are located in the reference section of your library, and they do not circulate. (This means you must use them in the library; you may not check them out.) There are encyclopedias on both general and specific subjects, and a you'll find a list of these on page 158.

You can also survey a topic by reading a book or article that treats your topic in a general way. Textbooks often provide a useful overview as well. (You will learn to locate books and periodicals in the library later in this chapter.)

Here are some important points to consider while reading about your topic:

- Pay attention to **key words** associated with your topic. You may want to use these key words to help you search for relevant books and periodical articles later on.
- As you read, think about ways in which you can **limit your topic** (make it more specific). For example, the Business student wants to write a paper on Apple Computer, but he can't possibly write all about it in 5–10 pages. Reading a subject encyclopedia article will help him find a specific **subtopic** that interests him.
- Make a note of any **bibliographic information** (list of sources for further research), which is usually found at the end of the article.

Exercise 8:   Refer to the list of representative subject encyclopedias on page 158 at the end of this chapter. Write the name(s) of the encyclopedias you think would contain an article on each of the following topics. Then select one topic, and locate an encyclopedia article from the library.

1. The Civil War

   _____

2. Capital Punishment

   _____

3. Racism

   _____

4. The Great Depression

   _____

5. Stocks and Bonds

   _____

6. Martin Luther King

   _____

7. Earthquakes

   _____

8. The Appalachian Mountains

_____

9. Schizophrenia

_____

10. Early cave paintings

_____

Exercise 9:   Survey the topic you selected in Exercise 6 of this chapter on page 128, or select a new topic if you prefer.

1. Select an appropriate subject encyclopedia from the list at the end of this chapter and locate it in the reference section of your library. (If you have difficulty locating the encyclopedia you are looking for, ask a reference librarian for help.) Write the name of the encyclopedia below.

   _____

2. Find and read an article on your topic from this encyclopedia. Take notes below from that article. Write down key words, subtopics, and any bibliographic information provided.

   _____

   _____

   _____

   _____

Searching for Books

The next step in your search is to look for appropriate books on your topic. To do that, you will consult either a computerized catalog or a card catalog (if your library is not computerized).

You can search for a book on your topic in three ways, depending on the information you have:

1. By the **author**'s name. These are filed according to the author's **last name** (e.g., Hemingway, Ernest). Type in the computer (or look up in the card catalog) the author's last name, followed by the first name.
2. By the **title** of the book. Type in the computer (or look up in the card catalog) the title of the book (e.g., _The Sun Also Rises_).
3. By the **subject** of the book. Type the subject word or phrase that corresponds to your topic into the computer (e.g., Apple Computer). Consult the _Library of Congress Subject Headings_ for a list of appropriate terms used in the card catalog. Computerized catalogs will usually provide a cross-reference. Use the key words that you noted during your survey reading of your topic.

UP CLOSE: A COMPUTERIZED CARD CATALOG BOOK ENTRY

Here is a sample computerized catalog entry for a book on Apple Computer. The researcher wanted to find a book about one of the founders of Apple Computer, Inc.—Steve Jobs. He typed in "Jobs, Steven" in the computer and the following entry appeared on the computer screen. Note that entries from your library will probably be slightly different, but they will contain the same information.

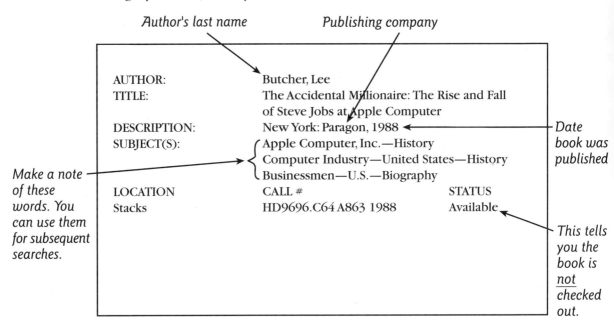

Author's last name   *Publishing company*

AUTHOR: Butcher, Lee
TITLE: The Accidental Millionaire: The Rise and Fall
                       of Steve Jobs at Apple Computer
DESCRIPTION: New York: Paragon, 1988   — *Date book was published*
SUBJECT(S):   Apple Computer, Inc.—History
                       Computer Industry—United States—History
                       Businessmen—U.S.—Biography

LOCATION   CALL #   STATUS
Stacks   HD9696.C64 A863 1988 Available

Make a note of these words. You can use them for subsequent searches.

This tells you the book is not checked out.

Exercise 10: Using the subjects listed in "Up Close: A Computerized Card Catalog Book Entry" on page 132, find at least two more books on the topic of Apple Computer, Inc. Note bibliographic information on a 3" × 5" index card, called a "reference card." Use the following format for your reference cards.

Call number   General Topic of Book

Author's last name, first name

Title of the book (or article)

Publisher, place of publication, date of publication, pages

Your notes (e.g., excellent source, good section on X topic, etc.)

Exercise 11: Find three books on the topic you selected in Exercise 6 of this chapter. Complete a reference card for each book. Keep these cards in a safe place because you will be using them throughout this chapter.

Searching for Periodical and Newspaper Articles

The next step in your search is to find periodical and newspaper articles. Magazines and journals are called "periodicals" because they are published on a regular (periodic) basis—weekly, monthly, quarterly. They are appropriate sources of information when you need current information for your paper, when your topic is specialized, and when you would like to find differing points of view on your topic.

The distinction between **magazines** and scholarly **journals** is an important one. Generally speaking, you will use articles from scholarly journals for your research paper because they are more suitable for academic writing. Here are some major differences between a magazine and a journal:

A Magazine	A Scholarly Journal
• Has shorter (one- or two-page) articles	• Has longer (five- or ten-page) articles
• Is aimed at the general public	• Is written for other researchers in the field
• Has articles that are of general interest	• Includes articles on current research in the field
• Is usually written by journalists whose names are not always given	• Is usually written by experts in the field who are almost always named
• Does not list references	• Usually includes citations and references
• Is indexed in a general periodical index (e.g., *Reader's Guide to Periodical Literature*)	• Is indexed in specialized subject indexes and databases (e.g., *PsycLit*)

Exercise 12:

1. Work with a partner. Look up the following titles of periodicals in the card catalog, and write down the call numbers. Some libraries have a separate listing for periodical call numbers. Ask a reference librarian to help you if necessary.

   NOTE: Periodical titles—but not individual periodical articles—are catalogued just like books, and they each have a call number. For example, *Time* magazine will be in the card catalog, but the article on the president in this week's *Time* magazine will not be in the card catalog.

   The Journal of Law and Education

   Call number: _____

   Magazine or journal?

   Fortune

   Call number: _____

   Magazine or journal?

TESOL Quarterly

Call number: _____

Magazine or journal?

The New Yorker

Call number: _____

Magazine or journal?

Signs

Call number: _____

Magazine or journal?

2. Find any volume of the periodicals listed above. Ask a reference librarian to help you locate the periodicals in the stacks if you have difficulty. Then examine each periodical to determine whether it is a magazine or a scholarly journal.

USING INDEXES

The card catalog does not list all the articles from all the journals published in the United States; as you can imagine, there are simply too many articles to catalog. Therefore, you must consult a **newspaper index** or **periodical index,** which lists references to articles from many different sources on various subjects.

There are two types of indexes:

1. A **general index** lists articles by subject that are aimed at a general audience and covers topics from a broad range of subjects. *The Reader's Guide to Periodical Literature* in print form and INFOTRAC in electronic form are the two most widely used general indexes. The *NY Times Index* will provide articles on very current issues.
2. A **specialized index** lists articles by subject that are intended to be read by a student or professional in a specific subject area. Of the many specialized indexes, the most commonly used electronic databases are listed in Part One of this chapter. Consult the list at the end of this chapter for the names of both print and computerized indexes.

Exercise 13:   Refer to the list of representative periodical indexes on page 159. Imagine that you are looking for periodical articles on the following topics. Write down beside each topic the name of at least one index that you think might have some articles on that topic. Then go to the library and locate those indexes, making notes of where to find them. This information will be very helpful for you when you begin your own search.

1. Dyslexia (a learning disorder) _____
2. Kurt Vonnegut (American author) _____

3. Pediatric AIDS _____

4. The making of the movie *Jurassic Park* _____

5. The Holocaust _____

6. Immigration laws _____

7. The real estate boom of the 1980s _____

8. The Prairie style of architecture _____

9. Watergate _____

10. The 1987 stock market crash _____

11. Your research topic: _____

ELECTRONIC DATABASES AND PRINT INDEXES

More and more libraries are making computerized databases—either on-line or on Compact Disc-Read Only Memory (CD-ROM)—available for students to use. As noted earlier, they are much easier to use than the bound, print indexes, but the principles for using both print and electronic indexes are very similar.

- **Begin with a key term.** By the time you consult a periodical index, you should know the terminology of your topic. These are the words you will be using over and over to look up information in indexes and catalogs.

    For example, the Business student writing about Apple Computer has narrowed his topic down to the founder of the company—**Steven Jobs,** the key term he will use to find periodical articles. Often this term will be too specific, and he may then have to use the broader term, **Apple Computer, Inc.**

- **Select appropriate subdivisions.** Most indexes have subdivisions, which divide a broad topic into more specific categories. When you are searching an index, you will need to locate not only the key word but also the subheading that seems most appropriate.

Electronic databases have made searching periodical indexes much easier for students.

Here are some of the 59 subdivisions that appeared in the electronic index, INFOTRAC, under the heading, "Apple Computer, Inc."

$\rightarrow$ Apple computer [This is the key *word.*]
        59 subdivisions

        achievements and awards
        acquisitions, mergers, divestments
        advertising
        buildings, facilities, etc.
        cases
        competitions
        computer programs
        data processing
        environmental policy
        finance
$\rightarrow$ history [This is a relevant *subdivision.*]
        innovations
        laws
        litigation
$\rightarrow$ management [Another relevant *subdivision*]
        market share
        marketing
$\rightarrow$ officials and employers [Another relevant *subdivision*]

Since the student intended to write about the founder of the company, he decided to look more closely at three of the subheadings—history, management, and officials and employers. Since this was from INFOTRAC, which is a computerized index, the article name and bibliographic information is not listed under the subheading. Instead, you select the subheading in the computer, and all citations for articles about that subheading will appear on the screen. When the student selected "history," the following entry appeared:

Database: INFOTRAC
Subject: Apple Computer, Inc.
Subdivision: history

Steve Jobs: Counterculture Hero. (Next Inc.) (Computerworld Special 25th Anniversary Edition: Twenty-Five People Who Changed the World) (Interview) James Daly, Computerworld, June 22, 1992 v26 n25 pS8(1)

- **Select appropriate articles.** Browse through the names of articles, and read any abstracts that are available. Look at the dates of the articles and their lengths to determine if they are current or in-depth enough for your paper. Here is an example of the abstract that accompanied the previous entry; the article contains useful information and provides cross-references at the end for other key terms to use in later searches.

Abstract: Steve Jobs and Steve Wozniak are the near-legendary founders of Apple Computer Inc., which they started in 1975. Apple was known for its counterculture image, and the Apple Macintosh, which was both user-friendly and technologically sophisticated, was one of the company's most notable successes. Soon after the introduction of the Macintosh, Jobs left Apple. In 1985, he started another company, which is Next Inc. At his new company, Jobs seems to want to carry on an Apple tradition, which has it that the best way to predict the future is to invent it. Jobs thinks of himself as a tool builder. He says tools bring out the creativity and intellect in people. He thinks that mistakes are not necessarily bad, because we learn from them, and he points out that mistakes are a part of risk taking. Jobs thinks that competitive advantage in the 1990s will not come from improvements that involve individual productivity. Rather Jobs points to group productivity and collaboration as the most critical issues of the coming decade.

Subjects: Computer industry - Personalities
Companies: NeXT Inc. - Officials and employees
Apple Computer Inc. - History
People: Jobs, Steve - Interviews

- **Write down relevant bibliographic information.** Always remember to fill out a reference card on each article that looks useful. Be sure to write the author's name, the title of the article, the journal name, the volume number, and the pages. (See Exercise 10 for a model reference card.)

UP CLOSE: A PERIODICAL INDEX ENTRY

title of article

subheading — (Japan)

Japanese education and its implications for U.S. education. N.K. Shimahara. bibl *Phi Delta Kappan* 66:418-21 F '85

title of journal —
Japanese education: how do they do it? M. I. White. *Principal* 64:16-20 Mr '85

The right to education in Japan. K. Aoki and M. M. McCarthy. bibl *J Law Educ* 13:441-52 Jl '84 — *date–July 1984*

volume number — *page numbers*

Look up the full title at the beginning of the index.

ABBREVATION OF PERIODICALS INDEXED

J Home Econ—Journal of Home Economics
J Ind Teach Educ—Journal of Industrial Teacher Education
J Instr Psychol—Journal of Instructional Psychology
J Law Educ—Journal of Law & Education
J Learn Disabil—Journal of Learning Disabilities

Exercise 14:   Make a reference card for each of the previous entries listed (in "Up Close: A Periodical Index Entry").

Exercise 15:   Do a search for periodical articles on your topic. Consult both a computerized and a printed index, if possible. Fill out at least five reference cards for pertinent articles. Indicate on your reference card why that particular article is pertinent to your research topic.

LOCATING PERIODICAL ARTICLES IN THE LIBRARY

Once you have identified appropriate periodical articles, you will need to find them in the library. It is important to remember that your library may not subscribe to the journal or magazine in which the article you want appears. (Many college libraries can arrange for "interlibrary loan," which means that they will procure a copy of the article from another library that does have the periodical you are looking for. This process may take a number of weeks, so be sure you make your request early in your search process.)

To find the call number of your periodical, consult the card catalog. Some libraries offer a separate "Serials Listing" of the library "holdings." (*Holdings* refers to the periodicals the library has.) Periodical articles appear in three forms, as follows:

- **Unbound Periodicals.** Recent (published within the last six months or so) periodicals are usually placed in the "Current Periodicals" section of the library, arranged by call number.
- **Bound Periodicals.** Less recent periodicals are bound in book form and shelved in the "Bound Periodicals" section of the library. Use the call number to locate your periodical, and then search for the volume number in which the article appears.
- **Microforms.** These include **microfiche** (4" × 6" sheets of film that hold up to 96 sheets of regular-sized paper) and **microfilm** (reels of 35mm film). Microforms require a machine to read them.

Periodicals can be current, bound, on microfilm or microfiche.

Exercise 16: Find the articles you selected for your research topic. Make photocopies of any articles that seem useful. Ask a reference librarian for help in any step of this process that may be difficult for you.

Using Other Sources of Information

Although you will probably find most of your information from books and periodical articles, it is important to know that your library has many other sources of information. These include **government publications,** which comprise reports, studies, statistics, and research published by the United States government and the United Nations on a variety of topics. Government publications are not cataloged in the main card catalog; they have their own system of call numbers and are shelved in a special area in the library. Ask a reference librarian to show you where government publications are located in your library.

SUMMARY OF STEPS IN CONDUCTING A SEARCH

1. Survey your topic by reading general reference material (e.g., an encyclopedia, a textbook).
2. Consult a card catalog to locate titles and the call number of books.
3. Consult appropriate periodical indexes and search for articles by your topic.
4. Consult the card catalog to find the call number of the periodicals you need.
5. Locate the periodicals in the stacks or in the microform section.

Gaining Expertise

Create a class file of information on one of the following topics. Brainstorm in small groups, and subdivide one of the topics below into a number of specific topics in a variety of disciplines. The first one has been divided for you. Work in pairs or small groups, and find relevant sources from the library on one of the specific topics. Create a bibliography, and make copies of periodical articles to put in the file.

- Ethics [Possible subdivisions: Legal ethics, business ethics, morality, etc.]
- Influential People
- Health
- The Environment

PART THREE: ORGANIZING YOUR RESEARCH

Armed with encyclopedia and periodical articles and books on your topic, you are ready to begin preparing for your research paper. This part of the process involves the following: limiting your topic; developing a thesis statement; evaluating, reading, and taking notes from your sources; and finally, creating an outline for your paper.

Limiting Your Topic

During the initial stages of your library search, you will have gained a general idea of your chosen topic. (Review Part One of this chapter on choosing an initial topic.) However, as you begin to do more in-depth reading, you will probably find that you need to adjust, refine, and sometimes even change your topic completely. As you gain expertise through reading in your area of inquiry, you will want your choice of topic to reflect your increased understanding.

Consider the example of the student writing about Apple Computer for his Business class. When he first began reading, he thought he might write something about how the Macintosh computer was developed, or a history of Apple's marketing strategy. As he began reading about the company, he discovered that one of the founders of Apple Computer—Steven Jobs—was a highly creative, controversial figure who had enormous impact on both Apple Computer, Inc. and the computer industry as a whole. As a result, he decided to focus his paper on this individual.

As he gathered sources and began to find out more about Steven Jobs, the student was faced with yet another decision. He was reading about many different aspects of this individual: his development, his management style, his entrepreneurial spirit, his relationship with Steve Wozniak, the co-founder and electronic wizard behind the computer, and on and on. The student realized that he had to select only one or two of those aspects. The following chart reflects this process of limiting his topic.

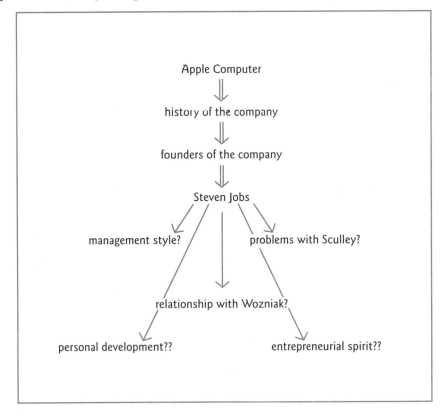

Here are some guidelines to help you limit a topic:

- **Select a specific aspect of your topic that interests you.** Above all else, consider your own interests. Choose something that you want to know more about. Your own interest will be an excellent motivator and will sustain you throughout the project.
- **Select an aspect that allows for depth of analysis and interpretation.** A research paper is more than a listing of facts; it includes an intelligent and interesting presentation of that information and reflects the writer's point of view. For example, some sources say that Steven Wozniak—not Steven Jobs—was the real genius behind Apple Computer. Other sources state that without Jobs the world would never have seen a Macintosh computer. The research writer will have to reconcile this conflicting information and present his own point of view, expressed in a **thesis statement** and well supported in his paper. (Writing a thesis statement will be discussed next.)
- **Select an aspect for which there is sufficient published information.** Avoid selecting an obscure aspect of a topic. For example, there will probably not be plentiful sources in your library on the topic, "Steven Jobs's Views on Total Quality Management."

WRITING A THESIS STATEMENT

Once you have limited your topic to a specific aspect, you will need to formulate a **thesis statement,** which is a sentence expressing the **specific topic** you have chosen as well as **your perspective** on that topic.

Thesis statement = Specific Topic + Your Perspective

For example, the Business student decided to limit his topic to Steven Jobs and his motivation in founding Apple Computer, Inc. A sentence such as "This paper will be about Steven Jobs and what motivated him to start Apple Computer, Inc." is **not** a thesis statement because it lacks the second part, **the perspective.** The sentence must be revised to reflect an indication of the writer's analysis of what motivated Steven Jobs. Was it money? Was it power? Was it creative spirit? The following thesis statement reflects a perspective:

Tentative thesis statement:

"Steven Jobs, one of the founders of Apple Computer, was driven to his success not by money or by power but by an entrepreneurial spirit of creativity and need for achievement."

The writer will have to persuade his reader that this statement is true; he will need to provide evidence to support his perspective of Jobs's motivation.

Since your thesis statement gives the reader an overall idea of what your paper is about, and also serves as a guiding principal for the contents of your paper, avoid limiting your statement to the following:

- **General information.** A thesis statement needs to express something that is not generally accepted as true by all people. For example, the statement, "English is spoken widely in the world," is factual. It would be very hard to write a five-page paper on this topic.
- **Lists and descriptions.** A thesis statement cannot simply list the parts of something. For example, the sentence, "There are four main approaches to learning a second language," is not a complete thesis statement because there is no analysis of which is the best approach—only a list of the four types.

Exercise 17: Read the following thesis statements. First, identify the specific topic and the perspective in each one. Next, discuss with a partner how a different writer might have used a different perspective for the sentence. Here is an example to follow:

Sample thesis statement: Although the TOEFL is used widely as an admissions tool for acceptance into colleges in the United States and Canada, it fails to provide useful information of an international student's ability to do written academic work.
Topic: the TOEFL as an admissions tool
Perspective: The TOEFL doesn't evaluate students' writing ability.
Alternative Perspective: Although the TOEFL is used widely as an admissions tool for acceptance into colleges in the United States and Canada, it evaluates a student's test-taking ability more accurately than it evaluates a student's ability to communicate in English.

Now, read and analyze the following thesis statements:

1. Young children who spend extensive time in day care may actually benefit; they may be better socialized and more cooperative when they enter elementary school.

   Topic: _____

   Perspective: _____

   Alternative Perspective: _____

   _____

   _____

2. The severe problems with violence in large urban areas of the United States may be traced mainly to the easy accessibility of automatic weapons.

   Topic: _____

   Perspective: _____

   Alternative Perspective: _____

   _____

   _____

3. Immigrants in the United States benefit from bilingual classes in school because mastery of the first language results in more efficient acquisition of a second language.

Topic: _____

Perspective: _____

Alternative Perspective: _____

_____

_____

4. AIDS research has not made substantial gains in discovering a vaccine mainly because the government has been slow to fund this research, owing to ingrained homophobic sentiment.

Topic: _____

Perspective: _____

Alternative Perspective: _____

_____

_____

Exercise 18: Evaluate the following thesis statements as acceptable or not acceptable for a 5–10-page paper. Base your judgement on the following criteria:

- Is the topic specific enough for a paper of this length?
- Is the perspective of the writer expressed? Does it provide more than just general information and lists?
- Is the thesis stated in a complete sentence (i.e., not as a title)?
- How could these thesis statements be improved?

1. English is important in our global world.
2. Apple Computer, Inc. started in the garage of two young long-haired men.
3. Abraham Lincoln was President of the United States during the Civil War.
4. Of all the factors leading to the economic prosperity enjoyed in California during the 1970s and 1980s, a healthy defense budget is probably the most important.
5. Despite recent reports to the contrary, the bulk of evidence indicates that there is no link between coffee and cancer.
6. There are three basic reasons why the use of corporal punishment for children is harmful.
7. "Type A" personalities suffer more cardiac arrests than "Type B" personalities.
8. There are many reasons why the "Lone Assassin Theory" is the best explanation for the killing of John F. Kennedy.

LEARNING STRATEGY

Forming Concepts: Keeping a reading journal of ideas, reactions, and impressions from your research sources will help you refine your research paper topic.

Exercise 19: Keep a reading journal during your research process. An inexpensive spiral or bound notebook will work well for this purpose. Use the journal to record any ideas, reactions, important information, or "leads" for your research. Record vocabulary words that are important or that you wish to remember in your journal. Explore your own thoughts and feelings about what you read. Since this writing will be principally for your own use and will not be corrected by your instructor, you do not need to worry excessively about correct grammar and punctuation.

Exercise 20: Write a thesis statement for the research topic you selected in Exercise 6 of this chapter.

Evaluating Sources

Once you have a tentative thesis statement in mind, you are ready to examine your sources more carefully. Examining the abstract (if there is one), the introduction, the headings, the conclusion, and the bibliography of works cited in the source will help you determine if a source is appropriate for your paper.

Here are some questions that you want to consider as you preview your articles:

- **Does the source address your specific topic?** It's not necessary for the entire source to be about your topic, but if there is useful information contained in the source, then you will want to use that source in your paper.
- **Is the source current enough?** It's very important to check the publication date of your article or book. If it is not a recent publication, be cautious in using the information.
- **Is the publication a reliable source?** You will want to use the most scholarly, respected authors in your field for your information. Once you begin reading about your topic, you will find that many articles cite the same authors. Be sure that you have read these important sources. You will also want to consider if the periodical is a scholarly or popular publication. [These were compared on page 133.]

Exercise 21: Work with a partner. Decide whether the following sources are appropriate for a paper on "The Motivation of Steven Jobs in Founding Apple Computer, Inc." Base your evaluation on the criteria listed above.

1. Peters, E. Bruce (December, 1985). "The conflict at Apple was almost inevitable." *Research and Development.*

   This article was written by Dr. Peters, head of International Sociotechnical Systems and adjunct professor at George Washington University. It describes the different management styles of Steven Jobs and John Sculley and explains why they were not compatible in managing Apple Computer, Inc. There is a bibliography at the end of the article.

   Comments: _____

2. Kahn, J. (April, 1984). "Steven Jobs of Apple Computer: The Missionary of Micros." *Inc.*

   This one-page article has the subheading, "Steven Jobs may, in fact, be the microcomputer industry's first rock 'n' roll superstar." There are many quotes from Jobs, no citations and no bibliography. The article was written before Jobs resigned from Apple.

Comments: _____

3. Quinlan, T., and S. Willett (1993). "Apple answers loss with complete reorganization." *Infoworld.*
   This brief article describes recent events at Apple several years after Jobs's resignation.

Comments: _____

4. Daly, J. (1992). "Steve Jobs: Counterculture hero." *Computerworld.*
   This interview with Steve Jobs appeared in the Computerworld special 25th anniversary edition, entitled "Twenty-Five People Who Changed the World." The interview explores Jobs's intentions for his new company and his philosophy on making mistakes and taking risks.

Comments: _____

5. Butcher, L. (1988). *Accidental millionaire: The rise and fall of Steve Jobs at Apple Computer.* New York: Paragon.
   This book writes about both Jobs and Wozniak, co-founders of Apple, Inc., and shows how it was Wozniak's ability to build the first Apple personal computer that made Apple famous.

Comments: _____

6. Sculley, J., and J. Byrne (1987). *Odyssey: Pepsi to Apple—a journey of adventure, ideas and the future.* New York: Harper & Row.
   This book was written by John Sculley, the manager brought in by Jobs and with whom Jobs had serious conflicts.

Comments: _____

Reading and Taking Notes

Reading sources for a research paper is quite different from reading a text for pleasure. When you read an article for your own amusement, you usually begin at the beginning and continue at a steady pace until you reach the end. However, when reading for a research paper, you rarely begin reading without previewing your source.

Here are tips to help you be more efficient in reading for your research paper:

- **Skim your source.** Look at introductory paragraphs, topic sentences, headings, the table of contents, and the index to locate information that is relevant to your topic.
- **Skip irrelevant material.** Read with a purpose—ask yourself as you approach every source, "Can I use this in my paper? Where can I use this in my paper?"
- **Take notes on index cards.** Once you have found a section that is related to the thesis of your paper, slow down your reading, take out your index cards and begin taking notes.

TYPES OF NOTE CARDS

It's very important that you take clear and accurate notes from your sources because you will be writing your paper from those notes, not the original sources. A simple system for taking notes on these cards is illustrated in the following examples:

UP CLOSE: NOTE CARDS

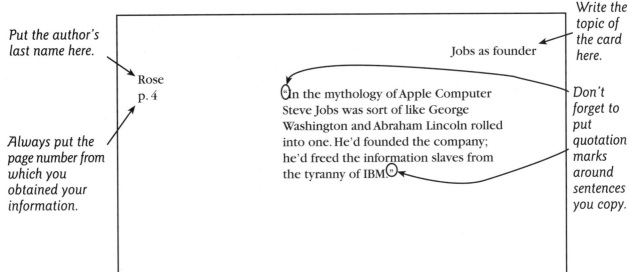

Put the author's last name here.

Always put the page number from which you obtained your information.

Write the topic of the card here.

Don't forget to put quotation marks around sentences you copy.

Rose
p. 4

Jobs as founder

"In the mythology of Apple Computer Steve Jobs was sort of like George Washington and Abraham Lincoln rolled into one. He'd founded the company; he'd freed the information slaves from the tyranny of IBM."

Sample Paraphrase Card

Paraphrase a section in a source that is important but not worth quoting. (Refer to Part Four of this chapter for more details on when to quote.) **Don't copy from the text directly unless you plan to use that text as a direct quote in your paper.**

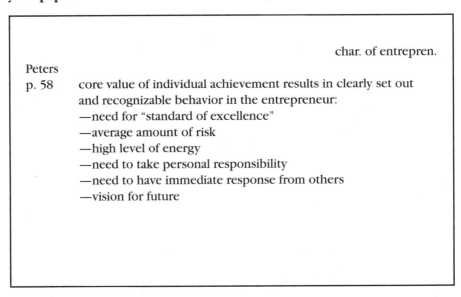

char. of entrepren.

Peters
p. 58

core value of individual achievement results in clearly set out and recognizable behavior in the entrepreneur:
—need for "standard of excellence"
—average amount of risk
—high level of energy
—need to take personal responsibility
—need to have immediate response from others
—vision for future

Sample Summary with Quotation Card

Summarize a text when you want to record the main points without including all the details. Summaries can also include brief quotations. A summary can be in abbreviated form (as the sample below) or in sentence form. If you write a sentence, be sure to use your own words.

Jobs's need to control

Moritz
p. 291   Jobs mostly interest. in <u>look</u> of Apple
- became VP of R&D, had control of major product dec.
- Jobs's influence increas. growth and
  "so did the force of the tactics he had used to push, goad, prod, cajole and coax Wozniak during the development of the Apple II."

Sample Summary of Longer Text

At other times, you will read a very long section in a book or article and summarize it on one card. Note how this was done below for the early life of Steven Jobs. The student summarized several pages into one note card.

Jobs's Bio/early life.

Butcher
p. 12–14
—born in 1956, in California
—A discipline prob at school
—excellent reader
—spoiled child, didn't get along w/peers
—often an outcast
—tinkered w/ electr. in garage, but
   wasn't as good as Wozniak, his friend
—became expert at finding electr. parts
—had interests in humanit, too
—exper. w/ drugs
—had girlfriend, Judy Smith

Sample Quotation Card

Always make a note of a sentence or two that you find worthy of quoting in your paper. Complete a separate card for each quote. Copy the passage directly onto your note card, being very careful to copy it exactly, to indicate the page number, and to put quotation marks around it. Check your copying for spelling, punctuation, and exact wording.

Jobs as founder

Rose
p. 4   "In the mythology of Apple Computer
         Steve Jobs was sort of like George
         Washington and Abraham Lincoln rolled
         into one. He'd founded the company;
         he'd freed the information slaves from
         the tyranny of IBM."

Exercise 22: Refer to the reading selection, "The Abuses of Power," by Susan Basow on page 112. Imagine that you are writing a paper on Power and Gender Roles and prepare four note cards as follows:

> One paraphrase card
> One quotation card
> One summary of a short passage in the longer passage
> One summary card of the entire passage

> *NOTE:* Use the page numbers from this text.

Exercise 23: Prepare note cards for your research paper. Write your notes on large index cards using the format described above. Include at least one example of the four types of cards described above. Be sure to turn in a separate card with your thesis statement and a bibliography card for each source cited in your note cards.

Writing an Outline

It's essential to have a tentative plan for your paper before you begin writing. There are several ways to create this plan—an informal outline, a formal outline, or short descriptions for each section of the paper. In all of these cases, you will be stating your thesis sentence and providing the main sections of your paper, together with some detail regarding supporting points.

SAMPLE OUTLINE

Consider the following tentative formal outline for the paper on Steve Jobs. Note that this outline is tentative; as the student reads more information, he or she will likely make some changes. Note also how the grammatical forms are parallel throughout the outline. This outline uses phrases, but you can also write an outline in complete sentences. The topics are indented as they become more specific. Begin the outline by using Roman numerals (I, II, etc.), followed by capital letters (A, B, etc.), followed by Arabic numerals (1, 2, etc.).

Thesis Statement: Steven Jobs embodied the qualities of a true entrepreneur, and it was these very qualities that led to both his stellar rise and his eventual demise at Apple Computer, Inc.

    I. Introduction
   II. Qualities of an entrepreneur
      A. Need for personal achievement
      B. Need for control
      C. Creative energy
      D. Desire for excellence
  III. History of Steven Jobs
      A. Early developmental factors
      B. Start-up of Apple
      C. Apple's initial success
      D. Conflict with John Sculley
         1. Apple's need for new managerial style
         2. Jobs's reluctance to relinquish control
  IV. Analysis of Jobs's rise and fall
      A. Need to build the best computer
      B. Need to have fun, be creative
      C. Arrogance
      D. Inability to work within a structure
    V. Conclusion

Exercise 24: Make a formal outline of the section Nonverbal Processes in "Basic Principles of Intercultural Communication" on page 75. Include the author's thesis statement.

Exercise 25: Use the above sample outline as a model to write an outline for your research paper. Be sure to include your thesis statement.

PART FOUR: CITING AND DOCUMENTING SOURCES

As you have already discovered, writing a research paper involves incorporating the ideas of many different sources into a paper written in your own words. If you copy other people's ideas or words without acknowledging the authors in some way, then you are guilty of **plagiarism.** You are saying to your reader, "I wrote this. These are my ideas and my own words." The word plagiarism actually comes from the Latin word for "kidnapper."

Perhaps you feel that your writing is greatly inferior to that of your source material, and it may be very tempting to copy material from other books and include it as though it were your own writing. Don't give in to that temptation. Plagiarism is considered a serious academic offense in the United States. Many students and academics have paid the consequences for plagiarizing. It's better to struggle with your imperfect English than to have perfect writing that is not your own.

This final section of the chapter will introduce you to ways in which you can avoid plagiarizing—by using direct quotations, by acknowledging sources in your paper, and by including a reference list of works cited in your paper.

Using Direct Quotations

LEARNING STRATEGY

Incorporating quotations from source texts can help you to present other people's ideas without plagiarizing.

A quotation is a group of words, sentences, or paragraphs that has been taken directly from a source text, enclosed in quotation marks (" ") and accompanied by some acknowledgment of the author and/or source text. Using appropriate quotations in both written and oral presentations can enhance your work tremendously.

Quotations can be incorporated into your paper in a number of ways. As a general rule, include an introductory phrase or sentence before quoting. A reporting phrase is often used. (See the section on summarizing in Chapter 3 for a list of reporting verbs.)

QUOTING PART OF A SENTENCE

In this case, you select a phrase—not a complete sentence—and introduce the quotation by using an introductory expression, as in the following example:

> As Jobs became more influential at Apple, he increased the "force of the tactics he had used to push, goad, prod, cajole, and coax Wozniak during the development of the Apple II" (Moritz, 1984, p. 24).

QUOTING A COMPLETE SENTENCE

When quoting a complete sentence, be sure you integrate it into your own writing with an appropriate introduction.

> Moritz (1984) clearly identified Jobs's inspiration for product planning: "He found Apple's prototype customer in the mirror, and the company came to develop computers that Jobs, at one time or another, decided he would like to own" (p. 291).

QUOTING A PARAGRAPH

When you use a quotation that is longer than three typewritten lines, then you should **block** and indent the entire quotation. Always introduce the quote with your own introductory remarks. This will alert the reader to the importance of the quoted material.

Rose (1989) described Jobs's role at Apple during the initial years.

> In the mythology of Apple Computer Steve Jobs was sort of like George Washington and Abraham Lincoln rolled into one. He'd founded the company; he'd freed the information slaves from the tyranny of IBM. (p. 4)

UP CLOSE: THE MECHANICS OF QUOTING

Enclose the quote in quotation marks.

Use a single quotation mark for a copied quote.

As Jobs became more influential at Apple, he increased the "force of the tactics he had used to push, goad, prod, cajole, and coax Wozniak during the development of the Apple II (Moritz, 1984, p. 24).

Put the period after the parenthetical citation.

Once Sculley took over Apple, the ambiance changed dramatically. As Moritz described it: "The word people used [for this change] was 'Scullification'."

This quote is longer than three lines. Indent and don't use quotation marks.

Rose (1989) described Jobs's role at Apple during the initial years.

> In the mythology of Apple Computer Steve Jobs was sort of like George Washington and Abraham Lincoln rolled into one. He'd founded the company; he'd freed the information slaves from the tyranny of IBM. (p. 4)

Use brackets to add words to a quote.

Exercise 26:   Find the errors in the following quotations. Refer to "Up Close: The Mechanics of Quoting" on page 151 for help.

1. Samovar and Porter (1991) have likened ethnocentrism to a "perceptual prism" "through which cultures interpret and judge all other groups."
2. Samovar and Porter caution us against the dangers of ethnocentrism. "If we allow ethnocentrism to interfere with our perceptions, our reactions, and our interactions, we will reduce the effectiveness of communication. To be successful, we must be vigilant to the ease with which we negatively judge the actions of others."
3. Bloom (1987) states that ethnocentrism is "As ubiquitous as the prohibition against incest between mother and son (p. 36)."

Knowing When to Use a Quotation

Be sure that you have a good reason for using a quote. Some students use quotes because they have difficulty putting the quote into their own words, but this is *not* a good reason to quote something!

Here are some cases in which using a quote is recommended:

1. **To provide support for a statement.** This is by far the most common use of quoted material. If you are presenting a point of view, it is wise to find a reputable scholar or expert in the field to support your ideas. For example, note how the following quote supports the author's idea that the environment contributes to the development of violent behavior:

> The role of the environment cannot be ignored in understanding violence in adolescents, as Pincus and Tucker (1985) state: "The violence experienced at home in early childhood is probably an important etiologic factor in the development of a propensity for violence" (p. 82).

2. **To use as a springboard for ideas.** Many writers begin with a quote as a starting point for a discussion that may agree or disagree with the quote. Note how the following example does this.

> "I wouldn't be surprised if cancer in early childhood was linked to messages of parental conflict or disapproval perceived even in the womb" (p. 75). This statement by Bernie Siegel (1987) illustrates our relentless, modern quest for explanations about the cause of disease and conquest over death.

3. **To express an idea or sentiment eloquently.** If you come across a sentence that you find very moving or well written in clear, vivid language, then by all means use it as a quotation to emphasize a point you want to make. Writers often use these quotes at the beginning or end of a piece of writing. Note the rich metaphors in Bloom's quote below.

> In describing the spiritual life of the contemporary American family, Bloom (1987) laments its lack of vitality: "It [the spiritual landscape] is as monochrome and unrelated to those who pass through it as are the barren steppes frequented by nomads who take their mere subsistence and move on" (p. 57).

Exercise 27: Work in pairs. Refer to the article, "The Abuses of Power," by Basow on page 112. Find a passage suitable for quoting for each of the three cases described above: for support, as a springboard for ideas, as an eloquently stated sentiment.

Exercise 28: Select one article from the sources you have gathered for your own research paper. Select three passages to quote from that article. Write useful introductory sections to integrate your quote smoothly into your paper. Pay careful attention to punctuation. Then write a brief explanation for each quote, describing why you selected the passage that you did.

Acknowledging Material That Is Not Quoted

Your paper will draw on information from a number of sources: your printed research material, your own personal knowledge, your beliefs and experiences, and so on. It is very important for you to distinguish carefully among all these sources and to acknowledge sources of information that do not spring from your own personal fund of knowledge, experiences, and beliefs.

In general, follow these guidelines for acknowledging information:

- **Acknowledge information taken from a printed source or oral presentation.** If you learn a new theory, a specific point of view, a conclusion from an experiment, or any other original information from a source other than your own ideas, you must state the author and date of that information in your paper. Even if you don't copy the author's exact words, the ideas belong to him or her and you must give the author credit for them.
- **Undocumented information that is available in a number of general reference books is considered general knowledge and does not need to be documented.** For example, an historical fact, a date of birth, or a definition for a word are all examples of common knowledge. If you are not sure whether it's general knowledge or not, consult someone. If you are still in doubt, document the source.
- **You do not need to document your own experimental results, critical analyses, personal experiences, or observations.** Any conclusions that you have formed on your own through analysis or experimentation do not need to be documented. Be absolutely certain, however, that these are your original ideas.

Exercise 29: Consider the following pieces of information. Put a check next to those that are general information and don't require documentation. Be ready to explain your answers.

1. Steven Jobs was born in 1956 in California.
2. The true talent behind the founding of Apple Computer, Inc., was the other Steven—not Jobs, but Wozniak.
3. John Sculley was invited to be President of Apple Computer because Steven Jobs realized that he could no longer manage the operation properly.
4. The original Apple computers were intended for educational purposes.
5. Wall Street had great disdain for Steven Jobs because they felt he was not "safe."

In-Text Citations

The actual way in which you acknowledge your sources will depend on the style format required by your course. As mentioned earlier, there are two principal types of documentation systems: the MLA (Modern Language Association) format and the APA (American Psychological Association) format. Generally speaking, courses in the humanities require papers to be written using MLA format, and social science courses employ APA format. Always check with your professor to be certain of the preferred format.

This final section will review certain principles of documentation using the APA format only. An MLA style sheet can be found in the Appendix of this book. It's highly recommended that you purchase the handbook for the format you will be using the most—*The MLA Handbook for Writers of Research Papers,* 3rd ed. (1988) or *The Publication Manual of the American Psychological Association,* 4th ed. (1994).

An in-text citation provides the author's name (or the title of the publication if there is no author stated) and the date of the publication. If the citation refers to a quotation, the page number on which the quotation appears in the original source is given. If the citation refers to unquoted material, then no page number is necessary.

In-text citation for a work by a single author:
In the following example, the author's name is part of the sentence, so only the date of publication is in parentheses:

Butcher (1988) believed that Jobs gained fame and fortune only by accident.

If the author's name is not part of the sentence, put both author and date in parentheses:

Jobs gained fame and fortune only by accident (Butcher, 1988).

If both author and date of publication are mentioned in the sentence, do not use parentheses:

Butcher's 1988 book, *The Accidental Millionaire,* explains how Jobs profited from Wozniak's expertise.

In-text citation of a work by two or more authors:
Follow the same guidelines as above, except list authors as they appear on the publication:

Ethnocentrism colors all of our judgments of others (Samovar and Porter, 1991).

In-text citation of a work by a corporate author:
When a government agency or corporate author is the source of a work, then list the full name of the agency as follows:

The American Medical Association (1994) has recently issued a statement regarding recent health care reforms.

In-text citation of a work with no author listed:
Brief newspaper and magazine articles often do not have an author listed. In this case, cite the first few words of the title of the article (enclosed in quotation marks) or book (underlined) and provide the year of the publication.

Mexican inmates in the U.S. will be returned to their own country ("U.S. Sends," 1993).

In-text citation of two or more works:

Often you will find more than one source that supports a point of view or provides a piece of information. In this case, list the sources alphabetically, separated by a semicolon (;):

> Aggressive behavior has an environmental basis (Basow, 1992; Pincus and Tucker, 1985).

Exercise 30:   Refer to the article "The Abuses of Power" on page 112 of Chapter 3. Find examples for as many of the types of in-text citation described above as possible.

Exercise 31:   Refer to the "Gaining Expertise" section from Part Three of Chapter 3 on page 116. Paraphrase and summarize the ideas presented in four of the short passages on stress. Write a sentence using an in-text citation for (1) a single author; (2) no author; (3) two or more works.

Exercise 32:   As you begin writing your research paper, bring in samples of in-text citations for your instructor to check for accuracy.

Compiling a Reference List

Include a reference list at the end of your research paper and before any appendices. It will allow your reader to locate the sources you cite, so all the sources you cited in the text of your paper must appear in your references. Do not include any sources that you may have read but did not cite in your paper. List the entries alphabetically by author (or by title of publication if there is no author listed), letter by letter.

This section will give examples in APA format of the most common types of entries college students will use. Undoubtedly, at one time or another you will have questions for which this book does not provide the answers. Consult the APA or MLA handbooks for a complete, detailed listing of all possible types of entries.

Reference to a book:

Notes:
(1) List only the first initial of the author's first name;
(2) Capitalize only the first letter of the book, (3) proper names, and (4) words after a colon;
(5) Indent the second and subsequent lines three spaces;
(6) Include edition information after the title;
(7) Put city of publishing company first, followed by the name of the publishing company;
(8) Use an ampersand (&) to list more than one author

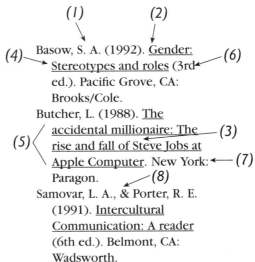

(1) *(2)*

(4) Basow, S. A. (1992). Gender: Stereotypes and roles (3rd ed.). Pacific Grove, CA: Brooks/Cole. *(6)*

(5) Butcher, L. (1988). The accidental millionaire: The rise and fall of Steve Jobs at Apple Computer. New York: Paragon. *(3)* *(7)*

Samovar, L. A., & Porter, R. E. (1991). Intercultural Communication: A reader (6th ed.). Belmont, CA: Wadsworth. *(8)*

Reference to a periodical article:

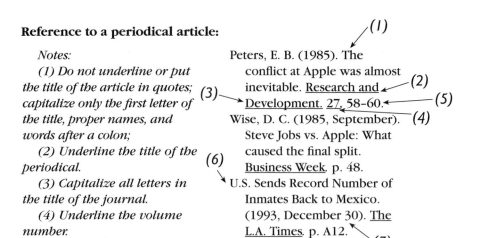

Notes:

(1) Do not underline or put the title of the article in quotes; capitalize only the first letter of the title, proper names, and words after a colon;

(2) Underline the title of the periodical.

(3) Capitalize all letters in the title of the journal.

(4) Underline the volume number.

(5) Include the page numbers of the article.

(6)Begin reference with title of publication if no author is listed.

(7)Include the month (and day) of an article for which there is no volume number.

Exercise 33: Transform the following sentences into references using the APA format listed above. (You may also use MLA format if permitted by your instructor. Refer to the MLA style sheet in the Appendix.)

1. Allan Bloom wrote a book called *The Closing of the American Mind* in 1987. It was published in New York by Simon and Schuster Publishing Company.
2. I read an article the other day by Bro Uttal. It appeared in the October 14, 1985 issue of *Fortune* magazine. It was two pages long and was on pages 119–120. The volume of the magazine was 112. The title was "The Adventures of Steve Jobs."
3. Did you see the article, "Removing Growths Found to Lower Colon Cancer Risk" in yesterday's paper? It was in the *Los Angeles Times* newspaper on page A12. That was Thursday, December 30, 1993.
4. You had better consult the <u>Publication Manual of the American Psychological Association</u> to answer your question. Look at the third edition. It's published in Washington, D.C. by the APA. It came out in 1983.
5. Write a reference entry for this book.

Exercise 34: Prepare a reference list of works that you intend to use in your research paper. Type the list, double-spaced. Exchange your reference list for that of another student and proofread it for errors. Then submit your list for your instructor to check.

Gaining Expertise

Activity One: Select one of the following questions and write a paragraph expressing your point of view, quoting selections from the paragraph to support your ideas or begin your paragraph. Pay special attention to the mechanics of incorporating the quotes into your paragraph. (See "Up Close: The Mechanics of Quoting" on page 151 for additional help.)

1. *Do men and women make decisions differently?*

"Many women feel it is natural to consult with their partners at every turn, while many men automatically make more decisions without consulting their partners. This may reflect a broad difference in conceptions of decision making. Women expect decisions to be discussed first and many by consensus. They appreciate the discussion itself as evidence of involvement and communication. But many men feel oppressed by lengthy discussions about what they see as minor decisions, and they feel hemmed in if they can't just act without talking first. When women try to initiate a freewheeling discussion by asking, 'What do you think?' men often think they are being asked to decide."

Source: *You Just Don't Understand: Women and Men in Conversation*
by Deborah Tannen, Ballantine Books, New York, 1990, p. 27.

2. *Is there a close relation between the mind and the body?*

"We don't yet understand all the ways in which brain chemicals are related to emotions and thoughts, but the salient point is that our state of mind has an immediate and direct effect on our state of body. We can change the body by dealing with how we feel. If we ignore our despair, the body receives a "die" message. If we deal with our pain and seek help, then the message is: "Living is difficult but desirable," and the immune system works to keep us alive."

Source: *Love, Medicine, and Miracles* by Bernie Siegel,
Harper & Row, N.Y. 1986, p. 69.

3. *Does worrying about grades help students to get better grades?*

"Students obsessed with A's tend not to get them. Certainly, A students care a great deal about their grades and a few are among the obsessed. But, unlike other grade-conscious students, better students spend more time thinking about their studies than their grades."

Source: *Acing College* by Joshua Halberstam, 1991,
Penguin Books, New York, p. 171.

4. *Which contributes more to a person's development—genetic factors or the environment?*

Today, most psychologists ascribe to what is called the **epigenetic model** of development (Gottlieb, 1970; Lerner, 1978; Plomin, DeFries & Fulker, 1988; Rowe, 1981). This point of view is an *interactionist* position, claiming that development *emerges* based on one's genetic history *and* one's experiences in the environment. A person's development is influenced by the forces of both nature and nurture, "experienced in an inseparable tangle" (McGraw, 1987, p. 103). To which we can add, with Robert Plomin, "The complex interplay between environment and genes is most apparent in the case of development" (Plomin, 1989, p. 110).

Source: *Psychology: An Introduction,* by Josh Gerow,
HarperCollins Publishers, New York, p. 388.

Activity Two: Prepare a reference list for the sources listed above. Refer to Part Four of this chapter for help.

You have now completed all the steps in compiling a research paper, and you are ready to complete the final draft of your paper. Type your draft, doublespaced, and include a title page, an outline, the text, and a list of references. Also include a preface to the paper, in which you do the following:

1. Acknowledge the help that you have received. Thank any classmates, friends, family, and teachers who helped you put this text together.
2. Describe the process of writing a research paper. What was it like for you? Which sections were easy to complete? Which ones were more challenging? Evaluate your own work. Indicate the sections of the paper you find to be particularly well done and point out those that might require additional attention.

REPRESENTATIVE SUBJECT ENCYCLOPEDIAS

SUBJECT	TITLE
Accounting	Accountant's Encyclopedia
Agriculture	McGraw-Hill Encyclopedia of Food, Agriculture, and Nutrition
Anthropology	Encyclopedia of Anthropology
	Peoples of the Earth
Art	Encyclopedia of World Art
	McGraw-Hill Dictionary of Art
Astronomy	Cambridge Encyclopedia of Astronomy
Bioethics	Encyclopedia of the Biological Sciences
Biology	Encyclopedia of the Biological Sciences
Black Studies	African-American Encyclopedia
Chemistry	Encyclopedia of Chemistry
Classics	Oxford Classical Dictionary
Computer Science	Encyclopedia of Computer Science and Technology
	Encyclopedia of Computer Science and Engineering
Criminal Justice	Encyclopedia of Crime and Justice
Economics	Encyclopedia of Economics
Education	International Encyclopedia of Education
Engineering	Encyclopedia of Environmental Science and Engineering
Finance	Encyclopedia of Banking and Finance
Geography	Worldmark Encyclopedia of the Nations
Geology	Cambridge Encyclopedia of the Earth Sciences
History	New Illustrated Encyclopedia of World History
Horticulture	The New York Botanical Garden Illustrated Encyclopedia of Horticulture
Law	Guide to American Law
Literature	Encyclopedia of World Literature in the 20th Century
Management	Encyclopedia of Management
Marketing	Encyclopedia of Advertising

Mathematics	Encyclopedic Dictionary of Mathematics
Medicine	Fishbein's Illustrated Medical and Health Encyclopedia
Music	The New Grove Dictionary of Music and Musicians
Philosophy	The Encyclopedia of Philosophy
Physical Education and Sports	Encyclopedia of Physical Education, Fitness, and Sports
Physics	Encyclopaedic Dictionary of Physics
Political Science	World Encyclopedia of Political Systems and Parties
Psychiatry and Psychology	International Encyclopedia of Psychiatry, Psychology, Psychoanalysis and Neurology
Real Estate	Arnold Encyclopedia of Real Estate
Religion	Encyclopedia of Religion and Ethics
Science and Technology	McGraw-Hill Encyclopedia of Science and Technology
Social Sciences	International Encyclopedia of the Social Sciences
Social Work	Encyclopedia of Social Work
Theater	McGraw-Hill Encyclopedia of World Drama
Zoology	Grzimeks Animal Life Encyclopedia

 **PERIODICAL INDEXES**

REPRESENTATIVE PERIODICAL
INDEXES

GENERAL PERIODICAL INDEXES—Located in General Reference

Humanities Index
Infotrac (Computer Index with printer)
Public Affairs Information Service
Reader's Guide to Periodical Literature
Social Sciences Index

FIELD	TITLE
Accounting	Accountants' Index
Anthropology	Abstracts in Anthropology
Art	Art Index
	RILA
Asian Studies	Bibliography of Asian Studies
Afro-American Studies	Index to Periodicals by and about Blacks
Business	Business Periodicals Index
	Predicasts F&S Index
Child Development	Child Development Abstracts and Bibliography
Children's Literature	Children's Literature Abstracts
Classic's	L'Annee philologique
Communication	Communication Abstracts
Criminal Justice	Criminal Justice Abstracts
	Criminal Justice Periodicals Index
Demographics	Population Index

Economics	Index of Economic Articles
	Journal of Economic Literature
Education	Business Education Index
	Current Index to Journals in Education
	Education Index
	Exceptional Child Education Resources
Film	Film Literature Index
History (U.S.)	America: History and Life
History (World)	Historical Abstracts
Humanities	American Humanities Index
	Arts and Humanities Citation Index
	Humanities Index
Information Science	Information Science Abstracts
Labor & Employment	Human Resources Abstracts
	Work Related Abstracts
Language	LLBA: Language & Language Behavior Abstracts
Language & Literature	MLA Bibliography
	Abstracts of English Studies
Latin American Studies	Hispanic-American Periodicals
Law	Current Law Index
Library Science	Library Literature
Music	Music Index
	Popular Music Periodicals Index
Personnel Management	Personnel Management Abstracts
	Work Related Abstracts
Philosophy	Philosopher's Index
Political Science	ABC Political Science & Government
	U.S. Political Science Documents
Popular Culture	Abstracts of Popular Culture
Psychology	Psychological Abstracts
Public Affairs	Public Affairs Information Service
Religion	Religion Index One: Periodicals
Social Sciences	Social Sciences Citation Index
	Social Sciences Index
Social Work	Social Work Research and Abstracts
Sociology	Sociological Abstracts
Women's Studies	Women's Studies Abstracts

SUBJECT PERIODICAL INDEXES LOCATED IN THE SCIENCE DEPARTMENT

Agriculture	Bibliography of Agriculture
Astronomy	Astronomy and Astrophysics
Biology	Biological Abstracts
	Biological and Agricultural Index
	Biological Abstracts/RRM
Chemistry	Chemical Abstracts
Computer Science	Computer and Control Abstracts
	Microcomputer Index

Consumer Info	Consumer Index to Product Information Sources
Energy	Energy Index and Abstracts
Engineering	Electrical & Electronics Abstracts
	Engineering Index
Environment	Environment Index and Abstracts
Food	Food Science and Technology
Geology	Bibliography and Index of Geology
Mathematics	Mathematical Reviews
Medicine	Cumulated Index Medicus
	Public Health, Social Medicine & Hygiene
Nursing	CINAHL, Cumulative Index to Nursing and
	Allied Health Literature
Nutrition	Nutrition Abstracts and Reviews
Oceanography	Oceanic Abstracts
Physics	Physics Abstracts
Psychology	Psychological Abstracts
Sciences	General Science Index
	Science Citation Index
Speech & Hearing	DSH Abstracts (Deafness, Speech, & Hearing)
Technology	Applied Science and Technology Index
Zoology	Zoological Record

MODERN LANGUAGES ASSOCIATION (MLA) STYLE SHEET

The following is a basic introduction to MLA style. Consult the MLA Handbook, available in the library as well as any college bookstore, for additional details.

Works Cited

List every source cited in your paper in alphabetical order on a separate page entitled "Works Cited." Be sure to indent the second line and subsequent lines of each entry.

Book—one author:

Basow, Susan. <u>Gender: Stereotypes and Roles</u> (3rd ed.). Pacific Grove, Calif.: Brooks/Cole, 1992.

Include the author's first name. Capitalize each main word of the title and underline the title. Put the date of publication at the end of the entry.

Book—two authors:

Samovar, Larry, and Richard Porter. <u>Intercultural Communication: A Reader</u> (6th ed.). Belmont, Calif.: Wadsworth, 1991.

Use the normal order (first name, last name) for the second author.

Periodical article—scholarly journal:

Peters, E. Bruce. "The Conflict at Apple Was Almost Inevitable." Research and
Development 27 (1985): 58-60.

*Enclose the article title in quotes and underline the name of the journal.
List the issue number of the journal, then the year of publication, and finally
the page numbers on which the article appears.*

Periodical article—popular magazine:

Wise, Deborah C. (1985, September). "Steve Jobs vs. Apple: What Caused the Final
Split." Business Week Sept. 1985: 48.

Be sure to include the month and year of publication.

Newspaper article—no author named:

"U.S. Sends Record Number of Inmates Back to Mexico." L.A. Times 30 Dec. 1993:
A12.

*Begin the entry with the title of the article. Indicate day, month and year
of the publication. The page number should include the section of the paper (A)
and the page number (12).*

In-Text Parenthetical Note

*The in-text note includes the author's last name and a page number. These are
enclosed in parentheses after a paraphrased or quoted section of your research
paper.*

A short quotation:

As Jobs became more influential at Apple, he increased the "force of the tactics he
had used to push, goad, prod, cajole and coax Wozniak during the development of
the Apple II" (Moritz 24).

*Enclose the quotation in quotation marks, follow it with the author's last
name and the page number on which the quote appears in parentheses. Put the
period for the sentence after the parenthetical note.*

Paraphrased material—the entire source:

Butcher believed that Jobs gained fame and fortune only by accident.

*If you are stating the general idea of a source, list only the author. Do not
enclose the author's name in parentheses if it is part of the sentence (as it is in
the above example).*

Paraphrased material—a specific section:

Jobs and Sculley were motivated by quite different needs (Peters 58).

*Include the author's last name and the page from which the material was
paraphrased.*

Paraphrased material—no author:

Mexican inmates in the U.S. will be returned to their own country ("U.S. Sends"
A12).

*Shorten the title of the article and enclose it, along with the page number,
in parentheses.*

Abridged   Reduced in length; condensed (e.g., an abridged dictionary)

Abstract   A brief summary of a book or article

Almanac   An annual publication with lists, charts, and tables of useful information

Archives   Written records of an organization or institution

Article   A report or essay in a newspaper, journal, or magazine

Atlas   A book of maps

Autobiography   An account that a person writes about his or her own life; a memoir

Bibliography   A list of books and articles in print on a specific subject

Biography   A written account of a person's life

Book review index   A listing of book reviews that have appeared in journals, magazines, and newspapers

Bound periodicals   A number of issues of journals or magazines bound together with a hard cover

Call number   The identification number that tells where to find a book on the library shelf (books and periodicals are arranged by call number)

Card catalog   Drawers with cards arranged alphabetically by author, title, and subject listing all the books in the library; each card has information about the book and the call number to help locate the book

CD-ROM (Compact disk with read-only memory)   A laser disk that can hold the equivalent of 1500 floppy disks (many periodical indexes are available on CD-ROM)

Checkout   The procedure of borrowing a book from the library

Circulating   A book that can be checked out of the library

Circulation desk   The area where you check out books, renew books, return books, pay fines for overdue books, place holds on books, and recall books

Closed stacks   Stacks closed to students. When a book is requested, a librarian gets it from the shelf.

Computer search   The search through a database for books and articles on a particular topic

Computerized catalog   An on-line system that lists all the books in the library collection by author, title, and subject, giving information about the book and the call number to help a student locate it. In many libraries, this system is replacing the card catalog.

Copyright   The legal right given to an author or publisher for exclusive publication and distribution

Dewey decimal system   A system of classification still used in some small, older libraries in the United States

Dictionary   A book containing lists of words, meanings, pronunciation, usage, and etymology of words. There are general and specialized dictionaries.

Due date   The date stamped inside a book when it is checked out of the library indicating when it must be returned

Encyclopedia   A collections of articles written by specialists and arranged in alphabetical order by subject. There are general and specialized encyclopedias, and they often contain bibliographies.

Etymology   The origin and historical development of a word

Fact books   Almanacs, yearbooks, and statistical abstracts

Fiction   A literary work that is not based on fact but came from the writer's imagination

Fine   The amount of money that has to be paid each day if a book is returned after the due date

Folio   A large book; folios are often shelved in a separate area of the library

Government publications   A collection of publications from the federal government, the state government, and possibly other governmental organizations such as the United Nations

Hold   After filling out a form at the circulation desk, a librarian will notify you when a book has been returned to the library and will keep it for you for a specified number of days

Indexes   Lists of articles from journals, magazines, and newspapers, arranged alphabetically by subject; author, title, and publication information; and in some indexes, abstracts

Index tables   Tables in the reference area where indexes are shelved

Interlibrary loan   Borrowing books through your library from another library

Journal   A publication containing articles on scholarly research

Librarian   A person trained in library science

Library of Congress   The national library of the United States in Washington, D.C., founded in 1800

Library of Congress classification system   The system of classification used in most university libraries, in which books are grouped together by subject, and each book is given a call number

Library of Congress subject headings (LCSH)   A complete list of terms used in the Library of Congress system of classification

Literature   Imaginative or creative writing in prose or verse

Magazine   A publication containing articles on popular or general subjects

Manuscript   A handwritten composition; the author's own handwritten or typewritten copy of a book, article, etc.

Maps   A representation of a region of the earth

Media   A means of mass communication: newspapers, magazines, television, etc.

Memoir   An account that a person writes about his or her own life; an autobiography

Microfiche   A 4" × 6" sheet of film with a series of micro-images

Microfilm   A roll of film with a series of micro-images

Microform   Photographic film with micro-images, often used to store periodicals and archival material

Noncirculating   Not be taken out of the library (referring to certain books or other materials)

Nonfiction   A literary work based on fact; not fiction

On-line   In a computer system

Open stacks   Stacks open to students, who can go to the shelves and get books without the assistance of a librarian

Overdue   Not returned to the library by the due date (referring to books or materials)

Pamphlet   A short, unbound printed work with a paper cover

Periodical   A publication that is published regularly—daily, weekly, monthly, etc.

Periodical index   References to articles found in periodicals, listed alphabetically by subject

Periodical printout   A listing of all periodicals held by a library; serial printout

Publication date   The year a book is put in print

Readers' Guide to Periodical Literature   An index of nearly 200 periodicals of general interest

Reference area   An area of the library that contains encyclopedias, dictionaries, factbooks, directories, and other sources containing practical and specific information

Reference books   Encyclopedias, dictionaries, factbooks, directories, and other sources containing practical and specific information

Reference desk   A section of the reference area where librarians are available to assist you

Reference stacks   Shelves holding noncirculating reference sources

Renew   Check out a book again that you currently have. You can only do this if no one else has placed a hold on it.

Reserve book room   An area where professors place books and articles for students to check out for short periods of time

Reshelving area   A holding area for books in the library that have not yet been put back on the shelves in proper call-number order

Serial printout   A listing of all periodicals held by a library; periodical printout

Special collection   A collection of rare books, manuscripts, archives, etc.

Stacks   The shelves that hold the library's books and bound periodicals

Statistical abstract   An annual publication with lists, charts, and tables of global statistics and facts

Study carrel A small private study area in the stacks of a library

Style manual   A book that gives writing rules and examples used to prepare research papers, dissertations, and articles for publication; available in the general reference area

Unabridged   Having the original length; not shortened or condensed (e.g., an unabridged dictionary)

Yearbook   An annual publication with lists, charts, and tables of information about the previous year

Communicating in Class

Chapter Theme: The Power of Advertising

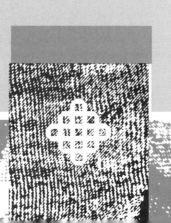

This final chapter will help you to develop your oral communication skills, very important tools for a successful student. Effective classroom communication will make a positive impression on the instructor and keep you actively engaged in class discussions. This chapter will provide you with information and practice in formal and informal communication in class. While you are developing these communication skills, you will also have the chance to learn more about the topic of advertising through exercises and discussions.

ACADEMIC TOPICS

- Participating in Class Discussions
- Giving Formal Presentations
- Presenting the Informative Talk
- Presenting the Persuasive Talk

CHAPTER THEME

The Power of Advertising

Making Cross-Cultural Connections

Exercise 1: Answer the following questions either orally or in writing in your journal, as instructed by your teacher.

1. Describe the flow of communication in a typical college class in your country. How often do students speak? Are there discussions? Do professors call on students directly? How do professors address the students? How do the students address their professors?
2. How is that style of classroom communication similar to or different from what you have observed in this country, either in your ESL classes or in classes with American students?

IT WORKS!
Learning Strategy:
Comparing
Academic Life

TAKING INVENTORY: YOUR COMMUNICATION COMFORT LEVEL

1. How comfortable are you communicating in English? Rate yourself from 1 (extremely uncomfortable) to 5 (completely at ease) for each of the following situations.

Asking a question in class	1	2	3	4	5
Answering the instructor's questions in class	1	2	3	4	5
Volunteering your own point of view in class	1	2	3	4	5
Disagreeing with another student's point of view during a class discussion	1	2	3	4	5
Asking the professor a question, privately, after class or during the break	1	2	3	4	5

| Striking up a conversation with another student in your class whom you don't know at all | 1 | 2 | 3 | 4 | 5 |
| Giving a speech in class | 1 | 2 | 3 | 4 | 5 |

2. Analyze your answers to question 1 above. What types of interactions are easy for you? Which ones are more difficult? Which would you like to improve?

PART ONE: PARTICIPATING IN CLASS DISCUSSIONS

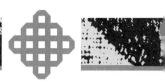

You will probably find that a percentage of your grade for many college courses will be based on something called "class participation." This means that the instructor bases some of your grade on how well you ask questions, offer comments, and participate in class discussions. As a non-native speaker of English, you will certainly have to make a special effort to contribute orally to your classes. Be sure to begin this effort on the first day of class because the longer you remain silent in class, the harder it will be for you to speak up.

If your instructor or another classmate says something that you cannot understand or if the instructor leaves out important information that you need to know, you don't need to "sit in the dark." You can ask the instructor to clarify what was said or to add important information that is missing. It's highly probable that if you are confused, then other students will be, too.

It's important to ask your questions at the appropriate time, however. Instructors find it especially annoying when students ask questions about topics unrelated to what they are discussing. Here is a common example. The professor is explaining an important but difficult theory. When she is finished, she says: "Are there any questions?" and a student asks, "When is the final exam?" The professor's invitation to ask questions refers only to the topic being discussed at that time—not to questions about the course in general.

> ## Threads
>
> **Professors seek, need, and appreciate student involvement in their class. We need applause, and the applause of the classroom is animated discussion.**
>
> Joshua Halberstam, Ph.D.

Asking for Clarification and Information

Here are some sample phrases you could use to ask for clarification and further information:

- "I'm sorry, but I didn't hear what you just said. Would you mind repeating it?"
- "I'm not sure what you mean by the term, 'disengage.' Could you define that for me?"
- "I'm not familiar with the novel that you are referring to. Would you take a moment to say something about it?"
- "Did you say when the final exam was going to be? I seem to have missed that information."
- "The syllabus states that we have two papers to write for this course. Could you tell us a little more about those papers?"

LEARNING STRATEGY

Managing Your Learning: Actively participating in your college classes will engage you more fully in the learning process and make a good impression on the instructor and other students.

Exercise 2:   Imagine that it's the first day of this class and your instructor gives you the following syllabus. You know that the information on a syllabus is important because it informs you of the course requirements and the basis for grading, so you read it carefully. You notice that the syllabus is missing some important information, and it is also unclear in places. Make a note of questions you have, and be ready to use some of the expressions above in asking your instructor for clarification and information.

STUDY SKILLS 101

INSTRUCTOR: Ms. Roberta Jones
OFFICE HOURS: Monday and Thursday
UNITS: 3

DESCRIPTION OF THE COURSE
This course is designed for the ESL student who is planning on entering a university. The course will provide students with instruction in the following areas: note-taking, test-taking, paper writing, APA format, library use, and oral skills for academic purposes.

REQUIREMENTS
Class participation
Completion of readings
Two papers
Midterm and final

READINGS
Readings will be put on reserve at the library, and a packet will be available at the copy shop. Be sure to come prepared, having read all the assigned readings for each class period.

EXAMINATIONS
There will be no make-up exams. Students must bring a note from their physician if they are unable to take an exam due to illness.

GRADING
Your grade will be based on the following percentages:
Class participation	20%
Completion of readings	25%
Two papers	25%
Midterm and final	25%

LEARNING STRATEGY

Personalizing: Identifying what you already know about a topic from personal experiences and knowledge can help you understand a new text more easily.

The readings in this chapter are on advertising in the United States. In order to prepare for them, think about the following questions and be ready to discuss your answers in pairs or small groups, or respond to them in writing in your journal.

1. Even though much of the advertising you see and read may seem ridiculous, it is carefully constructed and produced to persuade the greatest number of people to buy a certain product. What techniques do advertisers use to sell their products? Which ones do you think are the most effective? Which ones would you like to see eliminated?

2. Look at the ads pictured on page 167. What can you say about the images used?

3. Observe the advertising on television and in magazines. Describe some of the "stereotypes" used in this advertising to sell products. Are any of these stereotypes offensive to you? How are these stereotypes similar to or different from stereotypes used in advertising in your own country?

Exercise 3: Read the following excerpt on the psychology of advertising, making notes of terms or concepts that are unfamiliar to you. As you discuss in class the main ideas presented in the article, be ready to ask for clarification and information *when it is appropriate*. That is, don't ask the meaning of a vocabulary word that the professor is not using. Wait until that term comes up before raising your question, or wait until the professor asks, "Are there any questions?"

The psychology of ads

by Shirley Biagi

You make sure your buying decisions are based on several other sources of information besides advertising: friends, family, and your own experience, for example. To influence your choices, the advertising message must appeal to you for some reason, as you sift through the ads to make judgments and choose products. Humanities and human sciences professor Jib Fowles in his book, *Mass Advertising as Social Forecast,* enumerated 15 appeals, which he calls an "inventory of human motives" that advertisers commonly use in their commercials:

1. Need for sex. *Surprisingly, Fowles found that only 2 percent of the television ads he surveyed used this appeal. It may be too blatant, he concluded, and often detracts from the product.*

2. Need for affiliation. *The largest number of ads uses this approach. You are looking for friendship. Advertisers can also use this negatively, to make you worry that you'll lose friends if you don't use a certain product.*

3. Need to nurture. *Every time you see a puppy or a kitten or a child, the appeal is to your maternal or paternal instincts.*

4. Need for guidance. *A father or mother figure can appeal to your desire for someone to care for you, so you won't have to worry. Betty Crocker is a good example.*

5. Need to aggress. *We all have had a desire to get even, and some ads give you this satisfaction.*

6. **Need to achieve.** *The ability to accomplish something difficult and succeed identifies the product with winning. Sports figures as spokespersons project this image.*

7. **Need to dominate.** *The power we lack is what we can look for in a commercial: "Master the possibilities."*

8. **Need for prominence.** *We want to be admired and respected, to have high social status. Tasteful china and classic diamonds offer this potential.*

9. **Need for attention.** *We want people to notice us; we want to be looked at. Cosmetics are a natural for this approach.*

10. **Need for autonomy.** *Within a crowded environment, we want to be singled out, to be "a breed apart." This can also be used negatively. You may be left out if you don't use a particular product.*

11. **Need to escape.** *Flight is very appealing; you can imagine adventures you cannot have. The idea of escape is pleasurable.*

12. **Need to feel safe.** *To be free from threats, to be secure is the appeal of many insurance and bank ads.*

13. **Need for aesthetic sensations.** *Beauty attracts us, and classic art or dance makes us feel creative, enhanced.*

14. **Need to satisfy curiosity.** *Facts support our belief that information is quantifiable, and numbers and diagrams make our choices seem scientific.*

15. **Physiological needs.** *Fowles defines sex (#1) as a biological need, and so he catalogues our need to sleep, eat, and drink in this category. Advertisements for juicy pizza are especially appealing late at night.*

Media/Impact: An Introduction to Mass Media (1992) by Shirley Biagi, Wadsworth Publishing Co., Belmont, Calif., pp. 305-307.

Exercise 4:

1. Bring in a magazine advertisement to class that you consider to be either particularly persuasive or ineffective. Be ready to explain to a small group the category of appeal used in the advertisement and why you think it succeeds or fails in persuading the consumer to buy the product.

2. While your group members are presenting their advertisements, practice asking for clarification and information when there are words you don't understand or when you feel that important information is missing.

3. Choose one person from the group to be the observer, who will make a note when students ask for information and clarification and how they do it. Afterwards, the observers from each group will report their observations to the class.

Contributing to a Class Discussion

Threads

Even the most thick-skinned professor knows when he's not setting his class on fire. Students who make professors feel successful are rewarded with better grades.

Joshua Halberstam, Ph.D.

Many of your college classes will follow a lecture and/or class discussion format. The discussion segment of your class may be unplanned and informal as, for example, often happens when one student asks an interesting question and the instructor and other students join in on the discussion.

Other classes, usually smaller ones called "seminar classes," will be discussion-based. Students are expected to come to class prepared to discuss a reading or assigned topic. Their grades are based largely on their participation in the seminar discussions.

As you can tell, it is very important for students in American colleges to speak in class. Students who are shy or quiet often suffer the consequences of their silence in lowered grades.

SURVIVAL TIPS: CLASS DISCUSSIONS

How can non-native speakers of English do well in class discussions? Here are some helpful hints:

1. Be sure to contribute to the class discussion **at least once** during the class period.
2. If you know what the discussion will be based on (e.g., a reading, a specific topic), come to class **prepared,** preferably with a relevant question or comment written down.
3. If the discussion emerges spontaneously in class, listen to the other students very carefully and **respond** to what they have said. You can agree with what they have said, offer a personal experience, or add a piece of information.
4. In any case, be a **considerate listener.** Give the speaker your full attention. Avoid speaking while others are speaking, and if you wish to disagree, do so in a respectful way, without discounting the person's point of view entirely.

Using Discussion Techniques

Here are some techniques and expressions that may help you to communicate more effectively during a class discussion.

AGREEING

One effective way to contribute to a class discussion is to agree with something another student has said. You can begin your statement by saying you agree, then adding a minor additional fact or opinion. Here are some examples:

John's comment: "I am appalled by the stereotypic images of women on TV advertising."

Student responses:

"I agree with John. I believe that these images of women are truly outdated on television advertising."

"John has made an excellent point about gender stereotypes. I'd like to add that this is especially evident on daytime television."

DISAGREEING

It is acceptable to disagree with another student's opinion—and even with the instructor's—if you do it respectfully. It's usually a good idea to agree with one aspect of the speaker's point of view and then disagree with another. Note how the following speakers do that here:

"Although the image of women in advertising is not entirely up-to-date, I believe it's important to acknowledge the progress that the media has made in the past ten years."

"It's true that media's portrayal of women is a bit stereotypical. But, for that matter, I can't think of *any* portrayal that is true-to-life."

INTERRUPTING

Occasionally, you may find that you have a relevant example or essential piece of information to offer, and you need to interrupt the speaker to interject. It is not recommended that you do this often, but if you need to, here are some possible ways to do it politely.

"Excuse me for interrupting, but I wonder if anyone saw the car commercial on TV last night? The woman in that commercial was not stereotypical at all."

"Pardon my interruption, but I wonder if you are aware that the court recently ruled on this very issue?"

SOLICITING FEEDBACK

One way to gain support from other members of your class is to solicit agreement from other class members.

"It's my belief that consumer protection in advertising is too lax. Am I the only one who believes this?"

"What does everyone else think about the recent court ruling on truth in advertising?"

Exercise 5: Work in pairs or small groups, and practice the discussion techniques. Prepare an opinion statement for each of the topics below. Take turns asking, responding, agreeing, or disagreeing with your classmates' responses.

1. Many consumer groups believe that cigarette and alcohol advertising should be banned from television and print materials. What's your position on this?

   _____

   _____

   _____

2. Faith Popcorn, a respected marketer and trend forecaster in the United States, predicts a shift in advertising from taking advantage of the consumer through subtle manipulation of truth to protecting the consumer by emphasizing only truthful advertising. How important is it for you to have truthful advertising?

   _____

   _____

   _____

3. Some advertisements use nudity and highly sexualized images to sell their products. Calvin Klein and Guess!, for example, have been accused of this practice. What's your opinion about using sex to sell products?

   _____

   _____

   _____

4. Many consumers today want to know about a company's political, social, environmental, and even religious positions before they will buy their products. How important is a company's political or social reputation to you? If a company advertised that it was a socially aware organization, would that affect your decision to buy its products?

---

5. Refer to any of the questions in the previous section, "Taking Inventory: Your Own Thoughts."

Exercise 6:

1. Read the following selection on gender stereotypes in advertising and be prepared to discuss its contents in class. Mark up your text liberally, paying attention to the following:
   • Note what you agree with.
   • Note what you disagree with.
   • Add personal experience, anecdotes, or information.
   • Note what you would like to have clarified.
2. Form groups of six or seven students each. Select one student in each group to be the group leader, who will keep the discussion moving, asking questions and directing the group when necessary. Select two additional students to be the observers. Use the Observer's Grid (found at the end of this chapter) to note what was said, who participated, and some of the techniques that they used to agree, disagree, add information, ask for clarification, and so on.
3. After the discussion, ask the observers to share their observations with their group, describing the techniques used and commenting on the general flow of the discussion.

Gender stereotypes in advertising

by Susan Basow

Commercials The gender stereotypes are even more explicit in TV commercials than in regular programming, although women and men appear equally often as central characters (Bretl & Cantor, 1988; Ferrante, Haynes, & Kingsley, 1988; Lovdal, 1989, Osborn, 1989). Since the early 1970s, gender stereotyping has decreased somewhat, but women still are most often presented in the home in the role of wife and/or mother. When they are depicted as employed, their range of occupations is broader than it once was but is still traditionally feminine. Men, whose depiction as husband and/or father has increased, still are more frequently presented in other roles, especially ones in the business world. Women are most often seen in ads for food, and they are more likely than men to be shown using the products they advertise. Men are most often seen in ads for automotive products and alcohol. Women in commercials are much younger than the men, who can range between young and middle-aged. Relations between the sexes typically are portrayed in traditional ways. For example, detergent commercials still primarily depict a woman worrying about getting the dirt off her husband's clothes rather than vice versa. And women are presented as sex objects more frequently than men. On the other hand, men are increasingly likely to be the butt of jokes, especially when they show ignorance about nutrition and child care (Horovitz, 1989). . . .

The most striking difference between women and men in commercials is the fact that men predominate (83%–90%) as the authoritative, dominant voice-overs, even when the products are aimed at women.

Thus, again, the voice of authority is male, although research suggests that female voice-overs are just as effective (*Ms.,* February 1987, p. 30).

On children's shows, sexist stereotypes in commercials are rampant (Feldstein & Feldstein, 1982; O'Connor, 1989). Boys dominate both quantitatively and qualitatively. Boys are more likely to be portrayed in active roles, girls in passive ones. Indeed, commercials aimed at boys have a different format than commercials aimed at girls. Commercials aimed at boys have rapid action, frequent cuts, loud music, sound effects, and frequent scene changes. In contrast, commercials aimed at girls contain many fades and dissolves, background music, and female narration (R. L. Welch, Huston-Stein, Wright, & Plehal, 1979). Children as young as age 6 recognize these distinctions, which means that even if the content of a commercial doesn't sex type a product, the style in which it is produced might (A. C. Huston, Greer, Wright, Welch, & Ross, 1984). But most often the content is sex-typed as well. As discussed earlier, toys are markedly gender-labeled, with action toys tagged for boys, and domestic and cosmetic toys tagged for girls. Racism too is prevalent in children's commercials, with Black children almost always in supporting roles and other minority children completely invisible (O'Connor, 1989).

Thus, of all the television programming discussed so far, commercials are the most sexist.

Gender: Stereotypes and Roles (1992), 3rd edition, by Susan A. Basow, Brooks/Cole Publishing Company, p. 161.

Exercise 7: Have the class agree on a network news program to watch at home.

1. Pay special attention to the international news items. Come to class prepared to talk about the events in the world. Write down comments and questions that you have. Be ready to agree and disagree with the class on topics introduced during the news broadcast.
2. Pay attention to the advertisements shown during the program. Be ready to discuss whether there were any gender or ethnic stereotypes depicted in the advertising.

Working in Groups

It is common for instructors to ask students to complete a "group project," in which a group of students work together on a common project and are often assigned a group grade. There are many advantages in working collaboratively in this way. You are able to work with others, share information, and support one another. As you might imagine, however, there are some disadvantages as well, especially if some of the group members do not get along well or if one member is particularly irresponsible.

SURVIVAL TIPS: DEALING WITH GROUP WORK

Here are some hints on working successfully in a group:

• Divide the work up fairly. Don't take on more than your share, or don't assume that because the other students are native speakers of English that they should do more work than you.
• Be absolutely certain that you have understood what's expected of you. Ask for clarification until you are sure.
• Make a list of all members' telephone numbers so that you can contact each other if necessary.

- Set meeting times and objectives for the work that needs to be completed by each meeting time. Write this down and make sure that all members have a copy of it.
- Don't wait until the last minute to complete your piece of the project. If you know that you are someone who likes to do things early, volunteer to complete a part of the project that needs to be done early—e.g., the research. If you tend to do things at the last minute, agree to do some of the writing, editing, or typing.

Exercise 8: Form small groups. Prepare an audiotape or videotape advertisement to recruit international students for your school and target it to the international market. (You may limit your target to one country if all members of your group agree with the choice of a particular country or continent.)

Your final product should include the following:

1. A three- to five-minute audiotape (for the radio) or videotape (for television) advertising your school for the international market
2. A typed transcript of the advertisement
3. A written report describing your market, your advertising strategy, including the type of appeal, the cost of the advertisement, where and when it should be played, and any other pertinent information
4. A list of what each student in the group contributed to the project

Your grade for this project will be a group grade. Each student will receive the same grade as the others.

PART TWO: GIVING FORMAL PRESENTATIONS

LEARNING STRATEGY

Overcoming Limitations: Learning to speak clearly and persuasively in public will help you be a better student.

TAKING INVENTORY: YOUR OWN THOUGHTS

Think about a good speaker whom you have heard. What makes him or her an effective communicator? What are the characteristics of a good speaker?

Presenting in Class

College students are often asked to give **presentations** in front of the class. These range from summarizing a paper you have written, to reporting on an experiment you have done, to presenting a group project to the class. There's no question about it—most people find public speaking to be a very frightening experience. Take heart, because there are ways to overcome your own fear of speaking. Many shy, introverted people have become effective speakers, and so can you.

One of the most important aspects of being a good speaker is **preparation.** The more prepared you are, the better a speaker you will be. Here are some important points to consider before you give your presentation.

BEFORE THE PRESENTATION

1. **Analyze your audience.**

    Whom are you speaking to? What are their ages, their backgrounds, their interests, their educational levels, and so on? Successful speakers tailor their talks to the specific interests of their audience. If you are speaking to your engineering class, for example, you will use different examples than if you were speaking to your English literature class.

2. **Choose a topic that is important to you.**

    Select your topic carefully. Avoid speaking about something in which you have no interest. Your audience will detect that your heart is not in your topic.

3. **Prepare an outline of your talk.**

    Be sure to make notes for your talk, but don't write it out word for word. You are sure to forget some of the talk if you do that, and then you will have a difficult time finding your place on the page. It's better to make brief notes in the form of an outline and then to speak naturally from these notes.

4. **Practice your speech beforehand.**

    Practice giving your speech from your outline beforehand. Find a good friend who will listen, or do it in front of a mirror. Time it, and make sure it's neither too long nor too short. Try to avoid memorizing your speech, because it will sound artificial.

5. **Select colorful and appropriate examples.**

    After your talk, the audience will probably have forgotten much of what you have said, but they are likely to remember the examples and anecdotes you used to support your ideas. Choose them carefully.

PREPARING A TALK ON A PERSONAL TOPIC

Giving a short talk on a personal topic is an excellent way to practice speaking in front of other people. You know your topic (yourself) better than anyone else, and you can be enthusiastic and sincere when speaking.

Exercise 9: Choose one of the following topics and prepare a three- to five-minute talk. Complete "Part One: Choosing a Topic" of the "Worksheet for Preparing a Talk," which you will find at the end of this chapter.

Topics:
My first day at school
My favorite teacher
The person who has influenced me the most
My hometown and why it is special
My favorite (painting, song, food, restaurant, store) and why it's my favorite
The happiest day of my life
The saddest day of my life
My most memorable vacation
An automobile accident
My first date

DELIVERING A TALK

Once you have prepared all that you can for your presentation, the next step is to control your anxiety enough so that you can appear calm and confident in front of the audience.

Try to be yourself and speak as naturally as you can. If you are worried that other people may not understand you because of your foreign accent, be sure to **speak slowly.** The most common mistake that non-native speakers of English make when they are speaking in public is to speak too rapidly.

Here are some basic hints:

A good speaker is well-prepared and uses audiovisual props to keep the audience interested.

- **Establish rapport with your audience.** You can do this in many ways. Look at your audience, moving your eyes from face to face. If you have prepared adequately, you won't need to have your face buried in your notes. Whatever you do, *don't read from a written script.* Have you ever noticed how difficult it is to pay attention when someone is reading from their notes? It's much better to speak directly to your audience.
- **Speak slowly and clearly.** If you speak too rapidly, no one will be able to follow your ideas. Make a conscious effort to slow yourself down, and speak much more slowly than you ordinarily do. Pause between sentences and allow your audience to reflect on what you have said.
- **Use simple but colorful language.** The power of your speech will depend more on the images and examples you use than on the sentence structure and vocabulary. Keep it simple. Use only words that you know well and can pronounce easily. Define technical or complex words for your audience.
- **Begin your talk with a strong opening.** Avoid beginning your talk with an apology. Some students apologize for their poor English. This is not a customary or effective opening in the United States. It would be better to begin with a story or anecdote to attract the attention of your listeners. Remember, you want them to be interested in what you have to say, so say something interesting.
- **Use nonverbal communication.** The more lively and animated you are, the more you will engage your audience. Use gestures and facial expressions to maintain interest and demonstrate enthusiasm. Some speakers are very active—moving from place to place in the room.

Exercise 10: Read the following opening sections of a talk on "My First Day of School in the United States." Evaluate these openings and make suggestions for improvement.

1. "I'd like to begin my talk today by warning you that my English is sometimes hard to understand. So if you want me to repeat something, I will. Actually, that's why I am at this school. I need to learn English. I'll never forget my first day at this school—I was really scared. . . . "

   Comments: _____

   _____

   _____

2. "If you have trouble understanding my English, I'll certainly understand because I sure had trouble understanding your English on my first day of school at this university. I couldn't believe how jumbled the language sounded—as if someone had taken a tape and turned it on fast forward. . . . "

   Comments: _____

   _____

   _____

3. "Second-language acquisition is a complex process best accomplished before adolescence. Unfortunately, I had traveled well beyond that developmental stage before I decided to face the demons of mid-life, effect a difficult, but challenging career change, and tackle a second language. That's how I found myself mired in the intricacies of a foreign university."

   Comments: _____

   _____

   _____

Exercise 11: Now complete Parts Two and Three of the "Worksheet for Preparing a Talk" (page 190) for the personal topic you chose above.

Present your three- to five-minute speech in front of the class. If possible, tape the speech using a videocassette or audiocassette recorder. After your talk, ask each member of your audience to complete a copy of the Feedback Form at the end of this chapter.

Threads

If you've got anything to say, say it quickly, get to the point and stop, and give the other person a chance to talk.

Dale Carnegie

GIVING AN INFORMATIVE PRESENTATION

The informative speech is perhaps the most common type of presentation you will be asked to give in a college class. The purpose of an informative speech is to share information about a topic you have studied. Some examples of informative presentations include reporting on a paper you have written, presenting the results of an experiment or project you did, describing a process, technique, or method you have used, or giving the history of a corporation you're familiar with.

You will follow the same procedure for an informative speech as you did for a personal one. The main difference is that your subject matter will probably be a bit more academic, and you are likely to use information from other sources than your own personal experience.

AN INFORMATIVE TALK

When you make an outline for your informative presentation, follow these guidelines.

Opening:
- State the purpose of your talk very clearly.
- Let your audience know why this talk will be valuable to them.
- Use a question, quote, anecdote, or statistic to "grab" your listeners' attention.
  Expressions:
  - My topic today is . . .
  - I will be describing . . .
  - I chose this topic because . . .

  - First I'll _____ and then I'll _____ .

  - I think you'll find this to be useful for you because . . .

Main Points:
- Choose three or four main points that you will convey to your audience. Don't overload your listener with information.
- Choose one or two examples to support each of your main points. These examples can be stories, facts, statistics, research results, comments from experts.
- Use transitions between ideas. Show how one idea is related to another.
  Expressions:
  - This topic can be divided into three basic parts.
  - The first (step, point, argument) is . . .
  - The second one is . . .
  - Let's look at the final (step, point, argument)

Conclusion:
- Leave enough time at the end to summarize your talk. Point out what you want your audience to remember.
- Avoid ending with a weak statement such as "I guess that's all." Say something that sounds like a conclusion, so your audience will know that you have finished.
  Expressions:
  - In conclusion . . .
  - What conclusions can be made from this?
  - I hope that you have seen that . . .
  - As you can see, . . .

Exercise 12:   Read the following opening remarks for a talk on automobile advertising. Then answer the questions that follow.

"It's primetime on television, and the usual automobile advertisement interrupts your show. You think you've seen this a dozen times before—sleek car gracefully and smoothly gliding along a mountain road, shining in the sun. But wait, there's something different about this ad. As the car stops on a dime, you notice the profile of the person driving the car is not a man. It's a woman.

"Automobile advertisers have recently changed their strategies and have begun targeting both women and men. Some advertisers have begun looking exclusively at female markets. I'd like to briefly explore why this change has occurred."

Questions:
1. How did the speaker attract your attention?
2. What does the speaker say this talk will be about?
3. Who do you suppose the audience is? Why?
4. Do you find the opening remarks effective?

Exercise 13:   Your instructor will give an informative speech on three common characteristics of advertising in the United States. Use the Feedback Form (at the end of this chapter) to guide you as you identify the parts of the talk, and the techniques used for the opening, for support, and for the closing of the speech. Be ready to discuss the effectiveness of the talk with your class.

Exercise 14:   Prepare a 10-minute informative presentation of the research topic you studied in Chapter 4. If you have not yet completed that project, choose one of the topics below and consult the library for information.
Your oral presentation will include the following:

1. A written outline of your talk, to be given to the instructor the day of your talk.
2. At least *two* references to scholarly sources.
3. One overhead transparency or visual aid to assist you.
   Possible Topics:
   • The Effects of TV on Children
   • The Future of Electronic Home Shopping
   • The Rise of Cable Network News
   • "Court TV"—The Effects of Televising Trials
   • New Developments in TV Advertising
   • Ethnic Stereotypes on TV
   • Infomercials
   • Ted Turner's Contribution to the Media
   • Censorship and Television

GIVING A PERSUASIVE PRESENTATION

A persuasive presentation is one in which you try to convince others of your point of view. Examples of presentations that use persuasion are the following: a sales presentation to capture a market; a medical report extolling the virtues of a certain surgical procedure; a report on why one type of educational approach is superior to another.

At the heart of a persuasive presentation is an **assertion**—your opinion or point of view. You support your assertion by appealing to your audience's emotion and/or to their reasoning. For example, if you want to persuade someone to stop smoking, an **appeal to emotion** might include saying how much you love them and will miss them if they get lung cancer and die. An **appeal to reason** might include information on the number of deaths per year attributed to cigarette smoking.

There are times when an appeal to emotion is more effective. If you were trying to persuade your mother to quit smoking, which would you be more likely to appeal to—her emotions or her reason? When you develop a persuasive speech, you will want to consider your audience carefully and make the pitch that will have the greatest effect.

DISTINGUISHING AMONG FACTS, OPINIONS, AND BELIEFS

Persuasive arguments use facts, opinions, and beliefs. A **fact** is that which can be proved through verification and measurement. For example, "Smokers are at a high risk for lung cancer" is a fact because studies have been done to prove this.

An **opinion** is a judgment that is based on facts. For example, "Smoking is unhealthy" is an opinion that was developed from the studies and information on the ill effects of smoking on the health.

A **belief** is not based on facts. It is based on values, morals, and religious beliefs. For example, "Smoking is immoral" and "Abortion is murder" are beliefs because these statements cannot be proved. It is impossible to argue beliefs because there is no evidence to support them. Thus, it is not recommended that you develop an argument based solely on beliefs.

Exercise 15: Decide whether the following statements are beliefs, opinions, or facts.

1. Women live longer than men on the average.
2. Television viewing has reduced children's test scores.
3. Children watch 30 percent more television today than they did 15 years ago.
4. Fathers who abandon their children are irresponsible.
5. Fast food is bad for your health.
6. Women should not work when their children are young.
7. Men commit more violent crimes than women.
8. Men are more violent than women.
9. Parents should never hit their children.
10. Adults who were hit as children are more likely to hit their own children.

EVALUATING SUPPORT

An appeal to emotions addresses how people feel about something. It is important to avoid exaggerating your language and using words that are derogatory (e.g., "You should not vote for this policy because it is ridiculous and racist."). It's better to use language that will not insult your audience and will gather their support (e.g., "I advise you not to vote for this policy because its short-sighted approach will lead to more problems down the road.")

An appeal to reason presents an opinion supported by logical evidence such as facts, statistics, case examples, or expert opinions.

Make sure that your supporting evidence is accurate and relevant to your main point. In the argument against smoking, the following evidence is appropriate and true: smokers have higher rates of lung cancer and respiratory diseases; smoking in pregnant mothers has been linked with lower birth weights in infants; and the Surgeon General warns all smokers of the ill effects of smoking on all cigarette packages.

Don't confuse opinions and facts. Saying that smoking causes lung cancer is an opinion, not a fact, because it is impossible to prove that.

Don't ignore opposing arguments. If you say that only smoking is linked with lung cancer, you are ignoring some of the opposing arguments—air pollution, for example, has been linked with lung cancer.

Don't misquote your statistics or experts. If you say that the Surgeon General has "suggested" that smoking is hazardous to your health, then you are misquoting the expert. The warning on cigarette packages is much stronger than a suggestion.

Exercise 16: Work in pairs. Discuss possible arguments for or against the following statements. Provide an appeal to reason and one to emotion. Then suggest possible audiences for which each type of appeal would be effective.

Sample statement: Smoking should be prohibited on campus.

Appeal to reason: People who have never smoked, but who lived with smokers, developed lung cancer at an alarming rate.
Intended audience: Students on campus who risk being exposed to secondhand smoke.

Appeal to emotion: If we prohibit smoking, we'll be the first school in this city to set such a fine example.
Intended audience: The Board of Trustees, who are very concerned about the reputation of the school.

1. Alcohol should not be allowed at school functions.

   Appeal to reason: _____

   _____

   Intended audience: _____

   _____

Appeal to emotion: _____

_____

Intended audience: _____

_____

2. College football players who do not pass their classes should not be allowed to play for the football team.

   Appeal to reason: _____

   _____

   Intended audience: _____

   _____

   Appeal to emotion: _____

   _____

   Intended audience: _____

   _____

3. Students whose first language is not English should be given extra time to take their examinations.

   Appeal to reason: _____

   _____

   Intended audience: _____

   _____

   Appeal to emotion: _____

   _____

   Intended audience: _____

   _____

4. Class attendance should not be a part of a college student's final grade.

   Appeal to reason: _____

   _____

   Intended audience: _____

   _____

   Appeal to emotion: _____

   _____

   Intended audience: _____

   _____

AVOIDING PROBLEMS IN LOGIC

When you use logic to argue your point, be especially careful to avoid the following problems:

"Begging the question" means to state an opinion as if it were already proved:

> "If this school got rid of its ineffective teachers, then students would get better TOEFL scores."

The speaker thinks the teachers are ineffective, but he or she has not proved that fact. The entire argument is based on the speaker's opinion about the teachers.

A **non-sequitur** is a series of statements that are presented as if they are logically related, but they are not:

> "If more universities offered ESL classes, then students would work harder."

The connection between offering ESL classes and students working harder is illogical.

An **oversimplification** is an argument that is based on limited evidence. For example, some students jump to conclusions from one fact or statistic:

> "We took fewer units this year and got better grades, so universities should reduce the number of required units."

Black-and-white thinking divides things into only two categories without shades of gray:

> "There are two types of students on this campus—those who do drugs and fail classes and those who don't do drugs and succeed."

Clearly, there are some students who do drugs and do well and some who don't do drugs and fail. This is a form of **overgeneralizing.** When a speaker creates a stereotype based on limited evidence, he or she is guilty of this:

> "The highest grades in the class went to Asian students. Asians are such hard workers and good students."

This speaker has formulated an opinion of an entire ethnic group based on one observation (his or her class). It's very important to avoid making such generalizations.

Exercise 17:   Read the following statements and decide whether the logic in each argument is faulty or acceptable. If it is faulty, identify the error in logic, and rewrite the sentence to make it more acceptable.

1. Most of the students in my Chemistry class are men. Women aren't interested in Chemistry.
2. The government should regulate gun control. Then citizens would attend church more regularly.
3. The media should control the amount of violence shown on TV. Then children would not grow up to be criminals.
4. If abortion were illegal in this country, then girls would not get pregnant.
5. I don't bother voting. All politicians are corrupt anyway.

Exercise 18:   Select one of the following statements, and prepare a 5–10 minute persuasive speech arguing for or against the position. Use appeals to both emotions and logic. Prepare your speech carefully, following these steps:

- Research the topic in the library.
- Analyze your audience using the "Worksheet for Preparing a Talk" at the end of this chapter. Select appeals that are appropriate for your audience.
- Outline your talk carefully, paying special attention to the purpose of your talk and your main assertion. Use the worksheet at the end of the chapter.
- Select effective examples and arguments that will persuade your audience. Identify these as emotional or logical. Avoid the problems with logic described above.
- Prepare a strong opening and closing.

Possible topics:

- Explicitly violent or sexual rock music lyrics should be censored.
- Elderly parents who can no longer care for themselves should be placed in a nursing home.
- Terminally ill patients should be assisted in ending their lives.
- Animals should not be used for experimentation.
- Marijuana should be available to people for whom it is medicinally beneficial.

Gaining Expertise

Organize a debate with members of another class. Select a topic and have each class take an opposing position. Choose the debate team (five or six class members) and two judges from each class. Invite other faculty to judge as well, if possible.

Directions: Below is the self-evaluation check that you completed at the start of this chapter. Without looking back, rate yourself based on how you feel today.

1. How comfortable are you communicating in English? Rate yourself from 1 (extremely uncomfortable) to 5 (completely at ease) for each of the following situations.

Asking a question in class	1	2	3	4	5
Answering the instructor's questions in class	1	2	3	4	5
Volunteering your own point of view in class	1	2	3	4	5
Disagreeing with another student's point of view during a class discussion	1	2	3	4	5
Asking the professor a question, privately, after class or during the break	1	2	3	4	5
Striking up a conversation with another student in your class whom you don't know at all	1	2	3	4	5
Giving a speech in class	1	2	3	4	5

2. Now compare today's ratings with those you gave yourself at the start of this chapter. What has improved? What needs additional work?

OBSERVER'S GRID

Students' Names	Student Contributions			Other Comments
	Agree	Disagree	Info/Clarif	

WORKSHEET FOR PREPARING A TALK

Part One: Choosing a Topic

Describe the audience (age, interests, education)

_____

_____

_____

What is your topic?

_____

_____

_____

Why did you choose that topic?

_____

_____

_____

Why is it important to you?

_____

_____

_____

Why do you think your audience will be interested in it?

_____

_____

_____

Part Two: Making an Outline of Your Talk

Write a brief outline of your talk here. Put a star (*) next to your examples.

Opening Statements:

_____

_____

_____

Main Idea of Your Talk:

_____

_____

_____

Supporting Ideas:

_____

_____

_____

_____

_____

_____

_____

_____

_____

_____

Closing Remark(s):

_____

_____

_____

Part Three: Practicing Your Talk

How long will your talk be?

Make a note here of any reminders:

_____

_____

_____

FEEDBACK FORM

Presenter: _____

Topic: _____

Date: _____

Rate the speaker on the following categories:

The opening: (Did it attract your attention? Was it on the subject?)

1	2	3	4	5
Needs Improvement		Good		Excellent

Comments:

_____

_____

The organization: (Were you able to follow easily? Did the speaker develop ideas smoothly?)

1	2	3	4	5
Needs Improvement		Good		Excellent

Comments:

_____

_____

Use of support: (Did the speaker choose effective and clear examples? Were there enough of them? Were the speaker's arguments logical and relevant?)

1	2	3	4	5
Needs Improvement		Good		Excellent

Comments:

_____

_____

Language: (Was the language clear, easy to understand, at the level of the audience?)

1	2	3	4	5
Needs		Good		Excellent
Improvement				

Comments:

_____

_____

Presentation: (Did the speaker speak slowly and clearly? Did he or she make eye contact and use nonverbal communication?)

1	2	3	4	5
Needs		Good		Excellent
Improvement				

Comments:

_____

_____

Strengths: (What was the strongest element of this presentation?)

_____

_____

_____

Areas for improvement: (What elements require improvement?)

_____

_____

_____